"Chertkow and Feehan are the ideal n[...]
who want to navigate an ever-changi[...]

[...]s; I've worked on every side of it . . .
[...] up-to-date reference book for young
[...] and MTV/VH1 television personality

[...]cal guide for musicians that explains
[...] without a label. A must-read!"

—Derek Sivers, founder of CD Baby and HostBaby

"This is just the sort of zero-BS guide to modern artistic survival that should
be in every artist's handbag."   —Cory Doctorow

"Dear Parent: I hear your kid's band is starting to sound pretty good! The
band is getting regular practices in; they're gigging a bit; they've got a logo
and a Facebook page. How can you help them now? Have them take a look
at: *The Indie Band Survival Guide: The Complete Manual for the Do-It-
Yourself Musician* by Randy Chertkow and Jason Feehan."

—Laura Lamere, *Parenting Creative Kids*

"Chertkow and Feehan are plugged-in to the mercurial world that is the
music industry. Their straightforward approach to making your own rules in
a world without them is exactly what new and experienced artists need. . . .
I'm going to call the publisher to inquire about a quantity discount for
studios. Seriously. We should hand these out to every new client who comes
in the door."   —Garrett Haines, *Tape Op* magazine

"The internet is an extraordinary opportunity for musicians to make and
profit from their music. This clearly written and comprehensive book
shows exactly how. A perfect balance between the mess of the law and the
promise of the technology, it should be read by anyone who wants to take
their talent and share it—for the love of sharing, or for the profit."

—Lawrence Lessig, author of *Code*, professor at Stanford Law School,
founder of the Center for Internet and Society, and CEO of the Creative
Commons project

ALSO BY **RANDY CHERTKOW**
AND **JASON FEEHAN**

The Indie Band Survival Guide:
The Complete Manual for the
Do-It-Yourself Musician
(first and second editions)

Making Money with MUSIC

Randy Chertkow
& Jason Feehan

Generate Over 100
Revenue Streams,
Grow Your Fan Base,
and Thrive in Today's
Music Environment

ST. MARTIN'S GRIFFIN
NEW YORK

Dedicated to musicians everywhere

www.stmartins.com

The Library of Congress Cataloging-in-Publication Data is available upon request.

ISBN 978-1-250-19208-0 (hardcover)
ISBN 978-1-250-19209-7 (ebook)

Our books may be purchased in bulk for promotional, educational, or business use. Please contact your local bookseller or the Macmillan Corporate and Premium Sales Department at 1-800-221-7945, extension 5442, or by email at MacmillanSpecial Markets@macmillan.com.

First Edition: September 2018

10 9 8 7 6 5 4 3 2 1

CONTENTS

INTRODUCTION

"Dude, I owe you guys money!"

We had just finished the first part of our all-day talk when this excited musician, producer, and manager, who was making a living off his music, came up to us to share his story. Just a day before we were at SXSW interviewing music supervisors for an upcoming article series for *Electronic Musician* magazine, but, having been on a speaking tour around the country, we had scheduled one final talk before we headed back to our hometown of Chicago. "When I saw you were coming to town, I *had* to come to this event. My bestselling album is because of what I learned from you about marketing and piggybacking. It's all because of you."

It's successes and comments like these that keep us researching, writing, speaking, and teaching. It's been motivating us for over a decade since we first started, back when we gave away a free PDF from our band's website in 2006 called *The Indie Band Survival Guide*. After thousands of downloads, it caught on across the blogosphere, and next thing we knew, *Billboard* magazine interviewed us about it. Then the Associated Press and Reuters. Finally, publishers were interested in turning it into a book. While we didn't set out to do all this, we felt it was critical to help others. In a sense, we're similar to musicians who discover they're good at mixing and become mixing engineers for other musicians, except what we do is explain what to do in today's music industry in concepts and words we musicians understand.

And that's what we are: musicians who just did it ourselves through trial and error and then shared with the world what to do and what to avoid. Our band, Beatnik Turtle, has released over five hundred songs spanning twenty albums, licensed music to Disney and Viacom, and written music for TV, films, and theater, including Chicago's Second City. In 2007, we released a song every single day of the year from our website The SongOfTheDay.com. But after the book took off, we also became authors, journalists, instructors, public speakers, and consultants because so many reached out to us asking us to teach, write, and speak. It also helped that beyond being musicians, we also have expertise in law, IT, product management, marketing, and sales, all disciplines crucial to running a successful music business. One of us is an attorney, product manager, and project manager; the other a sales professional and an IT expert with a Master's in computer science.

The book you're holding was sparked by two things. The first was over five years ago when the Recording Academy's San Francisco chapter (the organization behind the GRAMMYs) flew us out to speak to their Music Business Night School, which helps teach musicians to succeed in today's music environment. Rather than do our usual talk based on the critically acclaimed *The Indie Band Survival Guide* and *The DIY Music Manual* (Random House) or our DIY articles for *Electronic Musician* magazine, we decided to create a new one focused solely on how musicians could turn on new revenue streams. We called the talk "Making Money with Music," and it was the highest rated of the year. This caused other chapters and music organizations around the country to bring us out to give the presentation.

The second spark was a government study completed by the city of Austin, the live music capital of the world. We learned about this pioneering survey after one of our "Making Money with Music" talks in Austin. Backstage at the event, we met Don Pitts (soundmusiccities.com), who was the head of the Austin music office at that time. He had commissioned the first-of-its-kind music survey (bit.ly/austincensus) so he could get a data-driven look into the actual health of Austin's music economy.

The study revealed how music contributed billions of dollars in revenue to Austin by driving tourism, restaurant traffic, and music venue ticket sales, as well as how it supported many secondary businesses and jobs. But while the hotel and entertainment businesses were thriving, the census also revealed the stark reality that musicians were barely making a living in the new music environment. Over 80 percent of musicians reported difficulty making money, and this was having an "extreme or strong impact" on their livelihood and whether they stuck with music as a career. Nearly one-third of the over 1,800 musicians who answered the survey were earning $15,000 or less per year in pretax income (including all income sources). And approximately three-fourths of them were earning below the Austin Metropolitan Statistical Area mean annual wage.

In short, the study's four critical findings were:

1. Musicians don't make enough money to support themselves (including finding it hard to afford housing).

2. Musicians lack the music business knowledge and skills required to make money with music within today's music industry.

3. Musicians lack access and knowledge to the necessary resources and services that can help.

4. Musicians find it difficult to network and collaborate with others in their industry.

There have been more studies in music cities around the world since, and the findings show the same thing: *musicians are struggling to make enough money with music.* This puts music cities and their interconnected businesses, services, tourism, and economic revenue at serious risk. This is why music cities are collectively waking up to the need to help musicians generate revenue. To us, this includes educating musicians on how today's music industry works, informing musicians how to tap into new revenue streams to make a sustainable business, connecting musicians with resources and networking opportunities within their cities, and creating more music and musician-friendly ordinances to promote a live music scene and community.

But cities themselves can't solve the musician revenue problem directly. Only musicians can register their songs to ensure they get all the royalties generated worldwide they're owed. Only musicians can determine their target audience and the best product and merchandise mix to sell at shows to maximize revenue. Only musicians can promote and publicize their releases and live events. They just need to learn how.

"It wasn't until we started having the right conversation with our local music community that we learned what musicians need to know more than anything else these days," says Pitts, "is what I call 'the fundamentals'—the basics on how to make money with music given the reality of today's tech-driven music environment. The field has changed, but musicians who learn the music business basics of this new music economy will thrive."

This book is our answer to the studies' findings. *Making Money with Music* gives musicians a clear understanding of what they need to do to succeed in this new music environment and create more music for the world. We know musicians can make a living at music because we've interviewed many who are paying the rent or mortgage with their music business. We've shared their lessons and methods and combined them with the best practices and frameworks here, within one book, so everyone can benefit.

Plus, this book has the resources and services musicians need today to tap the hundreds of income streams available to them. Because musicians can't be expected to know which services they need until they first understand the background, this book explains *what* they should do, *why* they should do it, and *how* they can use these services to do it for themselves. Learning how is as easy as following a recipe, and this book has dozens of how-to's in every area to help musicians increase their income whether they're solo artists, rappers, rock bands, DJs, EDM producers, or more.

By the time musicians are done reading this book, they'll have the framework to build a sustainable music business, the knowledge of over one hundred income streams now available, and the how-to instructions to unlock them. They only need to decide which to tackle first.

1

MAKING MONEY
WITH MUSIC

Imagine you just clicked "Submit" for worldwide distribution on your next EP and scheduled it to come out in six weeks to give you time to send pre-release copies to music reviewers. You've been announcing it for a while to your fans via social media, which has generated good buzz. You also send a note to your top patronage funders that they will have access to the EP a week early, plus get bonus material, and tell the lower-tier funders they can do the same if they choose a higher tier to get the rewards. Your patronage is contributing enough of your monthly income to cover your rent.

Next, you log in to your performance rights organizations (PROs) and discover your streaming royalties are up this quarter; plus, you're getting more foreign royalties due to your last single catching on in the Netherlands. A DJ there loved one of your songs (you found him on the internet playing similar artists and you reached out to him), and thanks to him and his audience, it caught on in the region. You know this because you check your social media stats weekly and pay attention to where your fans are located. Plus, your social alert tools tell you when you are mentioned on websites or social media, and you saw a bunch of new posts about your music. According to the other stats sites, not only did your current song do well but there's more streaming of your back catalog too.

Taking a look at the video stats reminds you to also check your You-Tube advertising revenue, which is doing well, but bonus income is coming from a fan-made animated music video that generated millions of views. Even though the fan used your music without asking you, you think the video is great; plus, because you registered your song with You-Tube, you get the ad revenue from it.

After that, you check a licensing service you signed up for a couple of months ago and discover a TV show licensed one of your songs. The licensing fees will get deposited in your bank account, and yet all you did was upload a few of your tracks to their online music library. A TV music supervisor discovered it on her own and loved the track for her show, and the site handled the transaction and license for you. You check out another service you use and find out the beats, presets, and stems you created for the last release—the same one which took off in the Netherlands—is also selling. Turns out you have a dedicated set of musician fans who love buying what you created to use in their own music. You just uploaded them and announced they were available, and you can make more income off the same release.

Thinking about your last release reminds you to upload it to the vinyl crowdfunding site and announce it to your fans. The production run only gets made if the funding is reached, but once it does, you don't need to do anything—it automatically gets created and shipped to those who paid for it. Your fans funded the last two, so you think it's likely they'll fund this one too, and all you had to do was upload it and announce it.

Next, you take a look at the income you made from last night's live show. Not only did you sell out your show, your merch did well; you even sold two of your custom-decorated, high-quality, one-of-a-kind jackets for $250 each. There are always a few die-hard fans who love these custom items. You also see your pay-per-view income is up. The venue provided cameras and an audio feed from the soundboard, allowing you to sell access to a stream of your concert. Your fans on the internet, found all over the world (including the Netherlands), love watching your performances and chatting with one another on the feed even though they can't come to the show. In fact, some of the fans at the show bought the recording as well.

Then, before you head back to the studio to work on more music, you submit your set list to your PRO so you can get performance royalties out of the show as well.

You don't need to imagine this. You can do this for your music, today.

The example above, with its multiple, parallel income streams, shows just a fraction of what's possible today for your own music business. The power to get your music out to the world, find an audience, and make money is within your reach.

In fact, there are many advantages to today's music world you can use for your own music:

1. You have access to free or inexpensive music/video production technology to express and create your art.

Previously, only very expensive studios could record professional tracks or make video. But today, a smartphone has recording and editing capabilities that entire studios lacked before. Plus, many of the tools are inexpensive or even free. Musicians only need to decide they want to make music or videos: the technology is no longer a barrier.

2. You have a world hungry for fresh new music, content, and entertainment.

Nearly everyone is carrying a device that can let them experience your work, and they're spending most of their day using it to find new entertainment, news, and distractions. The addictions people have to their phones can work for you if you can give them what they want.

3. You have access to a universe of music and business services, tools, and other partners who want to help artists succeed.

Everything a label did for musicians is now available to you from free or inexpensive services you can tap into. This means you can handle music production, marketing, promotion, publicity, tour support, funding, and more. Plus, you'll get to retain the rights to your music and collect all the income your music generates. In fact, this book covers hundreds of services, sites, and tools that can help you succeed at every aspect of your music business. This will allow you to build a profitable business with just a small team, making signing to a label an optional choice.

4. You can distribute your music/videos worldwide in an instant.

Today, you can get your music and videos in streaming services, sales platforms, music and video sites, and stores more quickly and cheaply than ever before. And some of these options are free.

5. You have more places to get your music/videos discovered, heard, and seen by more people across the globe than ever before in history.

There are more audio and video options than ever to get your work in front of new audiences from sites like YouTube, TV stations, radio stations, internet forums, and more. And everyone in the world can access your work once they find out who you are.

6. You have the ability to collect all the royalties your music and videos generate worldwide.

Royalty collection agencies used to only be available to major artists and out of reach of most musicians. Today, services have popped up to let musicians access all these methods and collect all the royalties their music generates, worldwide. Because every artist is global from the moment they make their music available, musicians can make money from their popularity no matter where their music takes off.

7. You have access to powerful audience data to help you target people who want to hear your type of music.

Social media companies mine their databases of information about all their users in order to deliver ads. To encourage people to buy these ads, they often provide free info on your fans and followers, which used to be out of reach for artists in the past. This allows you to know exactly where your fans are located so you can tour in the right places or what their ages, genders, and interests are so you can get a deep understanding of who they are and what they want.

8. You have access to more opportunities to play live, including streaming your shows online, and powerful tools to know where to tour so you can pack venues.

Not only are there more places to perform live, but there are also many income streams available for each show (and many musicians aren't tapping all of them!). Also, video streaming is free, allowing artists to either let their worldwide fans watch the show for free or create pay-per-view events, providing yet another income stream for concerts you are already performing.

9. You have access to free publicity and real-time worldwide promotion for everything you do.

Each one of your fans has hundreds of followers, and if you can keep producing entertainment they want to talk about, you can spread your message instantly and organically. And due to the huge number of YouTube channels, blogs, and more, there are also more media targets than ever, and they are always hungry for something new or entertaining to cover.

10. You can create free and inexpensive products and merchandise for your music business, distribute them worldwide, and generate revenue.

Making merch is now free. With print-on-demand merchandise, you can now upload an image and offer to print it on nearly any type of merch imaginable: T-shirts, clothing, posters, and more. The fans pay for the production and shipping of each item, allowing you to make a profit on every sale. Or, if you dream up a new imaginative piece of merch, you can let manufacturers bid on it and mass-produce something that never existed before.

11. You can raise capital for your music business through more methods than ever before, including going directly to fans.

Today there are multiple opportunities to raise money from fans, businesses, banks, and other sources.

12. You have access to income based on your fame and the size of your fan base.

Once you have a fan base, you'll find companies will pay good money to reach them, and you get to decide which you'll accept or reject. This opens up new income streams to you, and they start generating income even if you have a small fan base.

13. You have more opportunities to license music than ever before.

Multimedia dominates today's world, which means music is a critical component in everything people are creating. This includes promotional videos, films, TV shows, advertising, movie trailers, apps, video games, and more. If you can connect with the people choosing the music, you'll find licensing opportunities for your music.

As exciting as all these changes are, they have had a profound effect on how musicians make money today. In fact, most musicians still only focus on generating money from traditional income streams, such as live music, music sales, and merchandise. But there are hundreds of income streams now available, and successful artists making a living off music today tap into and layer these sources to create a sustainable and profitable music business.

That's what *Making Money with Music* is about.

This book will help you build your music business and generate revenue in today's music environment. It provides strategies, frameworks, systems, hundreds of links and services, and how-to instructions. These are not only learnable, the basic skills are as easy to apply as following a recipe, and the advanced techniques are just the logical next steps once your basic business is in place.

If you are willing to put in what it takes to build your business, this book can show you:

1. Over one hundred income streams you can tap, seven business strategies you can implement right away, and *a method to start your music business for $0*.

2. Thirteen ways to compete for free and build experiences that drive fan loyalty and engagement into everything you do.

3. Ten qualities of an authentic, well-crafted persona that attracts fans, provides the basis for your products and merch, and opens up ten new income streams.

4. How to get distributed worldwide, even for free, so you can generate royalties, sales licensing opportunities, and grow your fan base globally.

5. How to register to collect all the royalties you are owed worldwide.

6. Forty-five categories of places to get your music heard and videos seen so you can get discovered, grow your fan base, generate revenue, and boost licensing opportunities.

7. How to leverage services and build a team so you can focus on the music or other activities.

8. A modern release strategy so you can stay on top of mind with fans throughout the year, grow your fan base, provide real reasons for people to cover you and your music, and generate revenue.

9. A marketing strategy that drives all promotion and publicity activities so you can reach new fans, generate more revenue, and drive press/media coverage worldwide. This includes fourteen $0 marketing strategies you can implement immediately and seven musician-focused marketing goals to focus your efforts.

10. A comprehensive online strategy that allows you to promote worldwide while minimizing the work so you can focus on the music or other revenue-generating activities.

11. Promotion campaigns to maximize exposure for your live shows, your music, your videos, and your patronage and crowdfunding.

12. Ten methods for raising money so you can fund your music production and projects.

WHO THIS BOOK IS FOR

This book is for *every* type of musician who wants to make money with music—no matter your genre or style and regardless if you're a solo artist, band, DJ, EDM producer, or any other. It also will help you whether you're just starting out, established, or even a professional. Contained in this book are the knowledge, strategies, frameworks, and how-to steps all musicians can apply to build, grow, and mature their music business and generate revenue with music.

For instance, if you're just starting out, there is a structured system to build your music business, including the initial sources of income you can tap into right away. There is even a way for you to build a music business for $0. If you're an established or professional musician, this book has tons of ideas, methods, and systems to boost your income; plus, the entire chapter "Advanced Income Techniques" has dozens of ideas to create more income streams.

This book is also an essential resource for *everyone who works in the music business*, including managers, bookers, labels, promoters, music business professionals, teachers, recording engineers, music video directors, filmmakers, and more, since it explains what each of these roles do and how to make income from each.

Also, because this book has revenue development built into every step of the musician's life cycle, it can be a critical resource for anyone striving to educate musicians, including music schools, music business schools, teachers, city music offices, cities, nongovernmental organizations, and nonprofits.

HOW THIS BOOK IS ORGANIZED

This book is meant to be a reference. You can jump to particular chapters or sections rather than read it cover to cover like other books, but if you do, take some time to first page through the book to get the idea of its organization so you can get an idea of all the music income possibilities. You don't have to do everything here, just like you don't need to cook every recipe in a cookbook, but you should be aware of what exists in today's music environment and decide which make sense for you when you're ready to tackle it. After all, there's no need to run a marketing campaign if you don't have an album for sale yet.

Each chapter is broken up to make it easy to navigate:

- **Book Sections**

  The chapters are organized into three sections that are in the order in which most musicians start their businesses: "Getting Prepared," "Getting Paid and Making Money," and "Releasing Your Music and Getting Noticed."

- **Chapters**

  Some chapters are strategy or planning chapters, but most are how-to's focused on taking action.

- **Goal**

  Each chapter begins with a high-level summary outlining the purpose of the chapter.

- **Team Roles and Responsibilities**

  The most successful musicians build a team of people and services around their business so they can focus on the music. The top of each chapter lists who you can delegate to if you've built a team.

- **What You Get Out of This**

  Read this section for a list of topics this chapter will cover.

- **Money Map**

Eleven chapters include illustrations outlining key income streams that chapter covers and unlocks for your music business.

- **Chapter Sections**

Each chapter groups the information into sections. For instance, chapter 5, "Your Music," contains five sections: making your music, recording and mixdown, mastering, preparing your music for distribution and release.

- **Subsections**

Each subsection covers a specific topic. Most of the subsections explain "How to Do X." Other subsections may be titled "Understanding X" or "The Top X Thing(s) You Should Do." These subsections will explain key concepts or provide context for the topic.

EVEN MORE RESOURCES AT MAKINGMONEYWITHMUSIC.COM

You're holding more than just a book. MakingMoneyWithMusic.com is a free portal to:

- A monthly Making Money with Music newsletter (makingmoney withmusic.com/newsletter).

- Links to the latest resources, services, links, and tools for each chapter, including clickable versions of every link within this book.

- Over two hundred free articles, additional how-to information, and interviews with thought leaders.

- Exclusive bonus material and downloadable forms.

- Additional tools and detailed how-to material to help you unlock *additional* revenue streams beyond the book as well as manage your music business.

CONCLUSION

If you had the money and power to bring together the top music professionals, business consultants, analysts, researchers, marketers, product managers, project managers, and attorneys into one room to help you build a sustainable music business in this new music environment, the advice and guidance in this book is what they'd produce. Our goal with this book is to help make you so successful in generating revenue you'll want to share your success with others and how you did it. And when you do, email us at contactus@makingmoneywithmusic.com or tell us in person at one of our talks.

PART 1
GETTING PREPARED

2

YOUR MUSIC BUSINESS

Goal: To form a business and create a profitable music business strategy.

Team Roles and Responsibilities: Manager, Attorney, Accountant, Business Banker

WHAT YOU GET OUT OF THIS
By the end of this chapter, you will:

1. Be able to build your music business for $0.

2. Know the single success formula for creating a profitable music business.

3. Know the thirteen qualities you should build into your music business to create experiences, live events, shows, products, and merchandise fans will value and pay for (and compete with free).

4. Have seven strategies you can implement to maximize the amount of money you can make.

5. Understand the three parts of every business transaction that affect how much money you can make.

6. Segment your audience into three tiers of customers to maximize fan-based revenue in everything you release or do.

7. Understand how to strategically use services and middlemen to minimize costs and maximize your cut.

8. Know how and why to form a business for your music so you can limit your liability, create the ground rules for your business, and manage the money you make.

INTRO

To succeed today, you must tap multiple income streams to build a sustainable and profitable music business. Think of this as a wall with hundreds of water faucets. Each one represents a revenue opportunity you can choose to tap. Some are relatively easy to turn on, while others require additional time or prerequisites. For instance, you can generate royalties from the performance of your music on streaming services by registering your music correctly so the PROs know who to send the checks to. We outline these steps in a future chapter, but the point is you can turn on this faucet *to collect royalties for your entire life* if you spend only an hour or two on a Saturday registering your music online.

Some of these revenue faucets may only drip at first, so your job is to turn these drips into a steady flow by creatively applying the steps we cover in this book. To continue with the royalty example above, you will need to apply the steps in the "Marketing" and "Get Heard and Seen" chapters so your music generates more royalties.

This is the way successful music managers think. They answer the tough questions about how to run the business and make it as profitable as possible, and you need to do the same for your own business. For example:

- How can I make the most money I can from my music so I can live off it?

- What can I build into my products, merch, shows, and experiences to make fans want to open their wallets to pay for it?

- Who in my fan base will pay me the most money, and how can I angle my business to cater to them?

- How can I compete against free?

- How can I make sure I can get paid by handling credit cards, checks, and cash, and keep track of it?

- How can I build a business structure that allows me to maximize income and minimize my taxes?

This chapter answers these questions and will get you into the manager mind-set so you can build and grow a successful music business.

KEY CONCEPTS
THE ONLY SUCCESS FORMULA YOU NEED TO KNOW
No matter what kind of business you have—whether it's a taco stand or a multinational oil company—there's just one formula that determines whether you're successful or not:

$$How\ Much\ You\ Make - How\ Much\ You\ Spend = How\ Much\ You\ Keep$$

When you work on turning music into a business, you need to work on all three parts of the equation:

- **Boost what you make.**

There are many ways to generate revenue beyond playing live or selling tracks, and to help you tap them, we've shared "Money Maps" at the beginning of most chapters of this book.

- **Reduce what you spend.**

No business can last if it spends more than it takes in. Successful musicians spend as little money as possible, and when they do, they make sure it makes them more money in return.

- **Keep more by limiting your taxes.**

Successful musicians track their expenses to write them off for tax purposes. This allows them to keep more of their profit.

THE THREE PARTS TO EVERY TRANSACTION
THAT WILL AFFECT HOW MUCH MONEY YOU CAN MAKE
Each time you earn money, it filters through a chain of people: the customer, a middleman, and you. Understanding how these three parts affect your income will help you maximize your revenue.

1. The customer.

It's important to identify and define your customer for each income stream as clearly as possible and know what their needs are so you can make the most revenue from each. For example, when you sell merch, your fans are the buyers, but when you license music, music supervisors and directors are your customers. You will market and sell differently to each.

2. The middleman.

In today's music industry, for most business activities, you'll be choosing your middleman, the services and partners who you will be working with to build your music business, before doing anything with your customers. You'll want to select each carefully, because they each take different fees or cuts of your revenue and have different strengths and weaknesses.

3. You.

Although third on the list, this is the first thing to set up correctly, since each business you work with will be asking for a tax ID so they can pay you. Depending on your country of origin, you need to decide whether they'll be paying you as an individual (a sole proprietor) or your business (corporation, limited liability corporation, or other legal entity). Your business structure will determine how you separate your business income and expenses from your personal taxes.

THE SEVEN REVENUE-STREAM MAXIMIZATION STRATEGIES

To maximize what you make from your music business, there are seven strategies you should apply to each new revenue stream:

1. Create multiple streams of income.

The most successful music businesses create multiple streams of income so they are not depending on just one or two. This book has over one hundred you can choose from so you can build a strong music business that can survive even if some decrease.

2. Blend both active and passive streams of income.

You make *active income* when you trade your time directly for money. This includes any jobs when you're getting paid an hourly rate or doing business that requires your presence, such as playing live shows. *Passive income* comes to you even when you're sleeping, such as when you receive royalty checks for a song you've written that was played on TV or radio. This is often called "*mailbox money.*" Successful musicians generate both kinds of income streams.

3. Layer inconsistent income streams on top of consistent and stable income streams.

Successful businesses are built upon a mix of stable and irregular income streams to create consistent income. For example, your album sales may not be the same month to month; YouTube may change how they recommend videos, altering your views; or your song might not get radio play next month. But your live music income might be stable throughout the year if you tour consistently.

4. Stack parallel streams of income.

There are many income streams that can be done in parallel. In fact, some even enhance one another. For example, when playing a show, an artist can leverage the following income-generating activities all at the *same show*: sell tickets to the show/make money off the door; sell your music on physical albums, download cards, or USB drives; sell merchandise such as clothing, posters, and more; sell the recording of the show; sell access to a live stream of the show; sell the live-streamed video of the show afterward; charge for access to the band (such as backstage access, hangout time, VIP seating, or after-show meals); sell advertising space on their stage backdrop to businesses/sponsorships; get royalties from the show by turning in their set lists to their performance rights organization ("PRO") like ASCAP or BMI; and more. And that's just for playing a live show, so you should always be on the lookout for new ones to add to each activity to maximize your potential share of wallet from your audience.

5. Use the sales funnel method and then segment your customers.

Only a small percentage of the people who hear your music will become paying customers. To get as many of these as possible, use the sales funnel method. At the top of the funnel are free or low-cost options for the audience to discover and experience your music—for example, a music video on YouTube or a song on a streaming site. Your goal is to bring them deeper into your world so they come to shows, buy merch, or become a patronage/crowdfunding supporter. Although a wide funnel can help more people experience your music, you'll want to be smart and aim it at your most likely fans (see chapter 14, "Marketing"). Once you have customers, you should group them into segments based upon how much they spend on you. From lowest to highest, these are usually called minnows, dolphins, and whales. Your whales usually provide 50–80 percent of all your income. Your products, shows, and support levels on patronage/crowdfunding need to have options for all these customer segments, plus provide "upsells" to drive your customers toward higher spending levels.

6. Boost income from successful revenue sources.

Successful businesses know what's working and where their revenue is coming from and then focus on boosting the income from those sources. This means you need good metrics so you know what your customers are spending money on so you can put your resources into what's already working. This could mean using marketing and promotion to boost a track that's blowing up or choosing to create more of your most popular merch.

7. Focus on developing your business customers or your fan base when starting your business.

Some businesses sell directly to consumers, such as McDonald's, and others focus on business customers, such as Sysco, which sells ingredients and supplies to restaurants. Most businesses focus on just one when they are starting, and some never develop the other kind of customers. The music business is no different, since you can focus on the traditional route of developing a fan base or provide music or services to businesses that use music. Each one opens up different income streams requiring different activities. Knowing up front which one to develop will help you decide where to put your time and resources—for example, whether to develop a killer live show or spend time at trade shows networking with people in the music business.

MUSIC BUSINESS CUSTOMER STRATEGIES
THE THIRTEEN QUALITIES A MUSIC BUSINESS SHOULD HAVE TO MAXIMIZE REVENUE (AND COMPETE WITH "FREE")

Fans have been able to copy music for free for well over a decade, and the streaming platforms that fans favor today will generate only a fraction of a penny per play. Meanwhile, there are endless numbers of musicians out there reaching out to the same fans. The question is: How can you make a sustainable music business when there are so many free options to get music, including your own?

While fans expect music to be free or easy to stream, they *are* willing to pay for the thirteen qualities below because they provide real value, connection, and loyalty to you as an artist:

1. Live experiences.

People are willing to pay for live experiences. Sure, they can listen to recorded music at any time, but live music creates an emotional experience and shared moment that can't be pirated or stolen. Experiences increasingly have driven today's entertainment business, and this is why you need more than just live shows. Fortunately, there are many types of live events you can create for your fans (see chapter 13, "Advanced Income Techniques"). In addition, fans are willing to spend money on mementos to capture the moment, which can give more value to the merch you sell.

2. Certainty *and* uncertainty.

People generally live in the sweet spot between their desire for certainty, where they feel comfortable, and uncertainty, where they can experience the unexpected. If your music and experiences are too predictable, you can bore your audience; if they're wildly unpredictable or different, you can repel them. Entertainment containing a healthy mixture of *both* familiarity and surprise will often attract interest, engagement, and a following, allowing you to maximize the amount of money you can make.

3. Connections.

Fans seek connections with the artists they love. Often this connection arises from your persona, which reflects how fans see themselves in what you produce. In addition, you can grow this connection by speaking directly to *their* identity through commonalities you share with them. This can be your music, of course, but also a shared interest, belief structure, philosophy, emotion, location, way of life, religion, or political cause. This can drive ideas for creating or framing your products, shows, and events. For example, if your merch has a lyric on it that reso-nates with fans, they'll be more inclined to buy it.

4. Authenticity.

Some of the most well-known songs are played by musicians who pour themselves and their feelings into their music. This cannot be easily manufactured or stolen, and if it's expressed in a way that resonates with your fans, it can be a powerful driver for your music and music business. This can be further boosted through connections, which provide an ex-tra layer on top of the authenticity.

5. Unique interpretations.

Once you are known for your style of music or performances, fans will appreciate your take on cover songs, culture, or other things. This also applies to your commentary on media, current events, and more. Even your opinions will matter to your fans once you are known to have a point of view they care about.

6. Stories.

Storytelling brings people together and underlies the entertainment we love the most. Most stories are about overcoming obstacles and the jour-ney toward obtaining a goal. Once people are hooked on a story, they stay engaged to relieve the suspense of finding out how it all turns out. Create a story out of your music, videos, and events or your own journey as an artist, and people will stay engaged to find out what comes next. Also, stories can create concepts for your products, merch, live shows, and nearly everything else you do.

7. Themes.

A theme is a dominating idea that may resonate with your audience and attract interest, controversy, or debate. A well-chosen theme can drive and underlie concepts for your albums, live shows, merch, experiences, persona, and more. For example, Pink Floyd's concept album *Dark Side of the Moon*, which centered on the theme of insanity, resonated with so many people that it stayed on the *Billboard* charts for 741 weeks. Themes pair up well with many other qualities in this list, especially sto-ries, connections, and unique interpretations.

8. Embodiment and actualization.

Your fans may love your cool logo on the header of your website, but once you put it on a T-shirt or a key chain, it becomes something fans can touch, hold, and share with others and they'll pay money to get these items. This is the main reason you can sell merch. Anytime you can embody an idea into a real object, it has value. If you can pair this with the connection quality above, you can boost your product and merch sales. Since there are services that allow you to easily create custom merch, there are a lot of opportunities to do this. This isn't limited to merch; you can also turn event ideas into real experiences. For example, our band took our Christmas album, *Santa Doesn't Like You*, and turned it into a series of unique "un-holiday" shows. The idea embodied in the album brought people into the door.

9. Personalized or customized products and events.

A song a wedding couple listened to when they met for the first time can be touching when played during a wedding reception, but a song specifically written for the couple based on the actual details of their lives can create an unforgettable moment. We did this recently for one couple, and we treasure the video that came out of it. Personalization can give value to your songwriting skills by creating tailored music for your customer's special event, advertising, movie, or other music needs. But songwriting isn't the only way; every time you autograph merch for someone, you're using this quality.

10. Rare products and experiences.

In 2008, Nine Inch Nails created only 2,500 "Ultra-Deluxe Limited Edition" copies of their "*Ghosts*" album for $300 each. The entire lot sold out in less than thirty hours of its release because there were so few available. After all, if it were just a box set, it would be unlikely to sell for $300. If you can create limited-edition products or one-of-a-kind merch, it will more likely sell out for a premium price. Shows and events can be rare as well, which is why farewell tours for major artists sell so many tickets.

11. Accessible and findable products, entertainment, and experiences.

That soda in your fridge was cheap, so why do you buy the one at the movie theater for triple the price? Accessibility means you can charge a premium for anything you can bring within the reach of your customers, and findability means they know where to get it. This is why you need to make sure fans can easily find and buy your products, merch, and experience-based events you sell online and at shows.

12. Consistently released entertainment and engagement.

If you're able to produce and release music, videos, live shows, and other events on a regular schedule, fans will get in the habit of checking back with you to see what you're doing next (see chapter 18, "Your Release Strategy," on how to release all that you do throughout the year). Paired up with patronage, storytelling, and any of the other qualities covered in this list, consistently releasing content can be a powerful driver to keep fans engaged and supporting you monetarily on a consistent basis.

13. Opportunities to support you.

Some of your fans want to buy into your dream and have a stake in what you come out with next. All you need to do is let them know how they can contribute. You can do this by raising money through patronage, crowd-funding, and other methods (see chapter 11, "Patronage, Crowdfunding, and Raising Money," on how to do this).

THE THREE CUSTOMER SEGMENTS MUSICIANS SHOULD UNDERSTAND (MINNOWS, DOLPHINS, AND WHALES) AND WAYS TO GET THEM TO SPEND MORE

While most businesses serve all customers, the most profitable ones cater to their highest-paying customers. For instance, the online gaming indus-try, an industry obsessed with making lightning-quick changes to their business based on analytical data, categorizes their customers into three segments: minnows, dolphins, and whales. These customer segments are classified by the amount of income they can make from each, targeting dif-ferent services, modules, and expansion packs at them. The whales get the most attention because they provide the majority of their income. Your own business should be run the same way, since whales are the superfans who love the music and art you create and have the funds to spend on you.

There are many aspects of your business where you can offer higher-priced options that could entice your customers to move up to a higher level of spending with you. Some options include:

- **Physical music products.**

Create exclusive, high-priced, limited-run editions of your music and videos. This may include creating special vinyl, CD, USB, DVD, or cassette tape editions of your music. For instance, the Flaming Lips once released a limited-run EP, which was a four-song USB drive contained within a seven-pound skull made of gummy bear material that they sold for $150.

- **Merchandise and special live show mementos.**

Create limited-run or high-end, high-quality branded merchandise and price it accordingly. You can also sell unique, one-of-a-kind items such as autographed musical gear, lyric and song notebooks, or more.

- **Live events and special access.**

Create and charge for special access to your live events, such as VIP seating, giving backstage passes, access to attend sound check, or direct streaming events and access.

- **Prerelease access and exclusives.**

Give your fans the option of "jumping to the head of the line" and giving them prerelease access to your music or videos or offer exclusive tracks you won't release publicly.

- **High-priced crowdfunding and patronage rewards.**

Create high-end rewards on crowdfunding or patronage sites to entice pledges. For instance, Amanda Palmer created two $10,000 rewards where she offered to paint a portrait of the fan as well as cook dinner—and both were filled. Other options include adding their names to your album credits, giving them shout-outs in the liner notes or videos, or other unique rewards.

- **Other services.**

Consider offering highly limited availability options, such as playing a house concert, creating a song, or offering other special services for your superfans.

MUSIC BUSINESS MIDDLEMAN STRATEGIES

UNDERSTANDING THE MIDDLEMEN AND SERVICES THAT POWER YOUR MUSIC BUSINESS

There is no longer a single music industry; instead, there are industries around music. Every aspect of what labels did for their signed musicians can be found in services, tools, apps, software, contractors, and professionals available to *all* musicians.

You need to strategically use these partners and services, since each is a business decision that costs money or takes a cut of every transaction you make. Your goal with these services is to get the most out of them by paying as little as possible for each, maximizing your income, and keeping your music business flexible so you can move to another service if a better deal becomes available. It's also important, since some middlemen can affect your rights and your ability to make money from your business in the future. For example, label agreements may require you to give up the rights to your music in return for an advance, promotion, and other services.

Don't always go with the cheapest option. Sometimes services that have a higher initial fee take less of a cut for each transaction, making you more in the long run if you have a larger customer base. Because of this, routinely review your partners to see if there are better options available.

HOW TO START A MUSIC BUSINESS FOR $0

Not only are today's services available to every musician, there are $0 options for nearly every category of what you need to get started. By paying $0 to start your music business, every sale will generate a profit, and they're low-risk.

Of course, free options have downsides. For example, for sales platforms, they will take a bigger cut of the transaction to make up for the fact that you're paying nothing up front. Because of this, these are excellent ways to *start* your music business, but once you generate enough funds from your profits, you can change to better service options.

Consider the following free options to start your music business, but note that this list consolidates free options throughout this book—each chapter will go into detail on how to use the services and tools mentioned below.

1. Get digital audio workstation (DAW) sound editing software for $0.

Besides sound software built into your operating system, such as Garage-Band (apple.com/mac/garageband), you can also use the free multitrack DAW Audacity (audacity.sourceforge.net) or the open-source Ardour (ardour.org) to work on your music.

2. Get worldwide digital music distribution on streaming services, iTunes, Google Play, Amazon, and other digital distributors for $0.

Distributors like RouteNote (routenote.com) can place your music into streaming services like Spotify and stores like iTunes, Google Play, and Amazon for no up-front costs, instead taking a percentage of any sale you make (on top of what the outlets keep). The percentage RouteNote keeps is higher than other distribution outlets, but they also let you switch to a subscription fee and keep the full amount of every sale after that point.

3. Get your music heard and videos seen for $0.

There are forty-five *categories* of ways to get your music heard and seen worldwide, all of which are free. Pair this up with the free marketing, promotion, and publicity techniques discussed in this book and you'll have a very effective $0 get-heard-and-seen campaign.

4. Make, sell, and ship products and merchandise for $0.

Print-on-demand sites like DistrictLines (districtlines.com), Spreadshirt (spreadshirt.com), Zazzle (zazzle.com), and CafePress (cafepress .com) let you create and sell all types of clothing, items, and other merchandise without any up-front costs. Usually, this only generates a small profit margin, but this technique lets you try out new designs for merchandise at no cost to see which ones sell.

5. Create, distribute, and fulfill orders for CDs and DVDs for $0.

To sell CDs and DVDs for $0, use print-on-demand services like CreateSpace (createspace.com). Simply create a free account, upload your content, and set the price, and the service will handle manufacturing, customer orders, and shipping for you. You'll keep the difference between the base cost and the price you set.

6. Get free websites for $0.

Services like Blogger (blogger.com), WordPress (wordpress.com), and more offer free websites and website builders to get you started, and keep in mind social media accounts are free as well.

7. Get graphics and photo-editing software for $0.

You will need to create many images, photos, and other graphics for your business. You can use free tools like Gimp (gimp.org), which is a full-featured photo-editing tool comparable to Photoshop.

8. Get video footage for your videos and video editors for $0.

It's already free to get your videos to fans using services like YouTube or Vimeo, but to make the video itself, you'll need your music, video clips, and a video editor. For clips, use the Creative Commons Search page (search.creativecommons.org) and choose "use for commercial purposes" for a powerful search engine across a huge number of services to find video footage to use. You can also use NASA (nasa.gov), C-SPAN (c-span.org), or other U.S. governmental bodies. Also see Archive.org (archive.org/details/movies) and Public Resource (public.resource.org). You can also use the video editors available on your operating systems or phones, or try the free and open-source OpenShot (openshot.org).

9. Stream your live shows and events for $0.

You can stream any live event you create for free with services like Periscope (pscp.tv), uStream (ustream.tv), Facebook Live (live.fb.com) or YouTube Live (youtube.com/live_dashboard).

10. Raise money for your music business for $0.

You raise money from your fans to support you, your music, or your next projects with no up-front costs. Patronage and crowdfunding sites like Patreon (patreon.com), Kickstarter (kickstarter.com), and more are all free to use. They take all the cuts on the backend of the payments.

11. Get income from the ad share of your music and videos on YouTube for $0.

YouTube allows you to collect ad revenue fees your music and videos generate. Services like Orfium (orfium.com/youtube-music-content-id -monetization) let you collect these with no up-front fees.

12. Get sound-recording performance royalties for $0.

It's free to join SoundExchange (soundexchange.com) and collect royalties for your U.S. streaming and digital radio play.

13. Get extra income from your fan base by using affiliate sales for $0.

Affiliate sales can give you an extra percentage off every piece of music and merch you sell and can even generate income by linking to products and services in online stores. There are many affiliate programs, and all are free to join.

14. Market your music for $0.

Many marketing techniques are free, and we cover these in a section called "The Top Fourteen $0 Marketing Strategies" (see chapter 14, "Marketing").

15. Get publicity and promote your music for $0.

You can distribute your press releases for free using Mi2N (mi2n.com) and Free Press Release (Free-Press-Release.com). Also, it's free to promote your music, videos, shows, products, and merchandise through social media.

16. Build a team and get help for $0.

You can find people with nearly every type of expertise to help you out for free on sites like Simbi (simbi.com). The experts don't necessarily require you to do something in exchange; instead, Simbi simply asks you to offer your talents to the community and help others.

17. Create a business for $0.

In the U.S., you can start doing business under your own name as a sole proprietorship. This requires no fees or annual licenses, so you can start making money immediately with your music. Also, business tools such as Google Docs (docs.google.com) are free, as are cloud-based accounting solutions such as Wave (waveapps.com) and SlickPie (slickpie .com).

MUSIC BUSINESS FORMATION
UNDERSTANDING WHEN YOU CROSS THE LINE
FROM HOBBY TO BUSINESS

Once you start making money with music, you've begun turning your hobby into a business. The income you make from this is taxable, and it might require you to register as a business, keep records, maintain good accounting books, and more. Most musicians end up doing business as a sole proprietorship. While this is a free option when starting out, as your music business grows, you may want to establish yourself as a legal business entity.

Moving from a hobby to a business gets you two significant benefits:

1. Tax benefits.

A business gets to write off money it spends to operate it; a hobby cannot. This includes deducting every legitimate business expense: your gear and software, your rehearsal and recording space, your fuel costs, hotel costs, meals, and more. Collecting and scanning your receipts is key, and the total amount you spend can offset the money you make, lowering the amount you're actually taxed on at the end of the year.

2. Limited legal liability.

If you structure your business as a separate entity, it might shield you from personal liability. This means you might protect your personal assets. For example, if your music business goes broke or is sued and owes money to other people (producers, distributors, etc.), it's the legal entity that will go bankrupt, not you.

If you want to establish a separate legal entity for your music business, you should also consider working with an accountant, an attorney, and/or a business banker to ensure your finances and the legal implications of your business structure are set up correctly.

WHY YOU SHOULD CREATE AN AGREEMENT FOR YOUR MUSIC BUSINESS

Many artists do business without any formal legal agreement between themselves and their team members. Although you can handle issues, negotiate business deals, and figure out the money situation on a case-by-case basis, this informal approach doesn't protect you from yourselves. For example, if a team or band member leaves, what do they get? Does the band get to continue to do business with the same name? Who owns that trademark?

Once money is involved, it's best to create an agreement to define up front who owns the various rights, who makes the ultimate decisions, and what happens when someone leaves or there's a dispute. Defining these in a written agreement sets everyone's expectations and helps to avoid disputes. Good agreements usually cover things we discuss throughout this book, such as:

- How and when is money paid out to members?

- How are profits, losses, and expenses handled?

- Who determines budgets and how money is spent?

- How are royalties and revenue administered and distributed?

- How are business decisions made and business disputes handled?

- Who's authorized to enter into agreements on behalf of the business?

- What happens when band or team members join or leave?

- Who owns your brand elements, artist or band name, trademarks, and likenesses?

- Who owns the copyrights to your compositions, sound recordings, videos, graphics, and more?

- Who owns the merchandising rights?

- Who owns the equipment and instruments paid for by the business?

The best time to create your agreement is when you get started, since everyone's excited and is probably on the same page. If you do it right, making an agreement shouldn't kill the free-flowing creativity that sparks great music or mess up the relationships that make any business work; it will simply lay out expectations clearly. After all, the best agreements are ones that you never need to use. Work with an attorney to draft the agreement.

HOW TO MAKE SURE YOUR BUSINESS CAN HANDLE MONEY

Once you get your music business under way, you will need to track your income and expenses, take payments, and handle invoicing. Consider the following:

1. Bookkeeping.

Your bookkeeping software will establish a balance sheet for your business; track expenses and income; handle invoicing and accounts receivable; and allow you to report taxes properly each year (with a goal of maximizing your reported expenses and saving you as much off your taxes as possible). You can do this with a spreadsheet and free invoice templates such as using Intuit's free invoice maker (quickbooks.intuit.com/r/free-invoice-template) or templates on Google Docs. But if your business grows, you'll eventually want bookkeeping software like Intuit's Quick-Books (quickbooks.intuit.com/self-employed) or the free cloud-based accounting solution Wave (waveapps.com) and SlickPie (slickpie.com).

2. Banking.

Your banker will help you set up checking, credit card, and savings accounts for your business. This makes it easier to keep your business finances separate from your personal finances, which helps you take deductions at the end of the year. Note that business banking accounts may come with their own fees, so be sure to shop around to find the best deals. Don't forget the ability to take checks, which you might need to be able to do based on the business you handle. Also, make sure you understand the fees for non-sufficient funds charges for bounced checks; if you take a lot of checks, minimizing these fees can be a big factor in your business.

3. Cash payments.

When you take cash sales, such as at a live show, you'll want to handle it properly. Be sure you have change on hand for live events. Also, you'll want to make sure the cash doesn't get commingled with personal funds so you can track your income and expenses. Finally, don't forget to provide a way to make out receipts for cash sales if customers ask for them.

4. Credit card and electronic payments.

If you have a smartphone, you can take payments using solutions like Square (square.com), Intuit's Go Payment (quickbooks.intuit.com

/payments/products/qb-gopayment/), and PayPal (paypal.com). You may also want to be able to take electronic payments using platforms like Zelle (zellepay.com), Apple Pay Cash (support.apple.com/explore /apple-pay-cash), or Venmo (venmo.com).

3

YOUR PERSONA

Goal: To create an authentic and consistent persona that represents your identity to the world, attracts fans, and forms the foundation of your brand.

Team Roles and Responsibilities: Marketer, Graphic Artist, Copywriter, Photographer, Video Producer/Manager, Web Designer/Webmaster, and Manager.

WHAT YOU GET OUT OF THIS
By the end of this chapter, you will:

1. Understand what a persona is and the ten qualities you should build into it.

2. Develop an authentic and well-crafted persona that can be distilled into branding elements that accurately and consistently represent you to the world.

3. Build a brand aligned with your persona, including a logo, colors, fonts, images, and so on to use in all aspects of your music business, including your online presences, products and merchandise, press/booking materials, and more.

4. Create a living chronicle of your background that you can maintain to capture your achievements and continually revise your brand, press/booking materials, online presences, and more.

5. Have three forms of your bio and a succinct music description you'll have at the ready.

6. Know how to get precleared and royalty-free photos, images, and graphics.

7. Have downloadable access to all your brand elements for yourself and your team.

8. Know ten ways to make money from your persona and brand.

MONEY MAP

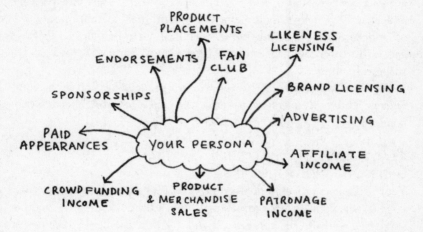

INTRO

Today, the people who have met you or seen you play live are probably a small fraction of the total number of people who have heard your music. The majority are those who discover you through digital means. To these potential fans, you will only be known through your music, name, and the identity you reflect through your website, logos, photos, blogs, videos, social presences, and avatars—that is to say, they will only know you through your persona.

Because of this, whether you like it or not, you have an image to manage. Ideally, you should not even start putting your music out into the world until you've come up with one. Skip this step, and you'll have a haphazard persona you don't control. If you keep changing your persona, it will only confuse people as to who you are and make it harder to attract fans to you and your music. But if you take control and design one, you'll find it easier to lure fans, grow a fan base, and build a community around you. It can also shape how the press and media see you, which makes it easier to get noticed and get the right type of coverage.

Your persona is also a key driver in ways you can make money with music. Ask yourself: Why would anyone buy a T-shirt from a musician? The answer isn't simply to "support them," because if that were true, you could just sell plain white T-shirts with nothing written on them. It's the brand elements of your persona that give your merchandise its value.

But it's not just about merchandise. A well-crafted persona and a growing fan base will open up additional income streams by attracting advertisers, sponsors, endorsement opportunities, affiliate sales, and other licensing opportunities (which we talk about in chapter 11, "Patronage, Crowdfunding, and Raising Money," and chapter 13, "Advanced Income Techniques").

In this chapter, we'll discuss how to design, develop, and refine your persona, and we'll cover how to create the concrete branding elements that convey it.

KEY CONCEPTS
UNDERSTANDING PERSONAS

Your persona is reflected through *expressions* such as your music, your appearance, your imagery, your story, tone, attitude, and more. It could simply be *you* with the volume cranked to "eleven" where you're larger than life, or be a subdued or specialized version of yourself that amplifies certain traits and moods you convey in your music. It could involve a costume like Deadmau5. And your persona doesn't even have to involve people; you could invent fictional animated characters like Gorillaz or the Japanese vocaloid 3-D computer character sensation Hatsune Miku.

The best personas are aligned to the music but aren't limited by music alone. A well-crafted persona encompasses everything you do, including how you appear onstage and offstage, the videos you produce, and the posts you write on your web and social presences. It also contains your brand within it by driving the concepts to distill into your brand elements like a logo and color scheme. Because of this, it drives merch and can even open up more ways to make money, such as charging for appearances, sponsorships, advertising, and more. Your persona can even become more valuable than the music, as the most successful music businesses are often lifestyle brands that expand into clothing lines, perfumes, or other non-music merch products.

Most importantly, people should see themselves reflected within your persona. This can draw people toward you. In fact, the best personas act as lures that attract like-minded fans. After all, the only reason fans would tattoo your logo on their arms is if it resonates with their own identities.

DEFINING YOUR PERSONA
THE TEN QUALITIES EVERY PERSONA SHOULD HAVE

As Andre Calihanna of Disc Makers says, "Your goal should be to wedge yourself into people's consciousness." Because your persona is a representation of your personality, you will want to manage it. To achieve this, use these ten qualities to make your persona effective and memorable:

1. Accuracy.
Your persona should give people a clear sense of what you and your music are about.

2. Impact.
Your persona should convey its message quickly and easily and be memorable. When it comes to words, this usually means brevity. When it comes to graphics, the image should represent you at a glance. When it comes to your appearance onstage or offstage, it should express your concept. The more impactful your logo, tagline, and other elements, the more likely your fans will promote it and purchase branded merchandise.

3. Repetition.
Repetition cements your persona in the mind of each person it meets.

4. Consistency.
Because repetition is the key to strengthening your persona, consistency is critical. Changing elements of your persona on a whim confuses the associations you've built up over time in people's minds. You waste your past persona and branding every time you make dramatic changes.

5. Pervasiveness.

To ensure repetition and consistency, brand everything in your control—your websites, albums, videos, social presences, press kits, posters, and so on.

6. Relatability.

A persona is about how your fans relate to you and how they see themselves in what you put out into the world.

7. Likability.

Your persona should make people like you or what you do. Note that even abrasive personas can be likable, so this doesn't mean you have to be nice.

8. Familiarity.

If your fans find something familiar within your persona to hook on to, you can generate instant connections to your audience.

9. Uniqueness.

A persona that doesn't stand out won't be noticed. There's a reason pictures of David Bowie from decades ago still represent an unmistakable persona.

10. Emotion.

The best personas can evoke feelings, moods, and emotions in others that increase a sense of connection and can create a stronger relationship with your fans.

HOW MAKING A CHRONICLE OF ACHIEVEMENTS CAN HELP YOU DEFINE YOUR PERSONA

To make it easier to talk about yourself as an artist and the music you make to the press and your fans, chronicle your music history and achievements. This will help build your story. Plus, it can provide insights about you and remind you of important parts of your history you may have forgotten. Once you've pulled this together, keep it up to date and use it to form the basis of future press kits, bios, and stories about yourself. We have done this for years and update ours each time we do a major release.

To do this, pull together all the information below about yourself and your musical career to date. The chronicle is not for public release; it's for creating marketing, publicity, booking, and promotional material to weave your story and make it easier to talk about what you've accomplished. Capture the following:

- **Music timeline:** Capture major dates in your music history, such as when you started making music, formed your band, released your albums, published your videos, had major performances, and so on.

- **Discography/list of releases:** Make a discography with every song, album, EP, and single you've released. Also, keep track of the total count of the number of songs you've both written and released.

- **Music videos:** Make a full list of music videos you've released.

- **Creative projects:** List any creative projects or collaborations that have used your music, such as other people's videos, films, podcasts, plays, and so on.

- **Publicity:** List out all the publications, articles, blogs, or other coverage you've gotten for you and your music (which you should be keeping track of as they come out), including any interviews. Also list the total number of outlets that have covered you.

- **Complete show calendar:** List all performances you've done. The total count of all the performances you've ever done shows off your stage experience.

- **Major venues you've played:** List famous venues you've played because it's useful for the story and marketing. For example, our band played live at Second City for a series of sketch comedy shows, and mentioning this fact often gets people interested in finding out more about us.

- **Places you've toured:** List all the countries and cities you've performed in (i.e., I've played in ten different countries . . .).

- **Each famous artist and person you have worked with:** List well-known people you've worked with, since these are always attention-getting in interviews.

- **Awards you've won.**

- **Every organization you belong to:** List music organizations, charities, and relevant associations.

- **Every artist, band, and producer you've worked with:** List all you've worked with, since they are a part of your story and can go on your timeline.

- **Everywhere your music was played:** Catalog radio stations, podcasts, TV, streaming radio, and wherever else your music has been played.

- **Instruments you play and music software you use:** List these to provide material for more technical or industry-facing press and media interviews.

- **Schools/music training programs you went to.**

- **Social media:** List your social media presences along with any notable follower, subscriber, or viewer counts.

One of the values of the chronicle is the number of items in each of the lists to make it easy to tell the world about your background. For example, being able to say you've toured in eighteen different countries, have charted eleven songs, have been interviewed by thirty-seven publications, and have generated over two million views of your videos can get you publicity, bookings, and more. This generates credibility, documents your expertise, and generates interest from press, media, and fans.

THE SIX QUESTIONS YOU CAN ANSWER TO DEVELOP A PERSONA

Whether your persona is an outrageous character or just another version of "you," creating a perception of how you want it to appear fleshes out the persona you are making. Answering these questions below can help you express the persona you want to create:

1. What is your persona's high concept?

A high concept is a one-sentence statement that explains your persona in terms your audience already understands. The producers of the movie

Alien explained it as "*Jaws* in space" to their potential funders. While *Alien* wasn't exactly like *Jaws*, it was accurate enough to get people to immediately understand what the movie would be like in just three words. And the band Gwar's high concept was a thrash metal band merged with *Heavy Metal* magazine–styled science fiction costumes and shows.

2. What clothes, hairstyle, and look does your persona have?

Answering this question helps you determine your style and how you appear. Also, the public tends to engage more with artists who stay in character. For some artists, such as the Residents or the Blue Man Group, remaining in character is an essential feature to evoke the emotions they want to project.

3. What is your persona's story?

The story behind your persona can help drive all your decisions and can help you answer all the questions below. If it's a character, you need to think through the background you want the media to know about him, her, or it. If your persona is just you, you will decide which parts of your personal story and background to emphasize.

4. What does your persona believe in? If you, in your persona, had to finish the following sentence, what would you say? "I/We believe _____."

If you can clearly express *why* you're doing what you're doing, fans will more easily relate to you. This can show fans how to find themselves in your persona if you make this belief statement public. A belief statement doesn't need to be serious, and it can be implied rather than stated outright. Juggalos, for example, just want to let their inner freak out.

5. What emotions do you want people to feel when they experience your persona?

Understanding the emotions you want to evoke helps you in very concrete ways to decide how to interact and which elements you use to represent your persona. For example, if the answer is "relaxed," you wouldn't want to write irate messages on your social media, and your color scheme shouldn't be an angry shade of red.

6. What one-word concept do you want people to think of when they interact with your persona? How do you want fans to describe your persona in one or two words if they were talking about you to their friends?

To test this out, ask a friend the one or two words they think of when they interact with it. You'll know you've succeeded if they answer with the same words.

HOW TO CHOOSE AN ARTIST NAME THAT IS UNIQUE TO YOU

More than anything, your artist or band name will be the number-one way people find and identify you. But choosing a name today is more complicated than it has been in the past. Every artist today is a global, digital musician.

Your name should represent the type of music you play, your energy, and style as performers, but it should also be unique to you so you can track mentions. It must also avoid any confusion with other musicians, products, or services. And since your name is what you'll be doing business under, you want to ensure it doesn't infringe on any existing trademarks or service marks. So if you're just starting out and still picking a name, follow these steps:

1. Check music services like Spotify, Apple Music, and others.

Check the name you'd like to use against Spotify, Apple Music, and other popular music services to see if the name is in use by another artist.

2. Perform a web and social media searches.

Use tools like Namechk (namechk.com) to ensure your name isn't associated with something else. Then check the name in your favorite search engine and other social media. Don't just focus on musicians or bands here, since you'll want to make sure you don't pick a name that can be confused with other company names, entities, or subjects.

3. Check band name databases.

Check the name you'd like to use against a band name source such as Bandname (Bandname.com) to see if someone may already have it. Bandname is free to check (though it charges a fee if you choose to register your name there).

4. Check a domain registrar.

Search on your name with a domain registrar such as Namecheap (namecheap.com) or GoDaddy (godaddy.com) to see if it's available. If it is, reserve it immediately by registering the domain. Note that the service Namechk mentioned above also checks domain names to ensure it's clear, but getting the domain is one of the most important steps in claiming a name that is unique to you.

5. Check your trademark office.

In the United States, you can search the U.S. Patent and Trademark Office (uspto.gov) and use the Trademark Electronic Search System (TESS). Note that not finding your name in use doesn't necessarily mean the name is clear to use, since the name could also be trademarked at the state level, rather than on the national level, or in other databases, since nearly every country maintains their own trademark program.

CREATING YOUR BRANDING ELEMENTS
HOW TO BUILD YOUR BRAND ELEMENTS

Because your persona is abstract, you make it concrete by expressing and distilling it through everything you release—your music, imagery, words, videos, and appearance. This is known as branding, and you'll want it to align with your persona.

Brands open up a lot of moneymaking opportunities and can grow your fan base. Once you have it, you'll be able to quickly create new merchandise, online presences, posts, imagery, posters, and more, as well as answer the press/media or apply for a gig. For example, if you have your logo and fonts ready to go, you could create a new show poster within minutes by grabbing any (legally cleared) image online and putting your logo and the show info on it.

1. Color palette.

Colors convey meaning and emotion, and they can do the same for your persona. A color palette consists of colors that work well with each other used in your logo, imagery, and merchandise. Colors also have an income element; your palette should specify both CMYK and RGB values (preferably Pantone colors) that limit your color choices but allow you to match the colors perfectly between computer screens and mass-manufactured merchandise. It also allows you to quickly create new merch your fans will immediately recognize as yours. If you want to experiment with color palettes, Adobe has a handy tool at color.adobe .com.

2. Logo.

A logo representing your persona should be line art in a vectorized layered file so it can be resized and reused repeatedly. The best logos are great for merch, apparel, and video, look good in both black and white and color, can be recognized from twenty feet away, and look good as a thumbnail image.

3. Mascot.

An optional character that represents your band. Preferably using line art in a vectorized layered file so it can be resized and reused repeatedly.

4. Avatar.

A square profile image that looks good when resized, in both small and large sizes for all your online profiles. Typically, this uses your logo or mascot but occasionally uses a personal picture.

5. Fonts.

Consistent fonts among your logo, website, press material, merchandise, and albums help tie all your materials and merchandise to your brand. The fonts you choose for your brand may not be as simple of a choice as you think. Your online fonts need to be available on every browser, but fonts within graphic images can come from custom sources and can make a real impact. A font is often as distinctive a part of a logo as the imagery. For a list of places to find fonts, see makingmoneywithmusic .com/resources.

6. Writing voice.

Similar to color, the words you choose also have meaning and convey tone, attitude, and emotion. This will affect how you write your bio, press and booking kits, website, and posts on social media. So if you make meditation music, the writing style should reflect it. It's especially important to choose a writing voice if you have multiple team members writing for you.

7. Bios, text, and copy.

You will probably spend more time writing about your music and persona than you do on nearly every other activity around your music. Once you have a voice in mind, you'll need to write bios, social media profiles, taglines, blogs, newsletters, stories, emails, descriptions, and more. We will cover how to create your bio in a section below.

8. Artist photos.

Formal artist photos for press and booking kits should be 8.5″ × 11″ in size. The photos should be in JPEG format at a minimum of three hundred dots per inch (DPI), and you should offer color and black-and-white versions. You may want other sizes for your web presences.

9. Brand style guide (optional).

Marketers generally create a brand style guide or brand bible that maps out the rules to apply to all graphics, fonts, text, and more so they're consistent across everything a business does. Style guides often lay out what *not* to do. It will contain the elements above such as the color palette and writing style. It becomes more important to make one once you work with graphic artists, web developers, or other professionals.

Although you may be tempted to create brand elements as you go along, you'll likely find waiting will slow you down and create inconsistencies. For instance, if you don't have your one-sentence bio and avatar created ahead of time, you may find yourself stuck coming up with a description for a social media profile on the fly or unable to upload an image that represents you. Worse, you may throw something up there that doesn't match your other presences. Avoid this by taking some time in advance to build out your brand elements.

WORKING WITH IMAGES, GRAPHICS, AND PHOTOS

There are a surprising number of graphic arts concepts you will need to become familiar with when you run a music business. If you don't have a basic knowledge of image formats and color formats, you may end up with files you can't use or rendered images that can't easily be modified, similar to getting the equivalent of an MP3 file when you really want the source tracks.

If you'd like to gain a further background in graphic arts concepts such as layered or flattened; vectored or rasterized; the difference between RGB and CMYK; Pantone; the rule of thirds; and more, see Making MoneyWithMusic.com/resources for a free detailed guide.

HOW TO FIND PRECLEARED AND ROYALTY-FREE PHOTOS, IMAGES, AND GRAPHICS TO USE

Unless you create everything from scratch, you'll probably be looking for photos, images, clip art, and other graphics to use to start building out the elements of your persona. The web may be filled with photos and artwork, but most of them are not copyright-free. If you want to make money with music and run a business, then you'll need to use artwork in the public domain, that is issued under a Creative Commons license allowing commercial use, or comes from services that produce royalty-free artwork and cost a onetime fee. To find precleared photos and artwork, do the following:

1. Check out free sources.

There are many free sources for photos, images, and graphics. Public domain images are always free to use, or seek out sites like Unsplash (unsplash.com) or Pexels (pexels.com) that allow royalty-free use of their images at no cost. There's also a great deal of material licensed under Creative Commons (CC) licenses that allow commercial use, while others require you to go back to the creator to get permission for the rights (so you need to check the license carefully). To find this, check out the Creative Commons Search page (search.creativecommons.org) and choose "use for commercial purposes" for a powerful search engine across a huge number of services to find images to use. Additionally, works created by the U.S. government, regardless where in the world you live, fall instantly into the public domain. As a result, any images created by NASA (nasa.gov) or other U.S. governmental bodies are available for you to use without permission. For more sites and resources, see MakingMoney WithMusic.com/resources.

2. Use content from image sites and services.

There are many services like iStockPhoto (istockphoto.com), Getty Images (gettyimages.com), and ClipArt.com (clipart.com/en) that will charge a onetime fee for the use of their images. For more sites and resources, see MakingMoneyWithMusic.com/resources.

3. Verify the terms.

Be sure to read the agreements carefully before downloading, buying, or using any images, photos, or graphics. The important thing about these services is that they come with a license allowing you to incorporate the image into your persona elements. You don't want to pay a royalty for every T-shirt you create with the image, for instance.

HOW TO CLEAR PHOTOS, IMAGES, AND GRAPHICS OWNED BY OTHERS SO YOU CAN USE THEM

If you fall in love with a photo, image, or graphic that is "all rights reserved," you can still clear it. The only step here is to contact the owner and ask. For instance, we found the perfect photo of sheep grazing in a field in New Zealand on Flickr we wanted for our first album. Since we needed permission, we contacted the photographer and explained we would like to use it for the back of our album and the number of copies we were going to make. While he could have charged us a fee to license his photo, he instead asked only for attribution on the album, which we were happy to provide. But be prepared to pay a fee to license the image if you reach out to a photographer.

HOW TO HIRE VIDEO PRODUCERS, PHOTOGRAPHERS, AND GRAPHIC ARTISTS AND OWN THE COPYRIGHT

When you decide to hire photographers, designers, graphic artists, video producers, or anyone else to do creative work for you, you'll want to use the right contracts and make sure you own the copyright when their work is complete. If you don't, and the photographer owns the photos afterward, every use you make of it might require another license from them. It gets even worse if you hire a graphic artist to create a logo and you don't even own your own logo!

Creative professionals you deal with often understand these provisions and will sometimes ask for an extra fee if you impose one on them (which is of course negotiable). Because of this, when you hire professionals, use the following steps:

1. Find a video producer, photographer, or graphic artist.
The best way to find these professionals is by referral. Photographers are often findable via other artists in your town. Because graphic artists can work remotely over the internet, consider using freelance sites like Upwork (upwork.com) or crowdsourcing sites like Crowdspring (crowd spring.com) or 99designs (99designs.com); or find artists you like at sites like DeviantArt (deviantart.com) and see if the artist does free-lance work.

2. Work-for-hire contracts.
Contractors who work for you must accept a work-for-hire contract for all the important image files you make for your business. This ensures you'll own the copyright of the work. Additionally, for photographers, you should make sure you get the full-resolution files from their camera. For graphic artists, make it clear you will get the vectorized, layered files (AI, PSD, or TIFF) as well as the final rendered versions. This allows you to take the files to other graphic artists to work with.

3. Include an optional clause that gives them attribution if they ask for it.
Attribution isn't always offered and depends on the type of work. For example, a photographer might want credit, but graphic artists may not require it.

Copyright ownership still applies even if you have a friend of yours take pictures for free or make some graphics for you. Whether you pay them or not doesn't matter; you'll still want to apply a work-for-hire for any work done for you. That said, sometimes a simple email with work-for-hire language they agree to in the thread can be enough to protect you.

HOW TO WRITE A COMPELLING MUSIC DESCRIPTION SO PEOPLE CHECK OUT YOUR MUSIC

You will need an accurate description of your music that grabs people and makes them want to check it out. One way is to use well-known artists that influenced you or are related to your music. Here's how to write a compelling description:

1. Compare yourself to three well-known artists.

Comparing yourself to well-known artists allows you to leverage their marketing efforts. When people search for those artists, your music might come up as a recommendation. Even better, the people who like the other artists will be just the sort of people who are most likely to become new fans of your music.

2. Make a description of your own.

This should emphasize your style, genre, and instrumentation. It should also be short. Ariel Hyatt, the founder of Cyber PR (cyberprmusic.com) told us her favorite description was from the bluegrass, rock, country, blues, jazz, and Cajun/zydeco band Leftover Salmon, who said they played "polyethnic Cajun slamgrass." It was accurate, summed up their energetic live show, and said everything in three words.

3. Use achievements and accolades.

If you've got an achievement such as receiving an award, getting some news coverage, playing at a famous venue, or charting, add it to the story. For example, we've successfully used: "We are a horn-based geek rock band that released a song each day for a year—365 songs." Also, you might have a few one-sentence alternatives aimed at a particular audience, including people you want to do business with. For a potential licensee, we say: "We've licensed music to Disney and Viacom, and written soundtracks to TV shows."

THE THREE FORMS OF YOUR BIO EVERY MUSICIAN SHOULD HAVE HANDY

You need an interesting and compelling way to introduce you and your music. This is usually done in a bio and is used in your press and booking kits as well as on your website. You should always have three versions of your bio ready to go:

1. A one-page bio.

The one-page bio should cover how you started, the music you play, what you're doing, and any accomplishments. It's best to write it in the third person because they are often copied and pasted into press coverage. The structure of a good one-page bio includes a first paragraph that has a description of who you are, your music description, and a story hook to keep them reading. In the body of the bio, use quotes from either the artist members or press clippings for more impact, and end it with contact info and links to find out more.

2. A one-paragraph bio.

This is a short bio that describes you and your music succinctly. You'll want to incorporate your music description within the first or second sentence. The purpose of this bio is to use it as an aid for the press and other websites so they can borrow from it to describe you to their audience in a quick way. It's also good for those websites, social networks, and web presences that provide a profile page with a character limit.

For example, our one-paragraph bio for Beatnik Turtle is: *Formed in 1997, Beatnik Turtle is a horn-powered geek rock band that's released over 500 songs spanning 20 albums, licensed music to Disney and Viacom, and has also written music for TV, films, and theater including at Chicago's Second City. In 2007, they released a song every single day of the year from their website TheSongOfTheDay.com.*

3. A one-sentence bio or elevator pitch.

This is a sentence or two that describes you and your music to someone within twenty seconds or less. It's usually used when you meet someone who asks you about your music. For example, our elevator pitch for Beatnik Turtle is, "We're horn-powered geek rock in the tradition of They Might Be Giants who has released 20 albums." The most common response we get is: "Wait, *twenty albums?*" which gives us a great opening to talk about our TheSongOfTheDay.com project and what we're working on lately. At that point, they're hooked, and we have them wanting to find out more.

If you need assistance in writing your bio, there are a variety of bio-writing services and writers who you can hire from sites such as Upwork (upwork.com) and Fiverr (fiverr.com), or services like Cyber PR (cyberprmusic.com/product/bio-writing). For more information about this, see MakingMoneyWithMusic.com/resources.

HOW TO ENSURE YOUR PERSONA ELEMENTS
ARE EASILY ACCESSIBLE

You'll want to have all your elements ready to go, since you'll be using these often. By having your bio, music descriptions, images, photos, and other brand elements accessible in the cloud, you'll save yourself time when you need to access them.

Google Docs is a perfect place for all your written brand materials—bios, press releases, testimonials, and other text. It also has a way to upload and share files. Dropbox (dropbox.com), Box (box.com), Evernote (evernote.com), and OneDrive (onedrive.com) are good services that provide storage and sharing for any type of file.

Make sure to store the final versions of images as well as the raw data files. Don't just have the JPG and GIF files handy. Keep the source files accessible so you can work with clothing and merchandise manufacturers or graphic artists when you need something changed quickly.

4

YOUR TEAM

Goal: To build and maintain a team of people and services that can help you succeed so you can focus on the music and build a profitable music business.

Team Roles and Responsibilities: Manager

WHAT YOU GET OUT OF THIS

By the end of this chapter, you will:

1. Have a framework outlining the roles and high-level activities required to manage your music business.

2. Build your own team and know how to keep them engaged and involved over time.

3. Understand how to delegate.

4. Understand networking techniques.

INTRO

Today, many tools, websites, and services automatically handle many of the tasks that used to require entire music label departments. This has enabled numerous successful DIY musicians to run music businesses with a minimal number of people. But even though they create the illusion they're doing it all themselves, most actually have a team behind them. Independent doesn't mean they're going solo; it means they have retained the rights to their music.

In fact, doing it yourself *doesn't* mean doing it *alone*.

The success of the business side of your music can depend entirely on your team and the network you build around it. Because of this, one of the most important skills musicians can develop is the ability to delegate so they can focus on the music and networking to grow their reach, business partners, and fan base.

You've heard the saying before: "It's not *what* you know, it's *who* you know." Or, as one of our friends puts it, "It's who you get to know" through networking. This is as true in music as it is in any other field. At the end of the day, despite all the advances in technology that have empowered the artist, it's not technology that will get your music discovered or making money, it's the people behind you.

KEY CONCEPTS
THE IMPORTANCE OF DOING ONE THING AT A TIME

There is a lot to juggle: music distribution, social media, merch, live shows, crowdfunding, music licensing, and more. And of course, you need to make the music in the first place.

You shouldn't—and can't—try to do it all at once. As a band with over twenty albums, multiple license deals, numerous gigs, press/media coverage, and a 365 song-of-the-day project, our advice is simple: *take it one step at a time.*

Your success will come from prioritizing what you work on so you can succeed. In fact, the most successful musicians we've interviewed are smart about what they choose to take on, and they do *not* do it all on their own. They do the following instead:

- **Make good decisions about what *not* to do.**
  Choose to focus on the critical tasks that are most likely to help you succeed, and skip the rest. For instance, you become more effective at prioritization when you base your decisions on a release plan, which structures what activities you need to do at what time (see chapter 18, "Your Release Strategy," for details).

- **Offload work to external services.**
Successful artists rely on external services, sites, and other digital tools to handle or speed up the work.

- **Build a team to help with the work.**
Not all tasks can or should be outsourced. You'll want to create a team to take on some of the work.

This is how most artists, including our own band, operate. For example, one member handled being our publicist, photographer, and graphic artist, while another managed our websites and social presences, and yet another took on booking and publishing. When we weren't playing live, we focused on music production, getting exposure, publicity, and media attention. Then, when it came to creating videos, only a handful of our band members were needed, and we'd share or trade off responsibilities (we all were camera people, for instance). And where we couldn't handle the activity, we would hire professionals, leverage services, or use web-based contractors to fill in the blanks, especially when the task could generate more money than it cost.

Successful teams are not built quickly. Some musicians who appear to be "overnight successes" took many years and a team of people behind the scenes to make it happen. But if you're smart about what tasks really need to get done and find ways to handle them, you'll be able to make money with music, build your fan base, and succeed faster in today's digital music industry.

THE THIRTY-FOUR MUSIC BUSINESS ROLES EVERY MUSICIAN NEEDS TO KNOW ABOUT

One way to think of your music business is to break it down into the roles you would normally hire if you were running a label. If you hired a full team, each role below represents the experts you'd call into the room to get their input and the necessary business or music activities completed.

Although this list contains the top thirty-four roles, don't be alarmed—it doesn't mean you need thirty-four people! The list below is grouped by categories, since it provides a convenient way to help you delegate a related group of role activities to a service or member of your team. Breaking it out in this way gives everyone a clearer idea of what they're taking on. Here are the categories and roles:

1. Music business.

• Manager: the person who oversees, coordinates, and manages the general business of the artist and the roles below and covers any gaps in the team.

• Attorney: the person who handles contracts and other legal issues.

• Accountant/bookkeeper: the person who keeps the financial books, does accounting for the artist, and understands royalties, licensing, and so on.

• Business banker: your bank's representative who sets up a separate account for managing your business's money and assists with credit and loans.

• Publisher: the person who shares ownership in the songwriter's composition, handles the registrations and administration (including the collection of money earned), and is tasked with exploiting the songwriter's song catalog to generate more royalties and licensing income, such as working with music supervisors and finding other licensing opportunities.

2. Music creation, recording, and production.

• Songwriters: the person or people who write(s) the music.

• Musicians: the person or people who perform(s) or records the music, which may include the songwriter(s).

• Recording producer: the person who produces the studio sessions and decides upon the sound, feel, and arrangements.

• Recording engineers: the people who handle the recording and mixing process in the studio.

• Mastering engineer: the person who masters the final mixes for distribution and release.

3. Live show production.

• Booking agent: the person who books the artist and negotiates with venues.

- Live event/tour manager: the person who schedules and manages your tours, arranges transportation and lodging, and manages venue expectations, the stage, and day-to-day live-event activities.

- Live-event promoter: the person who promotes the live event and gets people to come to the event.

- Live music producer: the person who produces the live show and rehearsal strategies and works with the artist and musicians on creating song arrangements for the stage.

- Store clerk: the people who sell your merchandise to fans at shows.

- Live sound engineer(s): the person or people who run(s) the sound at live shows.

- Lighting engineer(s): the person or people who run(s) the lights at live shows.

- Roadies: the people who help carry your gear to and from the stage.

4. Content creation and assets.

- Graphic artist: the person who creates the imagery and graphics.

- Copywriter: the person who writes copy for the artist's press kits, booking kits, bios, websites, liner notes, and more.

- Photographer: the person who takes pictures of the artist for press/media, album, EP, or single art, and more.

5. Product, merchandise, and distribution.

- Distributor: the person who distributes the music and videos to digital stores, streaming services, physical stores, and more.

- Product and merchandise manager: the person who is responsible for designing, creating, distributing, and selling the artist's products and merchandise.

6. Promotion, publicity, and getting heard and seen.

• Marketer: the person who is responsible for designing and managing the artist's persona and brand, coming up with marketing opportunities, and running marketing and advertising campaigns.

• Publicist: the person who works with the press/media and arranges interviews.

• Promoter: the person who gets the artist's music and videos played, heard, and seen.

• Web designer/webmaster: the person who creates and manages the artist's web, social, and mobile presences and promotional channels.

• Social media manager: the person who manages an artist's social media presences, posts updates, and maintains a consistent voice aligned to your persona.

7. Video production.

• Video producer: the person who produces all video content, manages the video production team and talent, and plans location shoots.

• Director: the person with the vision for the video and who directs the talent and crew.

• Editor and postproduction specialist: the person or people who sequence(s) the recorded video output, add(s) effects and color correction, and create(s) the final cut of the video aligned to the director's vision and input.

• Camera person and microphone operators.

• Crew: the people who assist the other video production roles in bringing the video to life.

• Actors and extras: other talent in the video production beyond the artist or musicians.

If you had to pick one of the thirty-four roles to fill, we'd suggest the manager role. This is because the manager's role is to ensure all the tasks get done, not simply the music business activities. Having a great manager you can trust has the added bonus of allowing you to focus on the music.

HOW TO BUILD AND MANAGE A TEAM AS A MUSICIAN
HOW TO FIND PEOPLE WITH THE SKILLS, TALENTS, AND NETWORKS YOU NEED

Fortunately, there are many options in finding the necessary skill sets or help in generating opportunities or exposure for your music. Consider the following:

1. Contact people within your reach.

When you're just starting out, your family and friends will usually be the first place to look for the skills and help you need. Don't be hesitant to ask for their assistance.

2. Network with people just outside of your reach.

Often the people who might help you are one degree away from who you already know.

3. Hire who you need through contracting sites or post a "Help Wanted" ad.

If you have the funds, sites such as Upwork (upwork.com), Fiverr (fiverr .com), and TaskRabbit (taskrabbit.com) specialize in connecting people in need of help with those who have the skills and experience you need. You can also post a "Help Wanted" ad on sites such as Craigslist (craigslist.org) for free. For tasks that can be done remotely, this approach can be very inexpensive, since talented people all over the world participate at these sites. We've consulted musicians who ran their entire music business by contracting for the skills they needed just through these sites alone.

4. Use directories or contact databases.

You can tap organizations that make lists of music business professionals, usually for a fee. Services like Music Registry (musicregistry .com), Songwriter 101 (songwriter101.com), and AllAccess (allaccess .com) can give you lists of people within each area of the music industry.

5. Barter for what you need.

Similar to contracting sites, services like Simbi (simbi.com) connect you with people with skills and experience, but rather than charge a fee, you trade services. All community members offer up their skills and then either exchange services directly one on one or use internal goodwill credits, known as *"simbi,"* to compensate one another. Since you don't need money to pay for anyone's services, this is low-cost, requiring only your time and effort.

HOW TO DELEGATE WORK TO OTHERS

Whether you're paying someone for certain services or you have someone—a family member, friend, band member, or fan—volunteering their time, there are three critical steps to follow to ensure you delegate the work and role correctly and set whoever is helping you up for success.

1. Be hyper-detailed about the steps.

Write out all the steps of the task or role so anyone you hand it to understands what to do. The more detailed the recipe, the more likely it'll get done correctly, and the more likely you can hand it to someone else if that person doesn't work out.

2. Check in often to see how they're doing.

Rather than wait for them to come back to you whenever they finish the work, at the beginning you should set up checkpoints along the way to ensure the person is on the right track. Plus, it'll give you a chance to make sure your instructions are clear and actionable. If anything is off, you can course correct quickly without frustrating the person helping you.

3. Assume some people will flake.

Successful delegation assumes some people won't succeed. Derek Sivers suggests having multiple people work on a task. For example, more than one person can book or work on a get-heard campaign. Just make sure they coordinate so they don't get in one another's way.

Delegation can be difficult because it's hard to trust others to get tasks done at first, and it's also a skill that takes time to develop. It's a good idea to begin delegating early in your career, even if it's only small tasks to friends of yours. This will make you more comfortable when you need to delegate bigger parts of your business when you achieve a higher level of success and can no longer tackle everything yourself.

HOW TO LET SOMEONE GO WHEN THEY'RE NOT WORKING OUT

Letting someone go is never an easy task; it caused our own band the most drama out of anything we handled. But while we worked hard to keep everyone together, we found our band always thrived after bringing in new people. It was better for the musicians who left, because their creative directions didn't match and they were able to work on other projects rather than staying with something that no longer worked for them.

This isn't just true for musicians; it's also true for your team. Producer Wally Lockhard III, who founded Urban Grind TV (urbangrindtv.com) and also runs a recording studio, always sets clear expectations for every job and makes sure people commit to it as he hires them in. After telling them what they need to do, Lockhard tells them, "The day you can't fill it, just tell me and I will find someone else. It's nothing on you. But I will hold you to it if you promise to fill it."

Still, delivering the news and dropping someone from your team is not easy. We suggest the following when you let someone go:

1. Make a clear decision and then let them go.

Phasing someone out slowly often doesn't work for either party. The most respectful thing to do is to cut the cord once you've decided. If you keep them in the role, it stops you from looking for other musicians or team members and stops them from finding something new.

2. Don't burn bridges.

You never know if you'll need to work together again. In fact, you should make the experience as positive as possible and see if you can keep the connection that might work out again in the future.

3. Follow your agreement (if you have one).

Dealing with separations is the primary reason for the band agreements we discussed in chapter 2, "Your Music Business." If you've built one, follow what it says, and it will make it easier for you to split.

THE FOUR EFFECTIVE WAYS TO ATTRACT PEOPLE TO YOUR TEAM AND KEEP THEM INVOLVED

One of the best ways to succeed in keeping everyone on your team or within your network invested in your goals and projects is when they know they're contributing to something they care about. This means making them feel valued and giving them credit for their work, both privately and publicly. Our band kept a consistent team for years by following the methods below, all of which are free.

1. Give credit by putting their name in lights.

Just like at the end of any movie, you need credits on everything you release. When people help you, thank and credit them publicly by doing any of the following:

- Mention them in your blog posts.

- Give a shout-out on social media.

- Link to their website or personal social media.

- Add them to any liner notes, video descriptions, your website, or on services where you register credit information as discussed in chapter 5, "Your Music."

2. Celebrate and acknowledge successes.

Theater groups throw a cast party at the close of every run. You should do this too whenever you reach a milestone, such as completing a tour, releasing an album, or celebrating a big achievement. We also found the celebration was the perfect opportunity to talk about the next project we needed their help on, since they were already excited about what we had just accomplished as a team. Whether you throw a celebration or not, be sure to send a thank-you email to everyone involved and acknowledge each person's part in the success.

3. Promote the work of any creatives who help you.

If any of your team members are creatives, offer to introduce their work to your fan base. Creatives are more likely to work with you if they know they'll get exposure in helping you out. You can promote their work through your sites and social media or collaborate on a project. For example, we offered to be the house band for a sketch comedy group, the Dolphins of Damnation. In turn, they got a time slot at Chicago's Second City because they were able to say they had a live band with an established fan base. Together, we got to play in front of an audience made up of both our fans and theirs as well as anyone else who came to Second City to see a sketch comedy show.

4. Help others with something they need.

Another way to show appreciation for someone's help and to continue to keep them involved in what you're doing is to simply help them with something *they* need. It doesn't even have to be with music. For instance, as successful indie musician and podcaster George Hrab (georgehrab .com) noted, he has helped people who helped him by cleaning their garages, painting their houses, or helping them move. By taking time out of his schedule to help those who helped him, George showed how much he valued their help on his music and career and deepened the trust and relationship between them.

NETWORKING STRATEGIES AND TECHNIQUES
THE TOP THREE REASONS WHY YOU NEED
TO GROW YOUR NETWORK

Nobody is born already knowing all the people who can help them achieve their goals. You need to build your network. This takes time, energy, social skills, and, yes, some courage at times, but the benefits far outweigh the costs. Here are three reasons why you always want to be expanding the people within your network. Note that people you meet might be able to help in multiple ways:

1. Filling team roles or providing specific help and skills.

As discussed above, to succeed at music today, you can't do it all yourself. Getting to know capable people who can help you fill the roles listed above will allow you to focus more time on your music and those activities you're best at.

2. Generating exposure for your music.

The more people who hear your music and learn about you, the more likely you'll be exposed to people who enjoy your type and style of music. This will grow your fan base and generate even more opportunities and publicity. All of this will boost how much money you can make.

3. Generating revenue for your music.

Building your music business requires growing your business contacts to generate additional income opportunities for you and your music beyond music sales, streaming, and merchandise. Some musicians get by working with just a few key businesses that keep them working throughout the year, but it helps to have a large network of connections in booking and venues, other industries including film and theater, and even government and nonprofits.

Of course, with #2 and #3 above, those people with access to the largest audiences or money-generating opportunities can be harder to connect with at first, but as you grow your fan base, accomplishments, and networking skills, it should get easier to reach up to them.

THE TWO SECRETS TO NETWORKING

The first secret of networking is: *it shouldn't start with strangers.* The people you already know within your arm's reach might know those people with the skills or connections you're looking for if you just talk to them about the help you're seeking. If they know someone who can help, they can introduce you to the person, which makes conversation much easier.

Still, there comes a time when this can run cold and you need to strike out on your own. The second secret is: *networking is about asking how you can help the person you hope will help you.* As George Hrab put it, the secret to getting other people to help you is "to find talented people and be really, really, really nice to them." People instinctively want to help those who help them—especially if you ask soon after helping. This simple technique is covered in the book *Influence: The Psychology of Persuasion* by Robert B. Cialdini, and it has benefited our band on many occasions.

For example, we did this when promoting *The Cheapass Album*, an album of songs based on game titles from the trendy board-game manufacturer called Cheapass Games. At the time of the release back in 2004, we discovered a niche podcast created by the people behind BoardGameGeek .com (a website generating over 2.5 million unique visitors a month). We wanted to get our band and our album about games featured on their podcast and website, but wondered how to do it when we didn't know the owners of the website. We did some research on the site and realized the podcast lacked its own theme song. That night, we emailed them and offered to create one for them. They were flattered and agreed to hear what we could come up with. We quickly wrote one and sent them the demo, and they immediately adopted it for their podcast. As we had hoped, they talked about us in many episodes, which kept our name, our music, and our website in front of their listeners. We kept in contact with them and later took it a step further by creating more music, helping them with voice-over bumpers, and eventually created some off-the-wall public-service announcements. Their podcasts have been downloaded thousands of times, and they continue to be downloaded years later by new visitors.

If you already know the name(s) of the person or people you hope can help you, do a web search to get their background and what they're working on. Their social media alone could give you an up-to-the-minute insight into what's on their minds. This gives you a natural topic to start a conversation about, ideas on how you can help them, and provides you with angles on how you can work together, collaborate, or do business.

THE TOP SIX EFFECTIVE NETWORKING TECHNIQUES FOR MUSICIANS

To help you become an effective networker, here are six ways to network naturally and connect with others to help you and your music.

1. Share your vision and what you're trying to achieve as an artist.

People generally like being a part of something bigger than themselves. For instance, we pulled in a lot of talented people to help us with our TheSongOfTheDay.com project simply by talking about our audacious goal of releasing one song for every day of the year. Once they knew what we were attempting, they wanted to be a part of it. To this day, everyone who participated in the project and helped to make it a success still talks about what we achieved together. It's also a fantastic technique to use to build support and pledges for patronage or crowdfunding, which we'll discuss in chapter 11, "Patronage, Crowdfunding, and Raising Money."

2. Make any problems you're facing known so others can offer help.

People love to solve problems. If you share the challenges you're facing, you're more likely to get help from others. For example, when we were putting together the artwork for our second album, *Santa Doesn't Like You*, we lacked the software and know-how to get it in the format that the CD printing house required. We were stuck. Luckily, we started talking about our problem at a party where one of the guests overheard us. She revealed she was a graphic artist and had the software to create the files we needed. We didn't know her and had no idea she could do this; she was just someone we saw in our apartment building on occasion. All she asked for in return was to get a credit in the liner notes so she could use it as part of her portfolio. We were happy to do that and, thanks to her, got the album art done in time.

When we wanted to make a music video but lacked the equipment, we asked around. Soon, we not only had the equipment, we had friends willing to direct and act. When we talked about how hard it was to get booked, a friend said they could get us booked at a college outdoor festival. And when we were trying to figure out how best to get press for our TheSongOfTheDay.com project, a friend who overheard us said he'd mention it to one of his buddies who wrote for a popular Chicago blog at the time called *Gaper's Block* (gapersblock.com). We ended up with coverage.

3. Get an introduction to someone you want to meet from a connector within your network.

If you want to meet someone you don't have a connection to yet, try your network to see who might already know them. Finding a mutual connection who can introduce you makes everything easier. The business social site LinkedIn (LinkedIn.com) is built around this technique. "Can you introduce me?" is one of the most powerful phrases in networking.

For an example of how powerful this technique can be, our own band ended up using it to get booked for the Chicago leg of the International Pop Overthrow (InternationalPopOverthrow.com) festival, a roving festival showcasing power pop rock bands. We went the traditional route of sending in our music and press kit but never heard back. Months later, when the festival came to town, we discovered our friend Yvonne Doll of the band the Locals (LocalsRock.com) managed to get booked. When we told her we were hoping to be a part of the festival but never heard back, she arranged to have us meet David Bash, the festival organizer, after her set. David asked for our music, and the very next day, he contacted us to fill in for a last-minute cancellation. We jumped at the chance, had a great show, and thanked Yvonne for the introduction. We ended up playing the festival for many years after that, and David included our music on IPO compilation albums.

4. Ask around; use your social networks to ask who other people may know.

You never know who the people you already know are connected to unless you ask, and this includes your fans. Social media makes it even easier to ask your connections if they know a particular person or type of contact. For example, you can ask whether anyone knows any music supervisors or if they know anyone at a particular booking agency. This pairs up very well with making your goals known and getting introductions as noted above. You never know what skills your fans, followers, or connections may have, the opportunities they might be able create, or whether they're connected to other people who can generate significant exposure or revenue opportunities.

5. Call ahead: find someone who succeeded in what you want to do and ask how they did it.

Most people like talking about themselves, but they're even more flattered when they're recognized for achieving something difficult and asked how they did it. Plus, many are willing to mentor or share their knowledge if you simply reach out and ask them. Learning how they succeeded at something can help you save time by showing the way and the mistakes to avoid. For example, if you want to get into licensing your music for film or TV, finding another musician who licensed their music could provide huge clues as to what to do (and not to do). And while you have that person talking, you can ask them who else they know you should meet (and can introduce you to). They might be able connect you with the very people you need to know to succeed.

6. Network where you're the only musician so you stand out.

Most musicians only think to attend and network at music conferences and events, but you should also look for events where you're the only musician. That way you stand out (which is also a powerful marketing technique we discuss in depth in chapter 14, "Marketing"). For example, we've attended DragonCon (DragonCon.org), where podcasters, bloggers, filmmakers, and other creative people hang out—but usually not musicians. Most of these people need music, and since we were the only musicians attending the event, we generated many new opportunities and collaboration projects, which in turn expanded our exposure to new audiences and grew our fan base.

HOW TO NETWORK WITH MUSICIANS AND THE MUSIC INDUSTRY

Today's music industry is filled with more musicians who are doing it themselves. The support, advice, and knowledge sharing between musicians can help you get your next gig or open up new revenue-generating opportunities. Use these options to connect with musicians and others in the music business:

1. Connect with musicians online.

Visit Subreddits such as "We Are the Music Makers" (reddit.com/r/WeAreTheMusicMakers) and "Musicians" (reddit.com/r/musicians) or community sites like Just Plain Folks (jpfolks.com) to connect with other musicians online. But there are tons of options, so check out MakingMoneyWithMusic.com/resources for more.

2. Look for local musicians' hangouts.

It seems every town has a musician's' hangout, depending on the style of music. In our hometown of Chicago, we've made a ton of connections through the Old Town School of Folk Music (oldtownschool.org), which has classes on every genre of music (not just folk) and is a great hub for Chicago musicians, as well as the Bloom School of Jazz (BloomSchoolOfJazz.com). Same with Fort Knox Studios (fortknoxstudios.com), which has tons of rehearsal spaces and studios and acts as a hub for the Chicago music community. Your town may have similar hubs, so be sure to go there in person and connect with your local musicians.

3. Network at conferences.

There's a wealth of conferences where musicians network and get the latest information about this new music business or the latest gear. Within the U.S., conferences like South by Southwest (sxsw.com), NAMM (namm.org), and the Future of Music Coalition Summit (futureofmusic.org) bring musicians together. In Europe, there are just as many conferences, such as Midem (midem.com). Head to MakingMoneyWithMusic.com/resources for links to conferences of all kinds.

4. Consider joining musician unions.

We talk about music unions in the conclusion of the book, but they're worth mentioning here because they also provide great opportunities to connect. Some of the larger ones include AFM (afm.org/en), and SAG-AFTRA (sagaftra.org).

5. Check out the Recording Academy.

The Recording Academy (grammy.com) does far more than run the GRAMMY Awards; they also provide educational sessions and seminars, and not all of them are members-only. We've run many workshops for Academy chapters across the country, where they've created their own educational series, flying in speakers to discuss music topics. Besides this, they also bring in well-known producers, musicians, and engineers for panels where they discuss their experiences in the music business and their techniques.

6. Join local music organizations.

You should explore the music organizations in your area by searching for them on the web and see what they have to offer, as many of them have information as well as connections to the resources you may need. One of the notable ones we ran across is Musicians for Musicians (MFM) (musiciansformusicians.org) in New York, which we joined immediately once we learned they focused on helping musicians make money.

7. Explore music business incubators.

Search for music business incubators in your area or even remotely. We're members of 2112 in Chicago (2112inc.com), where we speak regularly and have an office. We've helped many businesses with free consulting, mentoring, and advice since we're members there. They also host talks that help musicians as well as businesses and have become a networking hub. They do accept remote members and have offices in Nashville, with plans to spread to other music cities. Explore the ones in your own city, and if you're in Chicago, feel free to reach out to us through 2112 to work with us as a mentor for your music business.

HOW TO STAY IN TOUCH WITH YOUR CONNECTIONS

Making a connection is a great start to your relationship, but it's only the beginning. You should stay in touch with people once you've brought them into your network. Mark Shiozaki has played many different roles in the music business, including engineering, DJing, producing, and more. He keeps a large database of connections that deliver him new business opportunities all the time. He suggests the following:

1. Keep a contact database and mark down all the important details.

Shiozaki uses an online database to keep track of his connections. He tracks who they are, what skills and connections they have, what they've done for him, and, most importantly, what he's done for *them*. If he sees they've done more for him, he works to repay the favors.

2. Reach out at least every six months (and talk on the phone or in person).

According to Shiozaki, emails don't count to keep you top of mind, and he schedules fifteen-minute calls with all his connections every six months just to see how they're doing and what they're working on to keep the connection warm. He usually schedules the calls while he's driving because it's easy to connect. This is especially important for people with a higher stature in the music business because they won't remember who you are if you're not connecting on a regular basis.

3. Ask them what they're working on and see if you can help.

When you talk to your contacts, ask them what they're working on so you can catch up. Also, see if you can help them with anything they're doing. This will make it easier if you want to ask them to do something for you in the future.

5

YOUR MUSIC

Goal: To create, record, and prepare your music for release ready for streaming, sales, royalties, licensing, and promotion.

Team Roles and Responsibilities: Songwriter(s), Musicians, Recording Producer, Recording Engineers, Mastering Engineer, Sound Recording Manager, and Manager

WHAT YOU GET OUT OF THIS
By the end of this chapter, you will:

1. Generate and record music so you can consistently release music throughout the year, drive engagement, and make more money from music.

2. Have high-quality, well-mixed, and mastered tracks ready for distribution and release and ready to be licensed for TV, film, advertising, and trailers.

3. Have properly tagged tracks with metadata to ensure any person listening to it knows who created it and where to find you so you can turn downloaders into fans.

4. Create documentation crediting everyone who helped with creating your music to avoid disputes, document ownership in songs and sound recordings, and for use in distribution, promotion, building credibility, and everyone's music résumé and chronicle.

MONEY MAP

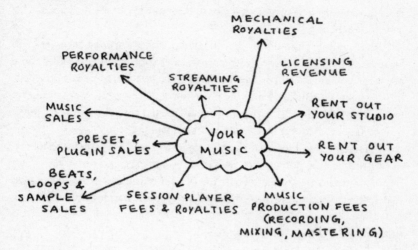

INTRO

Every musical idea or expression you have inside you can be brought to life today thanks to recording technology. Whatever you can dream up, you can record. Professional studio time used to cost tens or hundreds of thousands of dollars and required musicians to hire engineers and other professionals, but today it can all happen on your laptop. With your own computer, your studio time is free, allowing you to experiment at your own pace. And once you've created the music, because you're a digital musician, you can get your music discovered and heard by fans all over the world.

There's truly never been a better time to be a musician.

Your music forms the foundation of everything covered in this book. All other aspects of a music business grow from your creativity and musical output. Therefore, your own content is the most important asset you have.

If you want to build a following in today's music world, structure your music production process to create and release a steady flow of quality music. With people constantly looking at their phones to get the latest updates on social media while they wait in line at the store, releasing one album a year does not keep them engaged. And with streaming dominating the ways that fans listen to music, being active on the streaming platforms includes releasing music often. By releasing singles, then EPs, then albums over the course of a year, you'll create a steady beat of notifications about your new work. The artists who do this create more engagement with their fans, while getting more streams of their music played, and ultimately generating income.

But it's not just about fans. If you want to make the most revenue from your music, whether through streaming, sales, licensing, and more, there are steps you can perform *during production and postproduction* to enhance the possibilities of making more money. These steps are not extra work; they are the difference between musicians who want to make money from music and those who want to just make music.

This chapter will show you how to create a production process that maximizes the earning potential of each track you release and provide the best opportunities to grow your fan base out of your music. It will also cover how to directly make money from your studio and music making process.

PREPARING TO CREATE YOUR MUSIC
WHAT TO CONSIDER BEFORE YOU EVEN
HIT THE RECORD BUTTON

The digital world rewards musicians who produce regular and consistent releases of music. This means you need to think of your musical output differently from musicians of the past by making multiple versions and creating episodic releases of music, rather than releasing one big album on a yearly basis. This drives steady engagement, grows your fan base, and makes more money for you through streaming, royalties, sales, and more.

You should also try to release more music in general. Although it takes a lot of time and energy to convert a new person into a fan, it takes far less effort to get an existing fan to stream, watch, purchase, or support you through patronage or crowdfunding. This is where building a back catalog of music available for them to explore comes into play.

It's not necessary to always create new songs to do this. In fact, with each track you release, you can:

- Make a remix of your song.

- Create an acoustic/unplugged version.

- Create a live version.

- Do an a cappella version.

- Mix an instrumental version.

- Share the demo version.

- Release an outtake or wildly different version (different genre, style, etc.).

- Create a "making of" version.

- Export the stems for use in sales, remixes (so others can use your work and expose your music to their audience), and licensing for TV, film, advertising, or trailers.

Beyond releasing these versions directly to the public, you can also restrict the release of these versions as rewards for high-paying crowd-funding or patronage pledgers, or giveaways to your fans or street team.

Keep in mind, if you want to make the most money from the versions of music you create, there are other critical, repeatable steps to take for each release. For instance, if you're in the U.S., you can register the song and sound recordings with the U.S. Copyright Office to gain extra protections (see chapter 8, "Your Rights"). If your song has lyrics, you can add them to a lyrics database so services like Spotify and others can display them. You should also document who played and did what on each song and version of a song you release, since *every song* you create is an opportunity for you to make sales, boost streams, generate royalties, promote and market yourself and your music, and open up all potential income streams available to you. We'll show you how to do all of this in this chapter, but it starts first with capturing the information at the start.

WHAT TO CAPTURE WHILE YOU'RE CREATING AND RECORDING YOUR MUSIC TO ENSURE YOU MAKE MONEY, MAXIMIZE PROMOTION POSSIBILITIES, AND AVOID LEGAL DISPUTES

The time to capture who wrote what and who owns the final track is during the production process. We cover details about how copyright works in chapter 8, "Your Rights," but this boils down to doing two things during production:

1. Use "Song and Sound Recording Split Agreements" to capture song ownership.

Song and sound recording split sheets are easy-to-use templated agreements that track who wrote what in a song and who owns what for a sound recording. These split agreements document the authorship between musicians so you can avoid disputes in the future as well as a way to document who gets what percentage of revenue. We'll talk more about how to use split sheets and what to capture in chapter 8, "Your Rights," but for now, know the best time to capture this information is at the songwriting or recording session. Waiting until after the song is released and generating revenue can lead to problems between songwriters, publishers, and sound recording owners, so capture this information early and make it a habit or use tools like Jammber (jammber.com) that not only helps track splits but also the payments afterward.

2. Use a spreadsheet or online services to capture song and sound recording credit information.

Every song and sound recording you release into the world should document everyone who was part of the track. We'll discuss credits in detail later in this chapter, but in short, you'll want to capture this information for every song and sound recording you create, as you'll end up uploading this credit information with public database sources for every release. Doing so:

- Ensures services like Spotify, Pandora, and Apple Music will display accurate information about your music.

- Offers information to fans so they can learn about you and discover the other music you make plus provides external social proof to media/press from a third party that you're legitimate and worth covering.

- Captures the royalty information to make it easier to register the tracks so everyone gets the royalties they're owed once it's released (see chapter 12, "Licensing and Royalties").

- Improves your credibility and visibility in the music industry, since music industry associations such as the National Academy of Recording Arts and Sciences (NARAS), which recognizes talent every year via the GRAMMYs, rely on credit information in these databases.

- Helps music supervisors discover who you are so they know who to contact for licensing (which we discuss in detail in chapter 12, "Licensing and Royalties").

Avoid any disputes and legal issues by performing the above steps throughout the music production process rather than trying to piece it together afterward. Doing so can help you generate income and promote the tracks as we'll outline all throughout this book.

UNDERSTANDING RECORDING STUDIO OPTIONS

Quality sound-recording equipment and software has become inexpensive enough to allow anyone to record music at high quality. Today, your choices are:

- **Professional studios.**

Professional studios aren't just spaces with top-notch equipment and gear; they also bring the recording talent and experience, such as sound engineers, mixers, and mastering engineers as well as access to producers, session musicians, and more, allowing you to focus on the music. There are also multiple recording spaces, access to specialized equipment not usually within your budget, and faster recording times.

Most studios charge by the hour, but some may have flat fees. Do your research so you get the best value and are satisfied with the results of your recording and the overall experience. Rehearse what you plan to record so you aren't figuring out what you want to do on the clock and have to spend extra money, bring extras of all your gear, and tune your instruments to each other, including the drums. You will also want to ensure you walk out with the raw master studio files. We've heard horror stories where disreputable studios would hold the master files hostage and ask for more money to release them.

- **Home studios.**

Technology has dramatically brought the cost of building a home studio to affordable levels. And once you put together a home studio in a basement, garage, or bedroom, the time you spend recording doesn't cost you anything more than it does in a professional studio. It also gives you freedom to create, record, and produce new music whenever you want, which can increase your release output and enables you to create regular and consistent releases of music. Other advantages include:

- The capability to create new sounds, since the studio and the recording technology today is as much an instrument as a guitar was in the past.

- The ability to produce many versions of your songs, including instrumentals, remixes, beats, and loops, giving you more content to release as well as more ways to make money with music.

- The option of creating additional content, including high-quality podcasts. Plus, if you add a camera (and possibly a green screen), your home music studio can double as a home video studio.

- The new skills you'll develop can be marketable within the music industry and also outside of it as media continues to converge.

- The ability to create new synth and other virtual instrument presets, patches, and plug-ins, all of which can be sold, which is another way you can make money with music.

The downside is that you have to rely on your own expertise and solve any equipment problems if something comes up. Also, you probably won't have access to all the vintage or professional equipment a professional studio may have, although we have some solutions for that (see below). That said, these downsides may actually be an advantage. As Gino Robair, musician, composer, and editor of *Electronic Musician*, put it, "If you create a home studio and learn to record, mix, master, and trouble-shoot on your own, you will build up your experience, improve your skills for your own music, and become marketable within the industry. If you can make other musicians' dreams come true by recording them, it opens up new opportunities and additional income streams beyond just being an artist. You can do both in parallel: make money on the side by recording and producing other musicians, while making money as your own artist."

There is a wealth of information sources about building a home studio, from magazines like *Electronic Musician* (emusician.com) and *Mix* (mixonline.com), to sites such as AudioFanZine (audiofanzine.com), books, and videos (at YouTube, CreativeLive, and more). Check Making MoneyWithMusic.com/resources for more links.

• Mobile studios.

With today's digital audio workstations (DAWs), all you need is a laptop and you will have your studio with you no matter where you carry it. There are many portable hardware microphone solutions available, including external devices with built-in sound processing that offloads the recording processing to the hardware, letting you record audio anywhere you want. With a good pair of headphones, you can mix music on the bus, train, or in a coffee shop. Plus, you can set up and record audio wherever you can find some space.

• Apps.

Today's music apps are incredibly versatile and powerful, allowing you to make music with just a smartphone or tablet. From staples like GarageBand through the more sophisticated audio production apps, you have the basics to make your music. Plus, there are microphone solutions that plug in directly to the phone to let you have decent recording fidelity to lay down tracks. This also lets you record live, whether it's a show or an on-the-spot street performance.

HOW TO FIND AND GET THE RIGHT GEAR FOR YOUR MUSIC

From buying new gear to renting the perfect instrument at just the right time, you have an enormous number of resources available to you to help you develop music. If you are making music on your computer, among the more exciting trends are the huge number of plug-ins, VSTs, and virtual instruments available to you to make the perfect sounds. Below are options outside of traditional stores for new equipment available to all musicians that are worth checking out:

1. Digital Audio Workstations (DAWs)

If you have a computer, just install a DAW and you have a studio. There are many available on the market, with some of the most popular being Ableton Live, Avid Pro Tools, FL Studio, Propellerhead Reason,

Steinberg Cubase, Apple Logic Pro X (and GarageBand), Cockos REAPER, and many more. If you're just getting started, try out the free Audacity (audacity.sourceforge.net), the world's most popular DAW. Or the open source Ardour (ardour.org).

2. Plug-in marketplaces.

Besides the huge number of marketplaces provided by DAW vendors like Ableton's Packs page (ableton.com/en/packs), there are also sites like Splice (splice.com) that provide rent-to-own options for software plug-ins. The list of places to get digital plug-ins and tools is long and changes often, so we have links to some of the top ones at MakingMoney WithMusic.com/resources.

3. Gear rental sites.

Music gear rental has gone far beyond just renting PAs from your local music store. If you need a particular instrument, check out musician-to-musician rental sites such as Sparkplug (sparkplug.it). These sites also have vintage gear available that you might not be able to find anywhere else. Plus, if you put up your own gear for rental, you can create a source of income from the gear you're not using right now.

4. Sample, loop, and sound design marketplaces.

There are a world of musicians creating beats and loops for other musicians to use to make their music. Sites like Beatport (beatport.com), BeatStars (beatstars.com), and AirBit (airbit.com) allow you to buy beats from other musicians and sell them if you decide to.

5. Used gear.

Although Craigslist (craigslist.org) and eBay (ebay.com) are always good sources for used gear, the internet has revolutionized this area too with sites like Reverb (reverb.com).

HOW TO FIND AND COLLABORATE WITH LOCAL MUSICIANS

There are always musicians looking to collaborate. Here are some ways to find them:

1. Ask for a referral.

By far, the best way to find musicians is from other musicians you already know.

2. Post an ad at a local store, music school, or studio.

In Chicago, where we live, one of the best places to find musicians is the Old Town School of Folk Music (oldtownschool.org), which has music classes of all types of instruments and styles. But don't forget music stores as well. When we needed a new drummer, we posted an ad at the Drum Pad, one of the largest drum stores in the region, and we connected with the perfect drummer for our group.

3. Go to where the party is.

You can head to the community sites where the people with the skills you're looking for congregate and hang out with one another. Besides Reddit forums, there are also websites dedicated to finding bass players at TalkBass (TalkBass.com) or drummers at DrummerCafe (DrummerCafe .com/forum/index.php).

4. Use musician classified sites.

You can post an ad in your area for sites like BandMix (bandmix.com), JamConnect (jamconnect.com), Musicians Wanted (musicianswanted .org), Musolist (musolist.com), or Craigslist (craigslist.org).

5. Go to contracting sites.

You can head to websites where the people with the skills you need post their availability for hire. Sites such as SoundBetter (soundbetter.com), Craigslist (craigslist.org), Upwork (upwork.com), and Fiverr (fiverr.com) specialize in this.

HOW TO FIND AND COLLABORATE WITH MUSICIANS OVER THE WEB

Thanks to the internet, a musician can record a part for you, or play with you live, anywhere in the world. You are no longer limited to finding musicians in your area to jam with. To collaborate with other musicians, try the following:

1. Virtual jam sessions.

Sites like JamKazam (jamkazam.com), Jammr (jammr.net), and eJam ming (ejamming.com), or programs like Jamulus (sourceforge.net /projects/llcon) allow you to jam live with other musicians using your computer and an internet connection.

2. Remixing sites.

If you like the idea of remixing, musicians all over the world like to share the source tracks to their songs and see what other musicians can do with them. You can use these sites to both play music or share your own. Try out ccMixter (ccmixter.org), but if you put your music up there, be prepared to put it under a Creative Commons license (which we talk about in chapter 8, "Your Rights.")

3. Track sharing sites.

Mix multitrack recording with a file-sharing site, and you get the ability to record songs with any musician who wants to take part. On these sites, entire songs are written one track at a time. One might record a bass part, another might record drums, and before long, there's a song with vocals and even background vocals by entirely different singers. All of this is done by musicians who have usually never met each other. Try sites like Blend (blend.io), BandHub (bandhub.com), or Kompoz (Kompoz.com) if you want to give this a try.

On each of these areas, there are new sites that pop up all the time, so we will track this at MakingMoneyWithMusic.com/resources.

HOW TO FIND SOMEBODY TO RECORD ANY INSTRUMENT FOR YOUR MUSIC (OR MAKE MONEY DOING THE SAME)

Many sites go beyond finding a bass player or a drummer, allowing you to hire brass sections, wind ensembles, vocalists, entire orchestras, or musicians who play rare instruments. You can also hire well-known studio musicians to record a track as well. The possibilities are endless—for a fee, of course. These services go beyond musicians too. You can even hire engineers to mix or master your songs if needed. To use a service like this, do the following:

1. Choose a service.

Try services like Airgigs (airgigs.com), Online Sessions (onlinesessions .com), and Session Players (sessionplayers.com), or if you need producers or other engineers, see sites like Treble.fm (treble.fm).

2. Search for the musician(s) with the skill set you need and connect.

Use the search to find the musician(s) with the skill set you need and reach out to them. Also note the distinction between union session players—

see AFM (afm.org), for an example—and others as to their expectations of session jobs. These services differ on engagement, but in general, you'll want to give the session player candidate a rough mixdown with an explanation of what you're looking for (style, mood, etc.).

3. Coordinate the recording.

Send the WAV file to your session player. Some sites will allow you to watch or hear the session through their service or communication tool like Skype, while others will just let you trade recorded tracks. Work closely with the session player to ensure you get the performance you need.

4. Get the WAV.

Once complete, the session player should send you the WAV file of the performance or the stems. You should also get any other source files that were captured depending on the program they used in case you need it.

You can use these techniques with any musicians in the world, if they're willing. You could even start a band where none of the band members live in the same city. Keep in mind, you can also become a session player and charge for your services. Simply sign up at one or all of the services and review the service's terms and you can open a new source of income for yourself.

HOW TO FIND PRECLEARED AND ROYALTY-FREE SAMPLES AND LOOPS

With the right combination of samples and loops, you can create the illusion of a full band backing you, or just enhance tracks with that little something extra that they need. While these tools have been around for a long time, many new sources will sell them royalty-free. These sources can add new dimensions to your music.

To find samples and loops that meet your needs (and are precleared so you can use them), do the following:

1. Check out free sources.

Public domain recordings are always free, and there are many sound sources licensed under Creative Commons (CC) (creativecommons.org) licenses, some of which allow commercial use, while others require you to go back to the creator to get permission (always read the license carefully). Check out ccMixter (ccmixter.org) and the Free Sound Project (freesound .org). Additionally, the Creative Commons site allows you to search multiple sites for material that can be incorporated into your music.

2. Research loop and sample services.

There are a wide variety of loop and sample sources like Splice (splice .com), Beatport (beatport.com), BeatStars (beatstars.com), and AirBit (airbit.com) that sell samples to use in your music. For more sample and loop resources, see MakingMoneyWithMusic.com/resources.

3. Verify the terms.

Be sure to read the agreements carefully before downloading, buying, or using them. You want a license that allows you to incorporate the audio into your own songs without paying for each use (royalty-free). Don't use music in your work you don't own and isn't precleared, or you will find it difficult to license your music for TV, film, and video games.

4. Record a cover version of the sample or audio loop.

Samples often have two owners: the songwriter and sound recording owner, which is usually the label. If you find a sample you like, you can create a cover of the sample so you own the sound recording. However, you will need to license the composition from the songwriter (see chapter 8, "Your Rights").

RECORDING YOUR MUSIC
MAXIMIZING THE AMOUNT OF SONGS YOU CAN RELEASE

Because the digital world rewards consistent and regular releases of music, it helps to structure your production sessions to create as much music as possible. It's music that drives your licensing, sales, and promotion. But also, it's in creating a high *quantity* of music that will hone your skills and raise the *quality* of music you write and produce. Try these techniques to make it easier for you to create more music:

1. Turn songwriting into a habit and get organized around a calendar.

As we talk about in detail in chapter 18, "Your Release Strategy," you should structure your releases around a calendar. You should do the same thing for songwriting and recording sessions so they become a habit.

2. Collaborate with other musicians.

It's important to get the business items and ground rules taken care of up front so the focus of every session can be on the music. For example, dealing with the split sheet arrangements up front will go a long way to building a collaborative and creative environment.

3. Create a music assembly line and divide responsibilities.

If you try to *record and produce* your music at the same time you're trying to *write and create* your music, you might choke off your creativity or end up doing both parts of the production process poorly. Each of these activities uses different parts of your brain, which have been shown to compete or stifle one another. Separate the songwriting sessions from the recording processes so each can be more productive. Also, if you record with a band or other musicians, you may want to arrange the production process so the others are working on what they're best at and then have them do one task at a time. For example, you could record on one day and mix down on another. This works even better if there are multiple people because you can then work in parallel; you can have some musicians songwriting while others record.

Having a schedule, a shared calendar, and assigned roles and responsibilities for tasks with different people made a huge difference in the amount of music our band, Beatnik Turtle, could produce for our TheSongOfTheDay.com project. We learned that arranging our music lives around a calendar created more output and higher-quality work.

CREATING ADDITIONAL CONTENT FOR RELEASE WHILE RECORDING YOUR MUSIC

Since your fans are interested in what goes on in the creation and recording stage, your production process can generate extra of material. Consider capturing the following while you make the music:

1. Take photos.

You can use these on social media as well as after the song is released as extra promotional materials.

2. Capture video.

Behind-the-scenes videos or montages about your group or for any "making of" release of your song can easily include this footage, and you can also blend it with the song release. For example, the group Pomplamoose would record every take of their recording and edit together a music video based on their best takes.

3. Live-stream the production process.

This is an excellent patronage reward to give to fans who pay extra. We tried this in the early days of streaming by pointing cameras that would follow us as we moved in our studio while we recorded an album, which added an extra "performance" aspect to the music production process.

4. Create waveform or automatic videos from the music.

Many DAW plug-ins on platforms like Ableton's Max for Live can take the waveforms of the audio and create a video for it. This could be one of the easiest ways for you to make an initial video of your music to share with fans or friends, and you can generate this before you move on to the next song during postproduction work.

5. Post social media updates.

When you sit down to work on your music, you can let your fans know that you've started a production session. These make much better updates than what you had for lunch, and if you do this regularly, they'll look forward to hearing you're working on new music for them.

PREPARING YOUR MUSIC FOR RELEASE
HOW TO FIND OUT IF PEOPLE WILL LIKE YOUR
MUSIC BEFORE RELEASE

Like film studios that try out screen edits of their movies against target audiences before committing to the final cut, you may want to let people listen to your music before releasing it. This can help you determine which track to promote, whether you should make a music video, whether to release the track as a single as opposed to a track on the album, figure out an EP or album track running order, or get advice from professionals on how you can improve the song or mix.

If you'd like to get this kind of evaluation, there are two categories of services. First, you can use critique sites that have music industry professionals on staff to rate and critique your music, such as Fluence (fluence.io). Additionally, Music Xray (musicxray.com) is a music opportunity site that includes a "Music Industry Professionals" review option for your music. Second, you can go direct to music fans to see what they think by using services like AudioKite (audiokite.com), TuneCore's Fan Reviews (tunecore.com/index/fanreviews), or ReverbNation's Crowd Review (reverbnation.com/band-promotion/crowd_review). Each of these services lets a group of listeners review, rate, and comment on your track. They also have filtering features that allow you to choose reviewers who might be into your genre and style of music or whether you want to have random listeners rate it.

UNDERSTANDING MASTERING AND WHY IT'S IMPORTANT

The difference between a mastered track and non-mastered track can be dramatic. It puts the polish on the final mix to make the track sound great whether it's played on a high-quality sound system, headphones, a TV, or hands-free speakers. Mastering engineers achieve this through the use of EQ, compression/limiting, volume normalization, smoothing, and other techniques. Mastering also plays a significant role in making a disparate collection of songs you recorded at different times, levels, and with varying instruments into a cohesive whole.

Normally, a mastering house will charge a flat or hourly rate. Read the agreement and make sure it doesn't give the house any rights to your music and that it clearly states you own the master recordings.

If you're not familiar with mastering, some mastering houses will offer to master a track for free, charging you only if you decide to use it.

HOW TO PREPARE FOR AND USE
A MASTERING HOUSE EFFECTIVELY

Follow these steps to prepare for your mastering session:

1. Send your mix to the mastering engineer and get their thoughts before the session.

If the mastering engineer is okay with it, send the track before the session to get feedback. They might even find something that will cause you to remix or rework the track. Plus, it lets them think about what they plan on doing for their session, which will get you a better result.

2. Bring multiple mixdowns of the same track.

Although mastering engineers can draw on a surprising variety of tricks to deal with mixdown issues, don't depend on them to fix mistakes within your mix. To help with getting the vocals at the right level in relationship with the music, some mastering engineers will ask you to mix down your track with the music and vocals on two different stereo tracks. Doing so allows them the flexibility to combine these separate stereo tracks so the vocals are heard perfectly above the mix. In fact, some mastering engineers request you bring an instrumental mix, a vocals-only mix, a combined vocals-and-instrumental mix, and two additional combined vocals and instrumental mixes with the vocals +1 or +2 dB higher and −1 or −2 dB lower.

3. Bring reference tracks.

Bring other tracks you've done to help the mastering engineer get an idea of what you sound like. You can also bring tracks from other artists you want your release to sound like.

4. Bring the right formats.

While most mastering houses want WAVs, confirm ahead of time what format they require. It's expensive to schedule a session and then show up with music in the wrong format. (Note: The right answer is *never* "MP3 files." MP3 is a lossy, low-quality version of your recording that no mastering house will use.)

5. Don't mix it "loud."

A mastering engineer can boost your track so it's "loud" (close to 0dB—the highest limit of a digital track), but it helps to give them lower-level mixes with headroom to work with. If you come in with a mix that's too loud, you've short-circuited their ability, and they may send you back to remix it. This is one of the reasons they request multiple mixes as described in #1 above.

6. Decide if you want to master for vinyl ahead of time.

If you are making a vinyl record, you have the option of telling the mastering engineer to produce a vinyl split master, which may get you better results for a vinyl production of album.

HOW TO INEXPENSIVELY MASTER YOUR TRACKS

There's still a lot of value to having someone outside the mixdown and pro-duction process get their ears on your music, bring out qualities to it that you might not have caught, and potentially find mixdown issues or pro-duction errors. But if you release a lot of music or just want to master for demos, it helps to have less expensive options for mastering. Everything you release should have some mastering done to it. For alternatives to pro-fessional mastering, try the following:

1. Use built-in mastering tools in your DAW.

Many DAWs have default plug-in chains that perform compression, EQ, and other effects that will perform a basic mastering polish to your final tracks. You should apply this to the master tracks at the end of the process, making sure that you do a good job with mixdown first. Just make sure to perform the mastering step before rendering the track.

2. Try automated mastering services.

Automated mastering tools like Landr (landr.com) have become available to musicians, allowing you to upload a raw track and hear the results im-mediately. This is far less expensive than professional mastering and is likely to get better results than using standard plug-ins in your DAW.

3. Buy your own mastering software.

iZotope's Ozone and T-RackS MAX are just two examples of mastering software you can purchase for your own studio. Doing this would require you to learn how to use the software and has an initial investment but would also mean that you can do a better postproduction process in your own studio.

HOW TO ENCODE AND NAME YOUR MUSIC TRACKS

You'll likely want your final tracks accessible both locally and in the cloud, since there will be numerous times when you'll need to link or send tracks for many of the activities we talk about in future chapters, such as digital distri-bution, media/press promotional campaigns, get-heard campaigns (sending tracks to podcasters, MP3 blogs, and more), rewards for crowdfunding/patronage pledgers, music supervisors, other licensees, and more. To make sure your tracks are playable by as many people as possible once released, we suggest you encode your final mastered tracks using the following settings:

1. Create a WAV file.

Create "16-Bit/Stereo/44.1 kHz WAV" files of all your music. You'll need higher-quality WAVs for your digital distributors, licensees, podcasters, YouTubers, or any book media producers who want to incorporate your music into their work. We like to be able to act quickly if we get a licensee or a request for our work, so we make sure every WAV file is accessible from the cloud.

2. Create low- and high-quality MP3s.

Create both low- and high-quality MP3s for song giveaways to the media, press, fans, and as incentives and rewards for patronage/crowdfunding. You can make a low-quality version by encoding it at "Constant Bitrate (CBR)/128 KB/Joint Stereo" and a high-quality version at "Constant Bitrate (CBR)/320 KB/Joint Stereo."

3. Name your files using "Artist Name-Song Title."

Make sure the file name of your WAVs and MP3s identifies you and the song title. This is especially important for WAV files, since they do not have ID3 tags and someone may want to license your music and have no other information to go on beyond the file name. We recommend the following standard: <band>-<trackname>.wav (e.g., Beatnik_Turtle-Pizza _The_Rock_Opera.wav)

THE TOP EIGHT THINGS YOU SHOULD DO TO PREPARE YOUR SONGS FOR RELEASE

Many musicians put off some of these postproduction steps, but the time to do them is before release. The best reason is that your track can generate royalties from the day it's released rather than missing out on them until you remember to register the tracks. An added bonus is you only have to do these once for each song you release, and then they're covered *for life*!

Some of the details behind these steps are found within other chapters of this book, but it's presented here as a checklist when you need to take care of them during the postproduction process:

1. Create an ISRC code for all the tracks you may release.

The International Standard Recording Code (ISRC) is an international standard to uniquely identify sound recordings and music video recordings. It's the ISRC code that allows you to collect royalties for streaming. You'll need one for each sound recording you release. See chapter 12, "Licensing and Royalties," for more details on the ISRC, including how to get one, but for now know the unique code for your sound recording can be generated when you finish postproduction and should be included within the ID3 tags of your MP3.

2. Create a song description and capture BPM, key, genre, and related info.

DJs, music supervisors and other licensees, MP3 bloggers, song websites, and more all want extended information about each song you release. Generate this info as you're rendering the song for release while it's fresh and easy to pull together.

3. Write out and save the lyrics.

Streaming sites like Spotify and Apple pick up their lyrics from outside sources like Genius (genius.com) or Musixmatch (musixmatch.com). To make sure that your tracks have lyrics that show up in these streaming sites, you'll need to enter the lyrics into these services. Also, this makes great material for your website and social media. Capture this during the preparation phase so they are ready to go.

4. Make an image for each sound recording.

One of the most important marketing items is the song's image. This usually will be your album, EP, or single cover, but it also could be your artist image. MP3s can store this image (discussed below), but digital distributors will want an image as well so it's displayed at stores and streaming services. Also, you'll want an image so you can promote your track on your website and on social media.

5. Tag all your MP3s.

While most of your music will be released through digital distributors so they're in every digital store and streaming service, you'll need MP3s as giveaways for the press/media, as crowdfunding/patronage rewards, sales from your site, and more. Any MP3 you release should be tagged so it promotes you. See the next section on tagging for more information.

6. Record and upload the credits.

Know who did what on each song you make, including production information, featured performers, and more. Credits databases like Tivo

Music Metadata (which powers AllMusic.com), MusicBrainz (Music Brainz.org), and Discogs (Discogs.com) want this information. It's these databases that services like Spotify, Apple Music, Pandora, and many others pull data from. See the credits sections below for detailed information on this important step.

7. In the U.S., register your copyright with the Copyright Office.
Whether you're in the U.S., Canada, the UK, Ireland, or Australia, your music is copyrighted at the moment you create and record it, but, in the U.S., if you register your copyrights with the U.S. Copyright Office within three months of release, you'll get additional statutory protections (see chapter 8, "Your Rights").

8. Register your releases with your performance rights organization (PRO).
No matter what country you're in, register each track you release with your PROs so you can get paid when your music is played (see chapter 12, "Licensing and Royalties").

HOW TO TAG YOUR MP3S SO THE WORLD CAN FIND YOU

Once you release an MP3 into the world, you never know where it might end up, even if you only meant to send it to one music reviewer. We therefore recommend you do the following for each MP3 you create to ensure it promotes you and your entire music catalog:

1. Determine which ID3 tagging tool to use.
When fans listen to MP3s of your music, the artist name, album, and song title display in the player based ID3 tags. These can be set using most MP3 players simply by entering the data into the properties of each song file. If you release a lot of music, you might want a more advanced tool to handle tagging many MP3s at once, such as Tag & Rename from Softpointer (softpointer.com/tr.htm) and Jaikoz (jthink.net/jaikoz/).

2. Tag all your MP3s.
At a minimum, fill out your artist name, track name, album name, your URL, the ISRC, the copyright information, and an image. Adding in BPM, genre, and key information as noted above is a plus, since DJs, music supervisors, and other licensees look for this information. Also,

keep in mind the comments field allows space for how to contact you as well as promoting your website or other social media channels—for example, "Come to beatnikturtle.com for more information and music" or "Visit TheSongOfTheDay.com for more free music!"

HOW TO PROTECT YOUR MUSIC FILES AND ENSURE THEY'RE BACKED UP

Your source files are one of the most important assets you own. Because of this, you need to make sure your files are backed up and available no matter what happens. As producer Wally Lockhard III told us, one of his artists lost his house and all his files in a fire. Another lost his files after he got robbed. His suggestion was, "A portable hard drive with all your files, lyric sheets, and music has got to be in your arsenal. And if you want to be a professional and have a zero-fail mission, you need two backup drives, because hard drives fail."

To make sure you never lose files, do the following:

1. Get multiple hard drive backups and put them in more than one location.
You can lose everything with one disaster unless you keep copies in separate locations.

2. Consider using shared storage sites.
Although music files are quite large, you can always use cloud storage services like Dropbox (dropbox.com), Box (box.com), or OneDrive (onedrive.com) to store the raw files.

3. Make sure to store all your data—lyrics, images, raw files, MP3s, WAVs, stems, and so on.
You should back up more than your music files. Also, don't just back up your final versions of tracks, images, and materials. If you only have final versions and you lose all the materials you used to make them, you won't be able to make changes to them in the future.

UNDERSTANDING SONG CREDITS

There's one aspect of the music industry that's in a dark age. Since the rise of digital music and the decline of LPs and CDs that featured liner notes, tracking the people behind the music became difficult. If the information in most sales platforms was all the credit information we could read, we'd only know of a band called Led Zeppelin and wouldn't know anything about a guitarist named Jimmy Page.

Credit websites—which are like the Internet Movie Database (imdb .com) of the music business—stepped in to fill this gap. You can make sure that they have the information that fans want to know. For every album, EP, or single track you release, you should document who did what and enter the credits, musicians, engineers, producers, and lyrics.

Updating this information to the right databases has many benefits. For example, it:

- Feeds music distribution sources and media services like Spotify, Apple Music, MTV, iTunes, and more as to who did what on a recording so fans can access the extended information.

- Informs potential licensees who you are so they know who to contact to license your music.

- Improves your credibility and visibility in the music industry, since music industry associations such as the Recording Academy, who recognize and vote on talent each year via the GRAMMYs, rely on these databases.

- Cements your accomplishments for historical and cultural purposes.

- Provides fans with ways to learn about you and discover the other music you make.

If your credit information is missing from these credit databases, then you and the musicians, lyricists, featured artists, and music production professionals you're working with are losing out. Registering your credits is not difficult and can be done in an evening if you get organized and collect all the required information in one place.

THE TOP NINE THINGS TO TRACK SO YOU GET YOUR CREDIT INFORMATION RIGHT

The time to collect your credit information is during the music creation and production process. At this point in time, the fields for recording credits are being added to new DAWs with tools like RIN-M (soundways

.com/rin). If your DAW has this, you should use the feature. Otherwise, track all your credits on a spreadsheet, or you can use tools like Jammber (jammber.com) to track everything.

At a minimum, the credits you should track include the following: vocalist, instrumentalist (list each instrument separately), songwriter, arranger, producer, engineer, and mastering engineer. Note that these credits match the categories of eligibility for the Recording Academy, among other organizations. (And if you're interested in becoming a voting member, you must have twelve qualifying tracks in at least one of the categories as found in grammypro.com/join.) You should also consider including photography, design, and art direction credits.

If you're a guest musician on someone else's track, you should insist your contributions are documented and registered at the same database services so your contribution can be properly credited. This could lead to more opportunities for you and lead people to learn more about you and discover your music or other work. Of course, you should extend the same courtesy to anyone who appears on your releases.

THE TOP ELEVEN PLACES TO REGISTER YOUR CREDIT METADATA INFORMATION

If you've been documenting the information above, it only takes an evening to register your credit information at the various database services of the music world. Keep in mind that while this work is administrative, it can be delegated to your manager or a team member. Also, some digital distribution partners can handle some of these credit registrations for you (see chapter 9, "Distribution and Streaming").

Below are the services where you should register your credit information (for new and previously released tracks). Note that most have quick-start guides on how to submit or update data and use their services.

1. TiVo & AllMusic.

If you had to choose just one place to upload your credit information, TiVo Music Metadata (business.tivo.com/products-solutions/data /music-metadata) is it. This tracks credit information for the music industry and sends data to music players like Windows Media Player, TV stations, and other music services. Search this database by using the website AllMusic (allmusic.com) and see if your information is already listed. If it is, check it over carefully, and keep an eye out for any errors or omissions that you can change by the "Submit Corrections" link on every page. If you're not in AllMusic or any credits are missing, follow the instructions AllMusic provides on their site.

2. MusicBrainz.

MusicBrainz (musicbrainz.org) is an open music database. Similar to the Rovi database service, MusicBrainz is used by many music sources, including BBC Music.

3. Discogs.

Similar to MusicBrainz, Discogs (Discogs.com) is a crowdsourced database of music started by tracking electronic music, but it moved beyond it to cover all genres.

4. Gracenote.

Gracenote (gracenote.com) is a service that tracks CD metadata and powers music players like iTunes and WinAmp with artist name, album name, and a track listing when you put in a CD. You can use iTunes or other CD music players to submit CD track info to their database.

5. FreeDB.

FreeDB (freedb.org) is an open-source version of Gracenote. To enter your information here, use one of the FreeDB-aware applications.

6. Genius.

Genius (genius.com) is the lyrics source for Spotify as well as other services, and it also provides annotations to the lyrics, so it's worth it to enter your lyrics here.

7. LyricFind.

LyricFind (lyricfind.com) is the source of the lyric information you see at AllMusic, as well as many other sites, apps, and media.

8. LyricWiki.

LyricWiki (lyrics.wikia.com/wiki/Lyrics_Wiki) is another lyrics information site. It bills itself as an open wiki website where anyone can get lyrics for any song by any artist.

9. Last.fm.

Last.fm (last.fm) collects listening information from fans and provides a page that displays Last.fm members who are listening to your music, offering a unique way to connect to fans.

10. Wikipedia.

Services like Spotify also pull data from Wikipedia, since it's yet another place where people find credit and biographical information about you and your music. If you have an entry, you'll want to make sure that it's up to date, accurate, and contains your latest discography. If you don't have a Wikipedia entry and want to add one, first enter your credits at other databases to provide external sources for the info.

11. Ultimate Guitar

Ultimate Guitar (ultimate-guitar.com) contains the guitar tabs to thousands of songs, and if you want to make it more likely that musicians will cover your songs, you can post tabs to your music there.

The more places that your name is found, the more legitimacy it creates for your music. There are services such as TuneRegistry (tuneregistry .com) that help musicians by providing automated ways to capture credit information for your music, as well as copyright, royalty, and other information. Keep a lookout for new ones as they appear, and check MakingMoneyWithMusic.com/resources for more sites and ideas as we add to it over time.

6

YOUR VIDEOS

Goal: To create, record, and prepare your videos for release for promotion, streaming, sales, royalties, and licensing.

Team Roles and Responsibilities: Video Producer, Director, Editor and Postproduction Specialist, Cameraperson and Microphone Operators, Crew, Actors and Extras, Graphic Artist, Web Designer/Webmaster, and Manager

WHAT YOU GET OUT OF THIS
By the end of this chapter, you will:

1. Generate and record videos so you can promote you and your music, drive engagement, and make additional revenue.

2. Understand legal considerations whenever you create videos.

3. Have high-quality videos ready for YouTube distribution and streaming.

4. Create an optimized YouTube channel for your music.

5. Know video techniques to better promote your music, live events, and your products and merchandise as well as to maximize your chances of getting picked up in YouTube's searches and being recommended.

6. Understand how to become a YouTube partner so you can collect ad revenue.

7. Know how to make money from your videos.

MONEY MAP

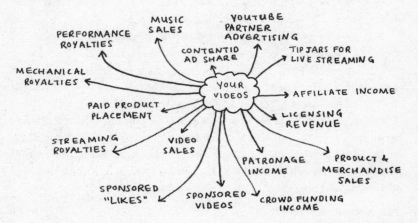

INTRO

There is no question video has taken over the internet. It's become one of the best and most powerful ways to discover new music. A staggering 1.3 billion people use YouTube daily, watching 3.25 billion hours per month (with 1 billion of those on mobile), many viewing sessions lasting over forty minutes at a time. In an average month, eight out of ten eighteen-to-forty-nine-year-olds watch YouTube, reaching more viewers in this age range than any cable network in the U.S. Plus, it's a global platform with 80 percent of views coming from outside the U.S. And sharing is built in; nearly 17 million people have connected a YouTube account to at least one social service such as Facebook and Twitter. In fact, every minute, more than five hundred tweets contain YouTube links, and each auto-shared tweet averages six new YouTube sessions.

Music plays a huge part in YouTube's success. In 2017, *"music"* was the most searched term on YouTube, and the second-most-searched term was *"song."* The channels with the most subscribers are all singers, and nine of the top ten most-viewed videos of all time are music videos. Of course, these are just YouTube stats, and with video being available in so many other platforms, this trend will only grow.

Besides the large viewership, video has become important for musicians for another, nearly hidden reason: sharing is built in to video services. It's easy and frictionless. Embedding, linking, or sharing video on your social networks is all just one click away. There's a reason the term *"viral video"* is so common but *"viral audio"* is not.

Because of this, video is the best way to engage your audience, social networks, and the internet to get your music heard. Everything you need is built in to video hosts, including sharing and subscriptions, and the best part is that you don't need to explain to your viewers how to share it; they already know how, and if they like it, they'll do it. Plus, it generates royalties and provides new revenue opportunities for your business. In this chapter, we'll talk about how to harness this incredibly powerful marketing tool, how to make videos, share them, and become part of the second video revolution in music since MTV—but this time, one that every musician can participate in.

KEY CONCEPTS
UNDERSTANDING VIDEOS AND VIDEO DISTRIBUTION PLATFORMS

Videos are the most easily shared form of your music, and it is worth your time to create videos. Consider the following:

- **Videos provide promotion *and* income.**
Videos get your music into the ears of new fans and generate revenue besides. They also drive merch, music sales, and more.

- **Videos can be viral.**
Sharing is built in to the platform, and people are already primed to look for viral videos to watch and share ones they think other people should watch.

- **Videos can be live or recorded.**
Grab your phone, fire up Periscope (pscp.tv), and point it at yourself with an instrument and you can start making live videos as well as making recorded videos.

- **Videos show off your persona.**

Your personality and brand are everywhere in your videos, and this only helps develop persona-related income streams.

- **Videos can boost everything else you do.**

You can use your videos to promote your music sales, shows, patronage, crowdfunding, and everything else you do. It's one of the most flexible communication channels you have.

If you do want to make videos on your own, you don't necessarily have to spend a lot of money, effort, or time on them to put out good video content. There are plenty of great options to create videos of your music shared below.

Also know that videos are a key part of your release strategy and provide some of the best content to offer your fans on a scheduled basis. Make it a part of your plan, and you can hook your fans on your music and bring them into the world of your content.

Today there's also a focus on live-streaming video with apps and services like Periscope (pscp.tv), Twitch (twitch.tv), Facebook Live (live.fb.com), and more. Because of this, live-streaming your day-to-day events—whether you're playing live in a venue, on the street, driving to your next gig, or in the studio working on your next song—are all ways to engage with your fan base. Plus, they open up revenue streams for your business. We discuss live streaming in chapter 16, "Get Gigs and Play Live."

Lastly, while this chapter will discuss YouTube, there are other channels such as Vimeo, Instagram, Snapchat, Facebook Video, and many more that you can use, and these are discussed throughout the book.

PREPARING TO CREATE YOUR VIDEOS
TWELVE TYPES OF VIDEOS YOU CAN MAKE

Often, the hardest part of tackling music videos is coming up with ideas about what type of video to make. Fortunately, not all videos need to be costly productions, and many types can be automated even as they come out with entertaining output based around your music and personality. Consider these many options to create videos.

1. Waveform or logo videos.

The most basic type of video is just the image for the song, album, or logo, sometimes animated in a simple way to spin or flip on the screen. Another option is to make a video of the waveform for your music generated by software, sometimes with your logos or images superimposed. The goal of these simple videos is to get your music up as simply and quickly as possible.

2. Traditional music videos.

These are usually bigger productions with musicians or actors made on a set or on location. If you choose this type, use good lighting, quality cameras, and solid video editing software. For a great example of these, check out how Pomplamoose (youtube.com/user/PomplamooseMusic) tackles them.

3. Animation.

There's no need for actors or even cameras if you use animation software to create a music video. Plus, animation is eye-catching. If you're a wiz with Poser (my.smithmicro.com/poser-3d-animation-software.html), Source Film Maker (SFM) (sourcefilmmaker.com), Miku Miku Dance (MMD) (learnmmd.com), or even Flash (flash.com), there's no limit to what you can do. Or try sites like GoAnimate (goanimate.com) or Wideo (wideo.co) to make drag-and-drop animations with ready-made images, and there are more options appearing for this all the time.

4. Mash-ups.

To create a mash-up, you use your music and combine it with other people's video footage—usually in a unique way. While you need to be aware of copyright issues, mash-up videos have been a popular way for fans to express themselves using video content from popular culture or other videos on YouTube. However, if you want to avoid any copyright issues, you can always use public domain video content, which we cover in a separate section below.

5. Still-photos video.

One of the quickest ways to upload a video for your music is to use video editing software to show static images or GIF animations while the music plays underneath. In fact, one of the most popular videos on You-

Tube, Nyan Cat, is just a tiny looped GIF animation of a cat flying in space while the song plays. The creator of this video didn't even make the GIF or write the song (although she did give credit to the creators), so it's also an example of a mash-up. But even the most basic video editing tools that come for free with your operating system have tools to sync groups of photos to video, including Ken Burns's effects (zoom in/out on the photos) and similar techniques.

6. Machinima.

Machinima is the art of staging video game action in real time and recording it to tell a story or make a music video. Video games like Halo, Minecraft, and World of Warcraft have been used in this way. Although there are potential copyright issues, it's become a separate video genre with its own fan base. Picking the right video game to use can create additional interest in your video even if potential fans have never heard of you as an artist.

7. Anime/animation music videos (AMV).

Fans of Japanese animation, called *anime*, like to mix their favorite music with clips from shows that they like, creating AMVs. They use their extensive knowledge of the shows to grab the perfect clips to sync the lips or action to the music. Like Machinima, this has become its own genre with its own subculture. Anime conventions even have awards for the best AMVs of the year, giving you an opportunity to tap a huge fan base if you create this type of content.

8. Live music videos.

If you play live, every show you perform is an opportunity to create new video content and exposure. Plus, this type of video can be shared with bookers to generate more gigs. Also, you aren't limited to recording live shows. For example, Nicki Bluhm and the Gramblers recorded live songs while driving in their van between gigs (bit.ly/van-video).

9. Automatically created videos via your DAW or video software.

Your DAW or video software may have ways to automatically create video based on the waveform or influenced by the music. For a music example, RokVid (ableton.com/en/packs/rokvid) for Ableton will take any video and morph it based on the music.

10. Live feeds.

With tools like Periscope (pscp.tv), Ustream (ustream.tv), YouNow (younow.com), and others, you can give fans a live feed of your life, travels, or even show a live feed of your studio work. For one of our albums, fans got a behind-the-scenes look when we live-streamed our recording, including a feed of the DAW software with the images of the studio musician showing in the corner. This allowed them to "be there" as we put it together and made them anticipate the album even more.

11. Behind-the-scenes content, vlogs, commentary videos, and reaction videos.

Using your smartphone, you can create regular, behind-the-scenes content about your life as a musician. After all, not all your uploaded videos need to be music videos. Some musicians actively engage with their fan base this way, answering questions or sharing what's on their mind. Others point a camera at themselves reacting to a release of other artists, videos, or media as they watch it for the first time or giving commentary.

12. Production videos.

Your musician fans often are interested in your production techniques. With screen-capture software, you can create tutorials or insights into your creative process.

Since some of these video types are easier to make than others, you may want to mix them up so the longer-production versions are scheduled in between a number of simpler ones so you can keep a regular release schedule. Make sure to think about production time as you put together your schedule.

UNDERSTANDING VIDEO PRODUCTION

Unless you love making videos and want to make it your primary social presence, your goal will be to focus on the music and to be smart about the time you spend on video. That said, there are a lot of great options available to you to get your videos filmed, including professional DSLRs, wearables such as GoPro cameras (gopro.com), smartphones, and drones. Below are some beginner options for making your own video productions:

1. Have a team member do it, or hire someone via the internet.

You should not need to derail your audio production to make videos if you can help it. Your best option is to get a team member to work on videos while the songwriters and recording engineers keep plugging away in the studio. Otherwise, keep in mind there's an entire internet full of people out there who are great at making videos and are available to make them for a fee on sites like Fiverr (fiverr.com), Upwork (upwork.com), or even Craigslist (craigslist.org).

2. Get a professional team.

If you want to make a video with you or musicians you work with, you can always hire a professional team to make and edit the music video for you. Although this costs more than doing it on your own, videos usually take a lot of effort, so hiring a team can get you a better-quality project with less of your personal time.

3. Do it yourself with mobile and apps tools.

If you have a smartphone, it probably has everything you need to do basic video production, including a camera, editor, and tools. Although you can get far more capabilities out of desktop software, if you're mobile, you can take a video anywhere and edit it on the spot. There are also apps that enhance the video process, which may help you keep multiple cameras synchronized or provide control software for external cameras.

4. Make your own video production studio.

A single decent-quality camera plus the editing software that comes with your computer can give you all you need to put together high-quality videos. Other free options include the free and open-source Open Shot (openshot.org). If you want to raise the bar even more, you can invest in decent editing software, such as Adobe Premiere or Final Cut, and put together a space with lighting and a green screen for special effects. If you can designate a space for recording, you can save time and make it easier to create your own productions.

High-quality audio is critical for all videos you create, since low-quality audio is far more noticeable and annoying to viewers than poor lighting. And if you do record audio for non-music videos, try using external mics rather than the built-in mic your camera or smartphone comes with. Lavalier mics are inexpensive and make a huge difference in audio quality, and the sound can be synched to match the video in postproduction, especially if you clap at the beginning of the video to provide a cue. As for the lighting, learning the basics of three-point lighting can go a long way to up your game on your videos.

UNDERSTANDING FILMING AND THE LAW

You need permission for all music, sound effects, video, locations, actors, and photos you use within your videos. Keep the following in mind as you make video:

- **Clearing all talent.**

Because of the right of publicity, you need to get the permission of anybody—actors, band members, team members, and extras—to use their likeness in your video. This is usually done through a short agreement in which the talent gives informed consent to be in your video, allows you to distribute the work, and releases all rights or claims they may have in the future. There are forms online if you search on "*talent release form*," but if you're just creating your first video, talk with your attorney.

- **Clearing locations.**

Like busking or street performances and block parties, you'll likely need a filming permit from the city if it's a public area, or, if you're shooting at a private location, you'll need permission of the owner. This, too, is done through a release. There are forms online if you search on "*location release form*," but you may also want to talk with your attorney.

- **Clearing any music and sound effects you don't own.**

Sometimes your videos may require music you don't create or own. If so, know you need to clear any music for your video you don't have the rights to (including recognizable music caught in the background). If you need to find other people's music, sites like Songtradr (songtradr.com) make it easy to find and license music directly from the artist. If, however, you choose to include yourself performing a cover song for your video, this requires contacting the author/publisher to negotiate a deal because there is no clearing service similar to Harry Fox (harryfox.com) or Loudr

(loudr.com) for handling synchronization licenses, since the law doesn't set a rate for this use.

HOW TO FIND PRECLEARED AND ROYALTY-FREE VIDEO FOOTAGE FOR YOUR VIDEOS

When it comes to using precleared video images, footage, and other graphics as well as video and photos, there are many options. Try the following:

1. Check out free sources.

There's a great deal of video material licensed under Creative Commons (CC) licenses, some of which allow commercial use. To find this, use the Creative Commons Search page (search.creativecommons.org) and choose "use for commercial purposes" for a powerful search engine across a huge number of services to find video footage to use, including from YouTube. Additionally, works created by the U.S. government, regardless where in the world you live, fall instantly into the public domain. As a result, any video footage created by NASA (nasa.gov), copyright-free material from C-SPAN (c-span.org), or other U.S. governmental bodies are available for you to use without permission. Also see Archive.org (archive.org/details/movies) and Public Resource (public.resource.org).

2. Use content from video sites and services.

There are sites that produce royalty-free video clips that can be used within your music videos, such as iStockPhoto (iStockPhoto.com /video) and Getty Images (GettyImages.com/Footage).

3. Verify the terms.

Be sure to read the agreements carefully before downloading, buying, or using them. The important point about these tools is that they must come with a license that allows you to mix the content with your own video royalty-free.

For more sites and resources, see MakingMoneyWithMusic.com/re sources. For precleared photos and images, see chapter 3, "Your Persona," and for precleared music and sound effects, see chapter 5, "Your Music."

RECORDING YOUR VIDEOS
HOW TO BULK UP YOUR PRESENCE ON YOUTUBE
Your videos are powerful marketing tools, not just for your music but for other videos you do. Your goal with a video channel is to keep them watching your videos to improve your watch time. This makes platforms like YouTube recommend your videos more often. When you sit down to make a video, you quickly realize that nearly everything that you've done to prepare your music business so far comes into play. Here's a checklist to go through before you do your video and get the most out of them:

1. Use the video formats which are optimized for YouTube.
Search for the latest YouTube suggestions for the best video format to upload. Note that YouTube currently prioritizes HD videos in their search, so you should upload HD if you can.

2. Brand your videos.
Nearly every aspect of your brand elements will be used in videos, especially the imagery, logos, and avatars. Consider adding a transparent version of your logo in the corner of the screen, called a bug or chyron, so no matter where your video ends up—promoted on some news or media site or streamed on a TV—viewers can figure out who created the video.

3. Create and use pre-roll and post-roll bumpers to promote other videos.
Pre-roll and post-roll bumpers or end rolls are extra video clips that appear before or after the music video. There are two reasons why you might want to add these tags. First of all, it's simple for your fans to rip the audio into an MP3. If there's extra audio material there, unrelated to the song, it makes it more likely they may purchase your track or stream it where it generates royalties for you rather than try to do some MP3 editing. Second, it allows you to plug your other videos, music, products, merch, or events.

4. Ask for a thumbs-up and to subscribe to your channel and receive notifications.
Subscription rates and thumbs-up rates do go up when you ask for them. Both of these improve your video's chances of being recommended and puts it higher up in search results.

5. Cross-promote within your video.

The time to cross-promote your other work is inside the video, not just in the description or cards. Besides the post-roll bumpers, if it's not a music video, promote inside the content itself. Always treat each video as if it's the first time a fan has run across your content, and use it as an opportunity to turn them on to other things you've done.

6. Prepare your audio.

One of the biggest mistakes you can make is to create a video before the audio is complete. It should be fully mastered, and the audio source for your video program should *not* be an MP3 file. YouTube will re-encode the audio, which will end up a low-quality result. Use the final mastered high-quality WAV files in your production. See chapter 5, "Your Music," for a complete rundown of everything that you need to do for recording, mixing, and mastering your music.

7. Use viral content techniques.

There's no one formula for making a video that will go viral, but if you look at ones that have gone viral before, you can find some trends you can build in. As Nice Peter—who created the wildly successful Epic Rap Battles of History channel (youtube.com/erb), which has over 2.8 billion views—advises, you want to make a video that makes people look cool when they share it. Besides asking your friends if they would want to share your video, you can also build in the following qualities that viral videos have in common: emotion, relevance, surprise, intensity, or something unique and never seen before.

PREPARING YOUR RECORDED VIDEOS FOR RELEASE
HOW TO OPTIMIZE YOUR YOUTUBE VIDEO CHANNEL
FOR VIEWS, PROMOTION, PUBLICITY, AND SALES

There are many techniques to boost subscriptions and views. Use the following for your own channels:

1. Brand your channel name and imagery.

Choose your video channel name so it matches your persona. Your brand elements help connect your videos with the rest of your persona and tell the viewer it's an official presence of yours. Once you have a channel, brand everything YouTube allows you to, including your top banner and other graphics.

2. Create an entertaining channel description.
Most music channels are entertainment, and your description should give the fans a feel for what it's about and get them to try out the videos. This is not the place to put your bio; the entire purpose for the channel description is to get fans to click and watch.

3. Create a custom URL.
Customize your channel's URL so it can be easily remembered and linked to.

4. Choose your most popular videos to be the introductory channel video.
The visitors most likely to watch the introductory video are people who have never seen you before. It should probably be your most popular video to maximize your chances of getting them to watch it all the way through and then check out other videos.

5. Use playlists to organize your channel.
You want to make it easy for your fans to find just what they want, so if you create multiple video projects, such as a vlog, music videos, live content, or "making of" content, organize these into playlists. Playlists are important, since the YouTube algorithm rewards your channel by how long someone watches your videos. Creating playlists up front gives lists you can promote and link to (rather than linking to a specific video).

6. Use your most popular videos to promote your other work.
People will usually discover you through your most popular videos. Think of them as front doors to your world. You can use them to promote everything you do. One of the better ways to do this is to add a card at the beginning of those popular videos, since fans might be rewatching them, and you might be able to direct them to another one of your videos so they can see something new. Keep in mind you can also use your popular videos to promote your music, products, merch, and events.

7. Register your music and videos with Content ID.

To get paid when your music is played on YouTube, register your music with Content ID and follow the steps in chapter 12, "Licensing and Royalties."

8. Follow YouTube's rules.

YouTube has the right to shut down your channel in an instant if you don't follow their terms and conditions, including copyright violations. You should be aware of what they are and follow them to avoid being closed down.

Since there's a lot of work to optimize and promote your channel and videos, we recommend sticking with one channel, rather than creating multiple channels for various projects, especially since you can organize your videos into playlists.

THE TOP TWELVE PREP TIPS TO INCREASE THE NUMBER OF VIEWS ON YOUTUBE

When you upload your videos to YouTube, there are many pre-steps to do to increase the numbers of views you can get once it's published.

1. Create a custom hero image for the video.

When you upload a video to YouTube, you can either choose a frame from your video or upload a custom thumbnail. This thumbnail allows you to have a click-friendly, easily viewable image that looks good viewed on a tiny mobile screen and is branded with your imagery. We recommend you create one for your videos, since it will help reinforce repetition and consistency of your persona.

2. Make each title clickbait.

You will get more clicks if you make the video title suggestive, sexy, bizarre, funny, or controversial. Test them out against friends to see which they like best.

3. Fill in keywords for each video.

YouTube uses keywords to help link similar videos with one another and provide recommendations to viewers. Choose all the keywords that match not only the music but the content of the video as well. For example, if you have a skateboard featured in your video, add *skateboard* as a key-word. Also, match the keywords to the title of the video, as this also helps the search engine. All this work maximizes searchability in Google as well.

4. Use video cards and end rolls to cross-promote and link to other videos on your channel.

With cards and end cards, you can make it more likely people will watch your other videos. The end cards are particularly effective, since they're easy to click and encourage binge-watching of your videos.

5. Begin each video description with calls to action.

Include a full video description, but start it with the call to action to cap-ture the impulse purchase, as many viewers only see the first line. For instance, include a link to buy the music or a live show ticket depending on what the video can promote. If you can, provide an affiliate link so that you get an extra cut.

6. Fill out the rest of the video descriptions with additional information.

Each bit of information you include can give YouTube's search algo-rithm more clues about how to bring your video up in its search results. Include lyrics to music videos, since sometimes casual listeners may know your song only from a lyric. Also include credits, since they might know your band members, and don't shy away from descriptions of what happens in the video for the same reason, since searches like "*the video with the guy who gets hit in the nuts*" is sometimes the only way they remember your video. Don't forget to cross-promote and link to re-lated playlists and videos in your channel so fans can find them (and it also gives the suggestion engine more clues about which videos are re-lated). And promote your sales of merch, high-quality versions of the video if you have them for sale, and other products you sell. Finally, ask for a thumbs-up and subscriptions.

7. Link to playlists, not individual videos.

While sometimes you'll want to link directly to another video on your channel, YouTube's search algorithm rewards the amount of time some-one stays on your channel. So to improve your videos' and channel's rankings, link to video playlists so your visitors spend more time on your channel and increase the number of views on more of your videos.

8. Cross-promote through comments.
Leave comments on videos by similar bands, musicians, and vloggers. You can also appear in each other's videos and cross-promote one another to each other's audiences.

9. Pay for promotion (if you want to).
If you want to spend money to promote your videos, Google makes it easy to run ad campaigns. You can use their AdWords feature (adwords .google.com) or even create video ads (adwords.google.com/home/how -it-works/video-ads).

10. Make sure your videos autopost to your blog and social presences.
If you use autoposting tools, every time you post a video, you will also automatically post a tweet and send a message to all your social presences (see chapter 7, "Your Online Presences").

11. Add captions.
Captions help your views for two reasons. First of all, they provide the search engine with more info about your video and make them more likely to come up when people search for parts of your video thus improving your ranking. Second, they make it more likely that viewers can watch the video if they have to keep the sound off or are in noisy environment, which is all too common if they are watching it on a mobile device.

12. Allow comments to drive rankings.
YouTube comments are unfortunately well known to be a magnet for trolls, so you might need to police your comments if you turn them on. However, comments can improve the ranking of your videos. If you can leave them on, it's worth doing so.

HOW TO BECOME A YOUTUBE PARTNER
YouTube makes their money off advertising on videos they distribute, and if you meet the requirements to become a YouTube partner, you can share in this ad revenue. The requirements can change, but they primarily

revolve around the total number of video views and subscribers you have to your channel, as well as the type of content you provide. This is an additional revenue source and worth striving for. To see how to join, search for their latest FAQ and follow their instructions if you qualify.

HOW TO USE STATISTICS ON YOUTUBE

There are a surprising number of statistics you can get out of your videos beyond just views. This is important because you can use the stats to direct your marketing and promotion campaigns, as well as which videos work and which don't.

Use the analytics tools YouTube provides to see detailed statistics using the analytics button next to each video. This gives you demographic information, how people clicked on your video, and location information for the viewers. Google has also opened up their system to allow other parties to get stats for you. They can go beyond what YouTube provides. Try VidStatsX (vidstatsx.com), SocialBlade (socialblade.com), or ChannelMeter (channelmeter.com) for more data on your videos.

7

YOUR ONLINE PRESENCES

Goal: To plan and organize your global web, social, and mobile presences to promote your work, grow your fan base, and make it easy for people to interact with you and promote you on their social media.

Team Roles and Responsibilities: Web Designer/Webmaster, Social Media Manager, Graphic Artist, Copywriter, Photographer, Video Producer, and Manager

WHAT YOU GET OUT OF THIS

By the end of this chapter, you will:

1. Have a comprehensive framework to build your social, mobile, and web presences for your music business.

2. Be able to share media and content once and post it to your presences automatically, making it easy for fans to get the latest posts no matter where they follow you.

3. Have a method for building an effective website for all audiences that focuses on conversions to maximize promotion, publicity, and revenue-generating opportunities for your business.

MONEY MAP

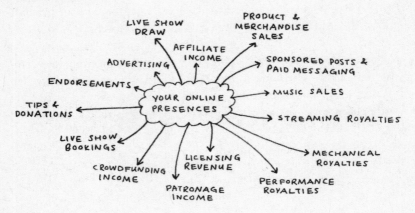

INTRO

Imagine you release a new single, post a blog entry about it, and then head into rehearsal. Shortly after, your autoposting tool tweets a link to your announcement and posts it to all your other social and mobile presences. When you take a break, you notice an email on your phone from your social networking alerting tool informing you someone retweeted your announcement, and another person posted a comment about your new album. You also get a Google Alert email with a link to an MP3 blog that reviewed your album! You sent it weeks ago, giving them a chance to check it out before release, and even though they never told you, they decided to review it, and your alert found it. You click the link, read the review on your phone, and share the good news to your fans and followers via your autoposting tool. This automatically takes your message and posts it to all social and mobile presences so your fans can get a link to the review. Instantly, you've turned all your presences into a coordinated communication channel to broadcast and share your accomplishment. Your five-minute break is over, and you head back to rehearsal to share the good news with the band.

This is the automated system for the web, social, and mobile world you'll be able to put together for yourself that will allow you to be active but spend *less time* on social media. When people talk about you, the alerts will come to you, and when you post something, it will post to every platform at once.

This chapter outlines everything you need to build a comprehensive set of presences for your music. And while these presences are powerful communication channels you control to send messages to your fan base (and we'll discuss how to monetize them in later chapters), *you don't need to do all of it*. While it's important to have an interconnected presence on many platforms, you should carefully consider which ones you want to invest time and effort in and maintain. Plus, this world is constantly changing with new services becoming must-have presences, and others are disappearing while taking your data with it, so your strategy must let you keep up to date with the changes while keeping it simple to let your fans find you no matter where they hang out.

KEY CONCEPTS
UNDERSTANDING CONTRACTS, WEB USER AGREEMENTS, AND PRIVACY POLICIES

All web, social, and mobile platforms require you to create an account and will eventually have you agree to a user agreement. When you signed up for these sites as an individual, you probably didn't bother reading them, but when you're working to make money with music, like any business, you need to start paying attention to these, since some may require you to give up certain rights.

You must ensure these agreements don't overreach and hamper any plans you have for your music, videos, or other content you upload. For example, the user agreements for music sites can be especially aggressive about copyrights, sometimes granting them the right to sell your music on compilation albums or to use it in other ways you might find objectionable. We routinely find websites that have bad user agreements and decide not to use them.

Also, if you're sharing images, music, and other content on the web, you should be aware of your own personal privacy rights, as well as the implications for your business. Photos you share often have GPS location data—and so while you're thinking you're sharing just the photo, you may be sharing your location embedded as metadata in the photo.

To avoid these kinds of problems, read the agreement of every website and service you use, and make sure you can live with it. If you are uncertain about the meanings behind any agreements, you should consult with your attorney.

THE SIX-POINT DIGITAL STRATEGY
HOW TO ORGANIZE YOUR WEBSITE, WEB PRESENCES,
AND SOCIAL NETWORKS

Here's a simple way to think about all your web presences and to organize your web strategy. You should have websites and services in each
of the categories below to make it easy for you to share music, videos,
photos, and text and stay on top of what people are saying about you no
matter where they're saying it. The following six categories will help
you determine what you need and which web presences you should
have:

1. Content hosts.

The goal is to choose just one host for each type of content: blog entries,
photos, videos, music, or others. Autoposting tools pick up the content
generated from content hosts and automatically share it with all your presences.

2. Outposts.

Outposts are places on the web where anyone can find you, such as websites, social networks, stores, mobile presences for your music, music
hosts, your own website, and even your Xbox Live account. With some
simple steps, most outposts pull from your automated feeds to get the latest news so they stay alive and fresh.

3. Autoposting tools.

Autoposting tools pick up feeds and automatically post them to your
outposts. With tools like Hootsuite (hootsuite.com), you will post just
once and spread the same data everywhere.

4. Conversion tools.

No matter where your audience finds you, the goal is to *convert* them
from casual visitors into fans and customers. Since you want to make
money with music, the presences you build should be aimed at getting
visitors to interact with your conversion tools. This means you should put
embedded streaming playlists or Play buttons; merch stores; links to buy
your music; and other conversion tools into your online presences. We
cover the concept of marketing goals and provide a full list of conversions
in detail in chapter 14, "Marketing."

5. Alert and notification tools.

Whether someone tweets about you, writes about you, or covers you in a story, you want to know about it. With alert and notification tools like Google Alerts (google.com/alerts), Mention (mention.com), and Social Oomph (socialoomph.com), you will get an email every time it happens.

6. Metrics tools.

Use metrics tools to get statistics such as how many people listened to your tracks across all music and video services, how many new social media follows you got last week, and the demographics of your audience. Rather than going to each site and counting them yourself, sites like Next Big Sound (nextbigsound.com) can consolidate all this information for you and produce reports.

HOW TO DETERMINE WHERE YOU NEED TO SIGN UP: A WEB STRATEGY CHECKLIST

Use the table below as a checklist to determine what kinds of places you can use to promote your music. You can also go to MakingMoneyWith Music.com/resources for tracking ideas and tools and clickable versions of all the links.

Web Strategy Checklist

Type	What	Description
Outpost	Domain Registrar	Domain registrars let you register your website domain name at sites like Namecheap (namecheap.com), GoDaddy (godaddy.com), or Gandi (gandi.net/en). For example, we own beatnikturtle.com and TheSongOfTheDay.com.
Outpost	Web Host	Choose a web host to host your domain. Many domain registrars provide this, too, but it's not required to use theirs even though they go out of their way to make it seem that way. You have free options like Blogger (blogger.com) and WordPress (wordpress.com), or hosting sites like HostBaby (hostbaby.com), ReverbNation (reverbnation.com), and Bandzoogle (band zoogle.com) to provide this, although there are numerous options.

Type	What	Description
Outpost	Web Platform or CMS	Many web hosts, like Bandzoogle (bandzoogle.com) or HostBaby (hostbaby.com) will provide a content management system, or CMS, for you. But you can also use solutions like WordPress (wordpress.com), Joomla (joomla.org), or Drupal (drupal.org).
Content Host, Outpost	Blog	Blogs are optional, but they are a good idea to have, as they make it simple to repost news to all the web presences you have. Your website may have a built-in blog, but there are advantages to using blog hosts like Blogger (blogger.com), Tumblr (tumblr.com), or WordPress (wordpress.com).
Content Host, Outpost	Photo and Image Hosts	Keep your photos and images in one place so you can easily make albums and share them to all your presences. Some examples include sites like Google Photos (photos.google.com), Flickr (flickr.com), and Photobucket (photobucket.com).
Content Host, Outpost	Video Host	While YouTube (youtube.com) dominates this space, and every musician should have a presence there, you may want to consider other high-end video hosts like Vimeo (vimeo.com), which has advanced video options.
Content Host, Outpost	Audio Host	You will want to consider having your music in places that aren't easily shareable so you have another place for fans to discover your music. Try sites like ReverbNation (reverbnation.com) or Bandcamp (bandcamp.com).
Outpost	Streaming Music Services	Streaming music services like Spotify and Apple Music are places where you can create a presence and playlists.
Outpost	Social Networks	You should be part of as many social networks as you can keep up with, including Twitter, Facebook (including a fan page), Instagram, and others.

Type	What	Description
Content Host, Outpost	Live Media Presence Sites	You can live-stream video to your fans with services such as YouTube Live, Facebook Live (live.fb.com), Periscope (pscp.tv), and many others. Also, services like Google Hangouts (hangouts.google.com) and Skype (skype.com) allow you to create two-way video chats.
Outpost	Location-Sharing Sites	While you may wish your location to remain private, some musicians may want to broadcast where they are using social sites like Four-square Swarm (swarmapp.com) or Facebook (facebook.com). This is especially useful when you are on tour.
Outpost	Mobile Pres-ences	Create your own mobile app for your music using services like GigRev (gigrev.com), Mobile Roadie (mobileroadie.com), Artist Ecard (artistecard.com), or Shoutem (shoutem.com).
Content Host, Outpost	Show Calendar and Event Log	You can keep show calendars in many different ways on your web presences, but it's best to do it through services like Eventful (eventful.com) or JamBase (jambase.com), where you can enter it once and share it through all your presences.
Conversion Tool	Music Store/ Streaming Platform	As we talk about in chapter 9, "Distribution and Streaming," you'll want embeddable streaming playlists and Play buttons and links to purchase your tracks online.
Conversion Tool	Merch Store	As we talk about in chapter 10, "Products and Merchandise," you'll want links to your merch platform or embeddable stores for merchandise. No matter whether you sell digital, physical, fulfillment, or on-demand services, you can easily drop in widgets, apps, or plug-ins to sell your merch directly to your fans from all your web presences.

Type	What	Description
Conversion Tool	Tips, Crowdfunding, and Patronage	As we discuss chapter 11, "Patronage, Crowd-funding, and Raising Money," tips, crowdfunding, and patronage all have conversion tools such as links, images, and videos to help you get more funders, patrons, and tippers from your audience. You can use services like PayPal (PayPal.Me) for this.
Conversion Tool	Mailing List	Capture new mailing list members using widgets so you can keep them informed of your activities and events through a newsletter. These work best when you can offer something for joining the list, such as free music or videos they can't get otherwise. You can use services like MailChimp (mailchimp.com), Constant Contact (constantcontact.com), ReverbNation (reverb nation.com), and Band Letter (bandletter.com).
Conversion Tool	Contact Tools	Use contact tools to embed email or contact forms in your web presences to make you easy to reach.
Conversion Tool	One-Click Sharing	Autoposting tools like ShareThis (sharethis .com) or Shareaholic (shareaholic.com) can make it easy for your fans to share your website, blog, and other content.
Autopost-ing Tool	Autoposting Solutions	One you create your content hosts, per above, use tools like Hootsuite (hootsuite.com) or SocialOomph (socialoomph.com) to automati-cally post the information to all your outposts. (And note that in some cases, you can get autoposting to occur without a tool.)
Alerts and Notifica-tions	Alerting Tools	Use alerting tools like Google Alerts (google .com/alerts) or Mention (mention.com) to send you notifications whenever you are talked about online. Set them up to watch for your artist name, your album or project names, the names of your band members, and the names of artists that are similar to yours (to get ideas about where to get mentioned yourself).

Type	What	Description
Alerts and Notifica-tions	Social Media Alerts	Tools like SocialOomph (socialoomph.com), Hootsuite (hootsuite.com), and TweetDeck (tweetdeck.com) allow you to get emails when someone tweets your name. You won't have to spend time searching this yourself and can just react to mentions when they happen.
Metrics Tool	Web Analytics	Tools like Google Analytics (google.com /analytics) allow you to hook metrics into your web presences to find out where your visitors came from, what they clicked on, and how long they stayed.
Metrics Tool	Artist Statistics Tools	Sites like Next Big Sound (nextbigsound.com) and ReverbNation (reverbnation.com) grab stats from multiple presences and combine them into a single dashboard to tell you how you've been doing. Also go directly to the bigger sites, such as Spotify for Artists (artists.spotify.com) and iTunes Connect (itunesconnect.apple.com).
Metrics Tool	Social Statistics Tools	If you have a Facebook fan page (facebook .com), you will get weekly stats as to how it's doing, but for some outposts, you can use other tools like Twitter Counter (twittercounter .com) and Klout (klout.com).
Helpful Hint	Login and Password Solutions	Keeping track of all the sites, logins, and passwords is a challenge. Use tools like Google Docs (docs.google.com/document/), where you can make a protected spreadsheet to keep track of it all, or for a more secure solution, use password tools like 1password.com (1password .com), or for a free solution for your desktop, try Password Gorilla (fpx.de/fp/Software/Gorilla).

HOW TO SET UP ALL YOUR PRESENCES SO YOU CAN "POST ONCE, SEND EVERYWHERE"

Autoposting tools allow you to post each type of content—like photos, videos, blogs, tweets, and more—just once and send the data to your outposts. For example, when you post a new video, the autoposting tools will automatically tweet a link to your new video. Autoposting tools are the reason your content will appear on all your outposts with no effort on your part.

To begin autoposting, choose a tool such as Hootsuite (hootsuite .com) or SocialOomph (socialoomph.com), set up an account, and tie it to your other feeds and outposts. Most autoposting tools include metrics, so you should explore each tool and see what it provides. Reviewing these metrics can help you understand if what you're posting or what service you're using is effective or if you need to make any adjustments.

YOUR WEBSITE

WHY YOU NEED A WEBSITE

The shortest marketing message that says the most about your music is your website URL. It can get them everything they need in a handful of letters. You will be putting it on T-shirts, stickers, albums, posters, and more.

Besides having your *own name* to send email from and put on your T-shirts, your website has many features social networks lack. While social networking sites usually succeed at making it easy to interact with fans, your fans aren't the only visitors to your website. For example, where in a Facebook fan page do you put booking information? Is there a good place to put song licensing info? How about a press page to show past media coverage and give facts about the artist so journalists can write about you? Social networking pages also provide limited options for format and design, since they want to brand themselves and display ads; the same ads compete with your music and try to send your hard-earned visitor somewhere else.

Your website also has powerful statistics social networks lack, such as when visitors arrived, how long they stayed, what they read, what they listened to and for how long, and who referred them to your page. Knowing who links to you and how many came there from a source can let you know how effective your publicity campaigns are.

Setting up a site doesn't have to be hard. Sites like Squarespace (square space.com), Wix (wix.com), and Shopify (shopify.com) allow you to quickly create a template-based website easily with your own domain name. Also, sites that originated as blog platforms, such as WordPress (wordpress.com) and Blogger (blogger.com), can be configured as websites as well, but for free. Some will even allow you to use your own domain name.

Finally, when building a site, be aware of search engine optimization (SEO), which means making your website search engine–friendly as well as making it fan-friendly. While the rules for SEO change often, if you can, use SEO plug-ins to your websites to handle building in the features search engines need to index your site and raise its ranking so they show up higher in search results. Since this is a deep topic with a lot of info, tools, and background, we cover more about it in MakingMoneyWithMusic .com/resources.

THE SEVEN AUDIENCES YOU SHOULD DESIGN YOUR WEBSITE TO HANDLE

Before you sit down to plan your site, understand this key point: your website is primarily a marketing tool. Even if you're just giving music away, you still need to convince your fans to download the music. Aim your website at getting your fans to *do something*: download music, talk about your music on their social networks, buy music or merch, come to see your show, license your music, or book you. Each of these conversions drives the design, text, and images on the pages of your site.

Here are the seven audiences you will likely find on your website:

1. Music fans

2. Live music fans

3. Bookers and talent buyers

4. The press and journalists

5. People who want to license your music

6. Sound people/stage crew

7. Random visitors

Each has a different expectation, and you want each of them to take a different action. See the table (page 127) "Your Audiences, What They Want, and What You Want Them to Do" to put this all together. Once you plan your website using this structure, you can put the conversion tools in the right places.

UNDERSTANDING THE IMPORTANCE OF MUSIC WEBSITE DESIGN

Designing a music website can seem confusing until you decide which audiences (listed above) you are targeting. Each of these audiences is coming to your site looking for something you will need to provide them, and then get them to take an action.

To meet this need, each page of your website should answer three questions:

1. Who is it for?

2. What do they want?

3. What do you want them to do when they get there?

The best pages satisfy visitors' needs while growing your fan base, bookings, sales, and show draw.

The *design* of each page should answer one other question: How do you want the visitor to *feel*? Never lose sight of the fact that a music website is primarily entertainment and is more than a pile of information and content. They should walk away *feeling* the way you want them to. This is even true of a bookings page; if you have an exciting show, the booking page should give them the info they need while making them feel pumped up.

The table on page 127 breaks this down for the most common music website audiences and answers these questions. Use this to help structure your own site.

THE TWENTY DIFFERENT PAGES YOU CAN PUT ON YOUR WEBSITE

Use the handy table on page 129 to decide what pages you want to have available on your website. You should only choose the pages you need for your site.

Note that not every page needs to be on your major navigation bar. Many of the pages on your site may be in a set of links from the bottom of the website for the detailed information.

YOUR MOST IMPORTANT PAGE: "CONTACT US"

No matter what content you put up, you need a Contact Us page. It's hard enough creating opportunities for yourself; you don't want to block the ones who come knocking. Almost all our best opportunities have come

Your Audiences, What They Want, and What You Want Them to Do

Audience	Expectations	Conversions	Site Features
Music Fans	Finding tour dates. Finding upcoming shows. Discovering latest projects. Buying your albums and merchandise. Listening to your music. Viewing photos and videos. Participating in the fan community.	Joining the mailing list. Subscribing to the blogs. Participating in the forum. Buying the albums and merchandise. Coming to shows. Telling friends about you.	News. Blog. Forum. About the Artist. Music. Photos. Videos. Store. Calendar and Event Announce- ments. Mailing List.
Live Music Fans	Finding the time, location, ticket price, other artists playing, and directions and map to the show. Knowing if there's any drink minimum.	Coming to the show. Bringing friends. Promoting the event. Discussing the event in the forum.	Calendar and Event Announce- ments. News. Blog. Forums. Mailing List.
Bookers and Talent Buyers	Finding booking info/booker contact info, tour and location info; artist performance history; fan and venue testimonials; flyers, bios, and other text and images.	Booking the artist.	Booker contact info. Testimonials. Calendar and Event Log. Music. Photos. Contact Us.

Audience	Expectations	Conversions	Site Features
The Press and Journalists	Downloading the press kit and press releases. Contact the artist for interviews. Finding images and credit info for the article.	Writing articles about the artist. Reviewing the latest album. Featuring the latest project. Contact you or your publicist for interviews.	Press Information. News. Music. Photos. Contact Us.
Sound People/ Stage Crew	Determining the style of music and instrumentation. Preparing for any special sound needs. Viewing stage plot and microphone layout.	Contacting you. Making you sound good onstage.	Stage Plots, Instrumentation, Sound/ Performance Information. Music. Contact Us.
People Who Want to License Your Music	Listening to songs. Requesting high-quality versions. Determining licensing requirements. Finding noncommercial use requirements. Determining pod-safe status.	Contacting you to license your songs.	Contact Us.
Random Visitors	Be entertained.	Listening to music. Watching videos. Buying albums and merchandise. Joining the mailing list. Subscribing to blogs.	Music. Photos. Videos. About the Artist. Store. News. Blog. Forum.

through the site this way. Gigs, music-licensing opportunities, interviews, and songwriting commissions have all come to our attention via the web form and email address on this page. You may include a phone number too, if you're comfortable releasing it. For instance, when ABC Family–Disney wanted to license one of our songs for a commercial, they

Music Website Pages

Content	Description
About the Artist	Basic information about the artist, style of music, similar groups, members and bios, instrumentation, hometown, and history.
News	Latest news. Place the latest story on the front page with older stories cycling to a separate news page. If possible, offer an RSS feed.
Blog	Offer one or more blogs with more personal perspectives, as well as an RSS feed for each.
Show Calendar and Event Log	Upcoming shows as well as a catalog of past shows and other events you've played.
Music	This should include all the music you've made available to the public. You can upload and link MP3 files or sample clips, use streaming players from services such as Spotify, Apple Music, Google Play, and others, or use embeddable music players from your audio host. Always provide music so they can listen immediately, but if you let fans download the music, try to get something in exchange, such as their email or contact information for your mailing list.
Store	All products and merch available for sale with photos and descriptions of each, or links or widgets from vendors.
Album Information	Information on each of your albums, including lyrics, liner notes, and possibly guitar tablature or full sheet music.
Photos	Albums of photos, recent performances, and other events.

Content	Description
Videos	This should include some of your top videos.
Information for the Press	This is your press kit and includes the artist bio, press releases, press-ready photos, logos and other images, press clippings, and contact info, including the press representative's email and phone number.
Information for Bookers	This is your booking kit and includes your booker's contact info and booking information, stage and microphone plot, and press-ready photos and images.
Testimonials	Quotes from fans, bookers, venues, and satisfied customers from corporate events, festivals, weddings, and parties.
Stage and Performance Information for Sound People	Stage and microphone plot, instrumentation, and any other information a sound person might need.
Forums	A place for fans to talk about you, arrange shared rides to your performances, coordinate grassroots promotion, and so on.
Mailing List Information	Information about your mailing list and an easy sign-up process.
Contact Us	Usually a web contact form, but it can be as simple as an email address.
Site Map	A map of the entire site to help people find what they want.
Legal Information	Any legal information, such as the copyright or Creative Commons license, privacy-policy statement (for your mailing list), and so on.
Links	Links to external sites, such as individual musician pages, other artists, favorite venues, and so on.
Artist-Only Area	Optional special protected section to store files or other artist-only materials.

left multiple voice mail messages with all the numbers we had posted in addition to emailing because they were under a deadline.

You should have the Contact Us link at the top or bottom of each page and built into your template so any new pages feature it automatically. If you use a web contact form rather than a direct email address, verify that it works properly.

UNDERSTANDING THE IMPORTANCE OF A PRIVACY POLICY

If people are going to be sharing their information with you, which they may do on your website, on your mailing list, or through giving information to any one of your web presences or conversion tools, then they'll want to know their private information is safe with you. With identity theft and spam on the rise, it's not hard to understand why. To set people at ease, you should create and post a policy for how you plan to handle the personal information you collect from them. It not only builds trust, having a privacy page on your website will improve its SEO.

Create a clear and concise policy that tells visitors and those signing up on your mailing list you won't share their information with any third parties for other purposes. Check with your attorney when setting and creating this policy so you understand the implications it has for your business. This policy should have its own page, which you should link to your mailing list signup page, store, and any other area where you ask for personal information.

BRINGING THE REAL WORLD INTO THE DIGITAL WORLD

HOW TO PUT QR CODES (LIKE SNAPCODES AND OTHER SOCIAL IDS) ON YOUR PROMOTIONAL MATERIALS, PRODUCTS, AND MERCHANDISE

Since you're a digital musician, your goal is to pull people back into your digital world even if they are encountering you at a show or in the street. Fortunately, you can turn fans in the real world into followers through the use of quick response codes, or QR codes. These are special bar codes smartphones and cameras can read that typically store URLs or other digital information.

Since most people have smartphones, use this to your advantage: add QR codes, Snapcodes, and other social IDs to as many of your physical presences as possible. For instance, add them to your physical products, merchandise, promotional material for your live shows, your merch table, and more. More and more services are creating QR codes. These include making QR codes out of your website, patronage site, and social presences with sites like QR Code Generator (goqr.me), music streaming sites like Spotify, and social media accounts.

8

YOUR RIGHTS

Goal: To understand and leverage your intellectual property rights so you can sell, license, promote, and protect your creative works and generate revenue for your music business.

Team Roles and Responsibilities: Manager, Attorney, Accountant/Bookkeeper, and Business Banker

WHAT YOU GET OUT OF THIS
By the end of this chapter, you will:

1. Have an overview of copyright law, trademark law, publicity rights, and merchandising rights so you can set up your business to make money from each of these as covered in the next section of the book, "Getting Paid and Making Money."

2. Know how and why to register all released song compositions and sound recordings with the copyright office for full statutory protections (U.S. and Canada only).

3. Create split sheets for each composition and sound recording to document ownership and properly distribute royalties.

4. Know how to get permission and clear copyrights for songs you want to cover, interpolations, samples, mash-ups, and loops.

5. Understand work-for-hire agreements.

6. Know how to register trademarks to protect your name, logo, and other brand elements.

INTRO

Nearly all the ways to make money from music are based on the legal rights you own in your music, imagery, and brand. While you don't need to become an expert in the law, you need to understand the basics because it forms the basis of the revenue-generating methods in the next section, "Getting Paid and Making Money." You also need to understand how to protect yourself if you use other people's work, play cover songs, or run into a contract with unfamiliar legal terms.

But once you understand the basics of the law, which we'll explain in plain language below, you can use it to both protect *and* promote your music and persona. You'll soon understand why it's generally safe to play cover songs in bars, but why you owe money if you make a version of someone else's song. You'll learn how to register copyrights of your own music and how this allows you to license and collect royalties for your music (which we detail in chapter 12, "Licensing and Royalties"). You'll understand how publicity, merchandising rights, and trademark law protect you and open up a wealth of additional revenue streams you can tap into.

UNDERSTANDING COPYRIGHT
UNDERSTANDING INTELLECTUAL PROPERTY

Under the law, your expression of original music is treated as property similar to real estate; you actually *own* your music. This means these expressions can be owned, sold, rented (licensed), gifted, or given away for free. Since this *intellectual property* forms the basis of how you can make money with music, you need to understand it so you can make money off it.

That said, musicians, compared to other types of artists, have their rights defined by some of the most convoluted intellectual property laws ever created, which come into play when you write a song, cover a song onstage, record a song of your own, and even if you hand your song to a filmmaker to use for free. Each of these activities has entirely different legal issues associated with it. The laws behind them were originally intended to protect record labels, music publishers, and other middlemen instead of independent artists who play the role of all these middlemen and own every aspect of their music. This is why you'll end up registering the same song multiple times to get all the royalties you're owed, as we'll cover in chapter 12, "Licensing and Royalties."

To help you navigate this, below is an overview of the intellectual property laws powering a large percentage of your income-generating methods in plain language. Plus, we'll outline the key differences between music-related laws in the U.S., Canada, the UK, Ireland, Australia, and New Zealand. Once you understand the basics, you will also realize why it's extremely important to document who owns these rights such as in a band agreement or other business formation documents, since they're the source of much of the money you'll be making as we discussed in detail in chapter 2, "Your Music Business."

HOW TO COPYRIGHT YOUR MUSIC (IT'S AUTOMATIC!)

Copyright protects "original works of authorship" whether they are literary, artistic, or musical. All the music you create, videos you make, and text you write is copyrightable. Thanks to an international copyright treaty dating back to 1886 between 174 countries (called the "Berne Convention for the Protection of Literary and Artistic Works"), whether you're in the U.S., Canada, the UK, Ireland, Australia, or New Zealand, you don't need to register your music with any governmental copyright office to get copyright protection. Copyright is created *automatically* when you:

1. Create and express something original.

Only an original work can be granted copyright protection. Note that copyright law doesn't protect the *ideas* underlying your work, just the unique way you express them. For instance, with music, the subject or theme underlying the lyrics wouldn't be granted copyright protection, but the lyrics themselves are granted protection. In disputes, the courts decide what's original.

2. Capture it in a fixed, tangible format.

There are multiple ways to capture your original music in a fixed format. This includes recording it in your DAW, video, captured as sheet music in a program or on paper, or even singing it into your voice mail.

Once you've met these two steps, congrats! The original work is now your property.

The length of your copyright depends on the copyright law in your country. In most countries, copyright lasts a minimum of life of the creator plus fifty years for most works (the song, the sound recording, written works, art). However, within the U.S., copyright lasts seventy years after your death, regardless of the type of work. If, however, you created a business entity and made the business the copyright owner, then the copyright may last either fifty, seventy, or, in the U.S., ninety-five years from its publication. This means you'll own the copyright to your original music for a long time, and that copyright should be treated as you would any property you own. For instance, you would want to include your copyright ownership in your will so the beneficiaries of your estate can continue to collect any revenue it may generate.

THE TOP TEN RIGHTS YOU GET UNDER COPYRIGHT LAW

When you own the copyright in some work, whether it's music, text, video, photos, images, and so on, you get a number of rights for it that can make you income. For instance, you can:

1. Reproduce your work.

2. Physically distribute your work.

3. Digitally distribute your work.

4. Broadcast and transmit your work.

5. Perform your work in public.

6. Make adaptations, modifications, and arrangements to the original work.

7. Create other derivative works based on the original work.

8. Publicly display the work.

9. Translate the work.

10. Use your work within an audiovisual work.

In general, no one can exercise any of the above rights without your permission (with some exceptions where you must give a compulsive license). You can also sue for infringement if someone infringes your rights. But most of the time, you'll be looking for ways to let others use your work in exchange for money, licensing it to them for specific purposes.

Note that countries outside of the U.S. allow their copyright owners one additional right: *the right to deny permission of use*. This is called *"moral rights."* Moral rights include the right to be identified as the creator of the work; the right to object to your work being used in a manner that's derogatory or you don't approve of, such as by a political party you don't support or for a cause you don't believe in; and the right to object to someone erroneously claiming they created the work.

Countries with moral rights grant them automatically; however, you must make it known you're the creator of the work. If you're a songwriter in Europe, depending on your country, this may mean these rights can never be transferred to others (assigned) or contracted away to someone else (waived). However, if you're in Canada, you do have the choice to assign or waive these rights if you so choose. Since this right doesn't exist in the U.S. for musical works, every election year some musicians object to their songs being associated with a particular party during their rallies but can't stop them from performing their song (they do, however, collect royalties for its use).

Lastly, "fair use" isn't a right under copyright. In fact, it's just an affirmative defense to an infringement claim. The fair-use defense allows the use of copyrighted works for specific uses, such as news reporting, commentary, teaching, and criticism (e.g., movie reviews). Claiming fair use to use someone's copyrighted work you don't have permission to use (such as sampling someone else's sound recording) doesn't automatically protect you from infringement claims, but it could possibly defend you from a lawsuit. At the end of the day, the courts decide what's "fair" based on the facts and a complicated legal test.

THE TWO TYPES OF COPYRIGHTS IN MUSIC: THE COMPOSITION AND THE SOUND RECORDING

When you create a new original song, you create two separate copyrights: the *composition* and the *sound recording*. Each generates separate income streams, and each can have different owners. If you're an independent artist, you have a copyright in the recording (the master) you created and a copyright in the composition (the song itself: the music, melody, and lyrics).

Note that if you make a remix or alternate versions of your compositions, such as an acoustic or live version, you'll get a new sound recording copyright for each one, but there will still be only one composition. If you create many different versions of your songs for release to generate streams and sales as we suggest in chapter 5, "Your Music," you'll probably have far more sound recording copyrights than composition copyrights.

If you are on a label, you will probably have to sign away the copyright to your sound recordings based on the recording agreement you have with them. While you lose the revenue streams associated with the sound recordings, they will usually promote your songs and you as an artist.

HOW TO KEEP TRACK OF WHO OWNS WHAT IN YOUR MUSIC: SPLIT SHEET AGREEMENTS

If you work with other musicians, you'll want to make sure to define who owns the compositions and sound recordings, since there's money at stake. You can do this using a song and sound recording split agreement so you can register them properly and make sure the associated licensing and royalties can get distributed to the right people.

Split sheets give you a written, signed record so you can avoid disputes and accurate split percentages to register your compositions and sound recordings. For song split agreements, this includes who wrote what and what percentage of the song they own. For sound recording split agreements, this includes who owns the masters. If there's ever a dispute, you can return to the split sheet everyone signed at the time. Plus, if need be, the written agreements can be used as evidence in a court of law. You'll refer back to your split agreements when you register the songs with the PROs to calculate the proper percentage ownerships in each song and master.

Since musicians collaborate with multiple people to get their music recorded, it's a good idea to capture the information below on a song-by-song and sound recording–by–sound recording basis. Or, if you're working with the same people often, you can negotiate an agreement that can apply to every song you create. Here's what to track in each of these split agreements:

1. The song split agreement (defining ownership of the composition).

When most musicians refer to a split sheet, this is the version they're usually talking about, as it's the most common. This agreement typically documents:

- The name of the agreement ("song split agreement") and an identification number that can be referred to in the future.

- The name of the song.

- The date of creation.

- Who the songwriter or writers are and who wrote what percentage of the music, lyrics, and melody. You can agree to split it any way you want: divide it equally between all those in the room at the time of creation or broken out by who contributed what part and how much to the song.

- Songwriter contact information (email, phone, address, etc.).

- Which PRO the songwriter is associated with and who their publisher is. (We discuss this in chapter 12, "Licensing and Royalties.")

- Signatures memorializing everyone is in agreement and the signature date.

2. The sound recording split agreement (defining ownership of the sound recording).

If you're an independent musician and are financing the production, you can decide to keep all the master rights, or you can split it with the musicians who work on it. If you decide to split your sound recording, capture the following suggested items:

- The name of the agreement ("sound recording split agreement") and an identification number that can be referred to in the future. Keep in mind you can have many more of these agreements, since songs typically have multiple sound recordings—demos, live versions, studio versions, remixes, and so on—all created over time on multiple computers or at different recording studios.

- The name of the composition and, if you own the song, a reference to the song split agreement that already would have documented who created what for the composition (this is where the identification number comes in).

- The name of the sound recording (give it a separate name from the composition because it might be a live version or remix).

- The date of creation.

- The studio where the sound recording was made.

- Document the ownership splits on who owns the sound recording masters.

- For each split, capture their PRO and publisher affiliation, including their SoundExchange PRO information (if in the U.S.).

- Who the producer is (if any), whether they were paid up front, whether they get a percentage ownership of the sound recording (known as *"points"*), and/or if they need to be included on a *revised* song split agreement due to their altering of an existing song.

- Who mastered the recording, whether they were paid up front (with a reference to their agreement), or whether they get a percentage ownership of the sound recording.

- Signatures memorializing everyone is in agreement and the signature date.

For downloadable split sheets, head to MakingMoneyWithMusic .com/resources. It's a good idea to have an attorney review or create the agreements for you so you can be confident in them going forward and understand them.

Once you agree to splitting composition or sound-recording percentages, you or someone on your team has to keep track of any money made in the future so everyone can get paid. And since copyright lasts the life of the last creator alive plus decades after, this is quite a commitment. This is why some artists hire musicians as a work-for-hire (which we talk about next) so they can own all the copyrights and have no future commitments.

Making sure everyone is paid in a timely manner is important, so you'll also want to define who on your team will be keeping track of the accounting and work out the timing of payments with everyone ahead of time. Note that your distribution partner may assist by allowing you to set up splits that automatically route your income to the right parties.

UNDERSTANDING WORK-FOR-HIRE AND COPYRIGHT

A work-for-hire contract provision assigns the copyright from the person creating the work to the party that hired them. Once these rights are given up, it removes the requirement to parcel out the percentages in song and sound recordings as discussed above. Normally, people charge a higher cost to give up their rights, since the creator is forgoing future licensing fees and royalties, but this is always negotiable. If you don't include a work-for-hire provision in writing ahead of time, the creator retains all copyright in their work even if you are paying them to create it.

Work-for-hire agreements should be in writing and must state both parties agree:

• Any works created by the other person is to be a "work made for hire." If you are in the U.S., many agreements cite Section 101 of the Copyright Act (17 U.S.C. 101) which defines what a work-for-hire is.

• The work and all rights contained within will be the sole and exclusive property of the hiring party throughout the world, without limitation, be royalty-free, and in perpetuity in exchange for the named fee.

• If for any reason the work is deemed not a work-for-hire under the law, the creator agrees to sell, assign, and transfer entire right, title, and interest in the copyrighted work and any registrations or renewals to the hiring party.

You'll want to use work-for-hire arrangements when you hire a photographer to take pictures; a graphic artist to design a logo for your online persona or T-shirt design; or any other creative work. If you don't, *they* will own the copyright and can charge you fees for each use. For example, if you hire a photographer and you don't agree up front in writing it's a work-for-hire arrangement, you would have to ask for permission and pay the photographer a fee for each use of their photo of you. This could add up, since you usually would want to use the photo as one of your key persona elements on your website, in your booking or press kit, on your album art, posters, and more. And if you hire a graphic designer to create a logo, you should own it.

WHAT TO DO IF SOMEONE WANTS TO HAVE YOU SIGN A WORK-FOR-HIRE AGREEMENT

If someone hires *you* to create music for them, you'll want to try to avoid signing a work-for-hire agreement and instead be flexible in *licensing* the work. This allows you to give them what they want while keeping the rights in the future. If someone hiring you to make music for them wants to specify a work-for-hire arrangement, try one or more of the following negotiation tactics. This may allow you to retain most of the rights or at least be properly compensated for a work-for-hire:

1. Create an extra up-front fee in exchange for giving up future income streams.

As noted above, giving up your copyright and the future publishing and licensing fees you could have made should come at a higher cost. It's worth emphasizing why it would be cheaper for them to let you retain the rights and instead license specific uses for them. If that doesn't work, then you should have a total work-for-hire dollar figure in mind before you negotiate, keeping in mind time value of money (you'll be asking them for a higher fee today on the chance it could have made you publishing and licensing fees in the future). If you know the total work-for-hire fee you'd be comfortable with giving up your rights ahead of time, it will help your negotiation so you settle on a price that's fairer to you.

2. Know what rights you have and be creative in how you license them.

Keep in mind that their use of what they're asking you to create for them may involve both the composition and the sound-recording copyrights. You may be able to argue that agreeing to a work-for-hire might cost them more money than if they allow you to license specific rights for them. Another possibility might be they only want a single mix of the song and sound recording you're creating for them. While they might own this song, they might not ask for or want the master tracks, since most people hiring musicians don't have DAWs or music software. This means you might be able to negotiate additional fees if they ever need to come back to you to adjust the mix, extend the song, or do additional work. If, however, they insist on a work-for-hire and the masters as well, you can make the masters an additional negotiation point and another fee.

3. Specify the attribution.

Note that even if you agree to a work-for-hire, you can always negotiate that they must credit you as being the artist or composer whenever they use the work, even though they own the copyright and have rights to use it.

These are just three tactics, and an attorney likely will have other ideas about how to negotiate with clients to let you retain the rights while they get the license they need. Like music, negotiating agreements is also a very creative process. As any lawyer will tell you, while it's a tactic to say an agreement is "boilerplate" and "standard," that doesn't mean you have to accept the terms "as is," so be clear about what you'll accept. The key is to get full financial value out of the work that you create.

HOW TO REGISTER YOUR COPYRIGHTS

In most countries, such as the UK, Ireland, Australia, and New Zealand, you don't need to register anything with a copyright office, since copyright is automatic under the Berne Convention, as we explained earlier in the chapter. That said, the U.S. and Canada will allow you to register your songs or sound recordings with them.

Registering your already copyrighted works with the U.S. Copyright Office (copyright.gov) or Canadian Copyright Office (cipo.ic.gc.ca/copyrights) creates a public record of your copyright claim by a recognized governmental authority. It's a way to declare to the world that on a certain date you created a song or sound recording. That's it. They won't listen to what you sent or compare it to other works in their system. Instead, all they do is create a file in their database outlining the details of your claim.

Note that registering in the U.S. enhances your rights as well if you do so before or within three months of publication. This gives you statutory benefits such as the right to sue for infringement, the right to sue the infringing party for attorney's fees and the fact you don't have to prove actual damages. Each of these are valid reasons to register your works before you release them.

Registration with the U.S. and Canadian Copyright Offices is not hard to do (you shouldn't need to hire a lawyer do this!), but it does cost money. Keep in mind this isn't required to make income from your music, such as selling or collecting royalties; it's only to protect it. But, should you choose to register your songs and sound recordings with one of these offices, we recommend doing so electronically.

Some things to keep in mind include:

1. Decide what songs and sound recordings you want to register.
You'll need to have the sound recordings (WAV or MP3) on hand, since you'll need to upload them during the electronic registration process. For both countries, typically you'd register your composition (U.S.: Form PA; Canada: Application for Registration of a Copyright in a Work) or your sound recording (U.S.: Form SR; Canada: Application for Registration of a Copyright in a Performer's Performance, Sound Recording or Communication Signal) and there's a fee for each.

In the U.S., if the same parties own *both* the composition and the sound recording, the office allows you to simply register Form SR, and, if you check the option to also register the composition, you'll get both with one form and fee. If different parties own the composition and sound recording, then this option isn't available, and you'll need to register and pay for both registrations (PA and SR).

2. Determine if you can register songs or sound recordings as a bundle.
You can save money by bundling your songs into a single compilation if it meets their requirements (usually that they have the same owners).

3. Save your application receipt and proof of registration.
Save your application (it should be saved automatically if done electronically) and any paperwork either of the copyright offices sends you (such as a certificate of registration) for proof.

Just as with music, copyright for text, artwork, photos, images, graphics, and video is automatic once you create anything original in a fixed, tangible format. However, if you want to ensure additional protection, you can register these works with the U.S. or Canadian Copyright Office as well. Typically, there's only one copyright owner (no complicated fifty-fifty splits between songwriters and publishers, for instance). Check out each site's instructions to learn how as well as other tips at MakingMoney WithMusic.com/resources.

CLEARING COPYRIGHT PERMISSIONS IN MUSIC YOU DON'T OWN
UNDERSTANDING INFRINGEMENT

If you want to make money with music, you'll want to avoid infringing on another's copyrighted work because lawsuits are expensive. It's a myth that there's an exception to copyright law that says it's not infringement if you only copy fewer than six measures or less than four seconds. The rule of thumb is, the more you copy, the more likely you're infringing. It's best to create original songs or properly license those songs/samples you don't own, which we explain how to do below.

HOW TO CLEAR THE RIGHTS OF SONGS YOU DON'T OWN
SO YOU CAN PLAY COVER SONGS LIVE

Fortunately, you don't need to clear cover songs before playing them live because copyright law built a "compulsory license" into the law. Once a song is published, copyright law allows anyone to cover it live, even if the songwriter and publisher don't want you to.

Live performance of a composition generates a performance royalty for the songwriter and publisher, and these are usually taken out of fees paid by venues, bars, restaurants, radio stations, and the like. If they haven't paid the license, *technically* you're on the hook to pay it as well, but PROs don't usually go after musicians because they often don't have the funds and are harder to find than the venues.

HOW TO CLEAR THE RIGHTS OF SONGS YOU DON'T OWN
SO YOU CAN RECORD COVER VERSIONS

You need to license the right to record other people's songs if they are not in the public domain. (If you want to see a list of songs that are free to cover, see listings like the Public Domain Information Project [pdinfo.com].)

The good news is anyone can record copyrighted songs that are published under a compulsory license. To do this, you need to pay for the right to make a copy of the song. In the U.S., there is a statute setting a maximum rate publishers can charge you per copy. This is set by the Copyright Office, and it changes over time so go to copyright.gov for the latest. Currently, it's 9.1 cents per copy for songs five minutes or less, and if the song is more than five minutes it's 1.75 cents per minute per copy. Note that it doesn't matter if you intend to give your version of the song away for free or use it as a promo; *you must have a license and pay for each copy you make.* Typically, it's at the maximum rate, but you can always try to negotiate for less. To clear a cover song, follow the steps below:

1. Determine how you will make your cover song available to the public.

You will likely need to pay a separate license fee for each method you use to make your song available: digital download, physical (CDs, vinyl, cassettes), ringtones, and interactive streaming.

2. Determine the number of copies you'll make of the cover song.

You'll need to pay a fee for *each copy* whether you sell them or not.

3. Determine where you will make your copies available.

The internet is global, but copyright is handled separately by each country, so you need to figure out where you want to distribute your cover. This means whichever rights-clearing methods you use must be valid within the countries you want to distribute the music.

4. Clear the rights by working out a deal with the song's publisher.

Track down the publisher of the song you want to cover and obtain a compulsory license. For instance, in the U.S., the steps are documented in Circular 73 (www.copyright.gov/circs/circ73.pdf) so you can send a "Notice of Intention." To find the publisher, try checking the U.S. Copyright Office online database, searching the internet, or checking the liner notes. You can also check the online databases of PROs (ASCAP, BMI, SESAC, etc.) and mechanical rights collection organizations, such as Harry Fox (we talk more about these organizations in chapter 12, "Licensing and Royalties"). The maximum you should have to pay is the statutory rate (though they may ask you for more!). If you get anything under that rate, you've gotten a bargain.

5. Clear the rights using a rights-clearing service.

If you're outside the U.S., your PRO might assist you to obtain a license. However, PROs in the U.S. do not do this. If you don't work a deal with the song's publisher on your own, there are rights-clearing services that can help you obtain a license. These services include Harry Fox's Song File service (songfile.com), Loudr (loudr.com), Easy Song Licensing (easysonglicensing.com), and Affordable Song Licensing (affordable songlicensing.com). Keep in mind each service charges administrative fees on top of what you'll need to pay the cover song's publisher. Also, most licenses will be at the maximum statutory rate. Lastly, know that your digital distributor, which we talk about in chapter 9, "Distribution and Streaming," may also help clear rights or partner with one of these services.

Note that there are limits on what a compulsory license allows. As Ilya Zlatkin, an attorney practicing in the areas of entertainment and media, says, "Anytime you take preexisting material and do anything even remotely original based on that material, you've technically created a *derivative work*. The question then becomes whether or not you need to license the preexisting work so you can exploit the derivative work." For instance, the law doesn't allow you to change the "basic melody or fundamental character of the work" beyond style and interpretation. So, if your recording changes the basic melody or fundamental character of the original song, then it's no longer allowable under a compulsory license. Although most covers fall under the style and interpretation exception, there's no bright-line rule explaining what exactly changes the "basic melody or fundamental character," and any disputes are handled by the courts. So if you think your recording is so far afield from the original song that the compulsory license requirements aren't met, you'd need to talk to the publisher and get permission to record your version (or use a rights-clearing service).

HOW TO CLEAR THE RIGHTS OF SOMEONE ELSE'S MELODY
SO YOU CAN RECORD IT WITHIN YOUR ORIGINAL SONG

When you change the fundamental character of an existing work, it becomes a derivative work. You can do this by covering a *part* of someone else's song or melody (with or without changed lyrics) and inserting it into your own original work. This is known as an interpolation. An example of this is Coolio's 1995 hip-hop classic, "Gangsta's Paradise," which used part of the melody from Stevie Wonder's 1976 classic song "Pastime Paradise." To be able to do an interpolation, you need to obtain permission from the original song's publisher (or use a rights-clearing service) and get permission to record your derivative version. This would require a license, and you'd both need to work out a fee (which wouldn't be limited by the statute like the compulsory license exception).

HOW TO CLEAR RIGHTS FOR SAMPLES, MASH-UPS,
AND LOOPS

Whenever you incorporate or mash-up actual recordings from someone else's song into your own music, such as samples or loops, you need permission from both the composition and sound recording owners. To avoid the hassle of getting a license from both the song publisher and the sound recording owner, you should use precleared and royalty-free samples and loops as discussed in chapter 5, "Your Music." If you can't or don't want to use these, then you'll need to do the following. But be warned, it can be a nightmare to pull off.

1. Contact the copyright owner of the sound recording and work out a deal.

You'll need to research and find out who owns the sound recording. Most likely this is the music label. Unlike recording or playing cover songs live, there is no compulsory license under copyright law for the sound recording. This means they can deny you permission and charge you whatever they want. Additionally, the owner may ask for a percentage of the income derived from your song and a bonus payment when a certain number of copies are sold or streamed.

2. Contact the publisher of the song and work out a deal.

If you're able to get a sample clearance license for the sound recording, you still need to get a license and pay the fee to the composition's publisher. If the sample you use is identifiable as the original song, you may be able to get a compulsory license. Just follow the steps of recording a cover song above. However, if you cut up the song in a way that's too dissimilar to the original—in a way that changes the "basic melody or fundamental character of the work"—then it could be considered a derivative work. That means the compulsory license method won't work and the publisher can deny you permission to use the song and charge you whatever they want.

TRADEMARKS AND SERVICE MARKS
UNDERSTANDING TRADEMARKS AND SERVICE MARKS

Since musicians now reach a global audience, protecting the expressions of your persona, such as your artist name and brand elements, is more of an issue than ever. Getting a trademark gives you a monopoly to do business using a common or unique word, phrase, or term for a specific, limited purpose. This is different from copyright law, which covers original works of expression, not common terms.

A trademark or service mark (for simplification, we'll stick with the word *trademark*, since both are essentially the same) is a distinctive word, phrase, symbol, or design that uniquely identifies your products and services in the mind of the public. For a musician, trademarks include brand elements we discussed in chapter 3, "Your Persona," such as your artist name, logo, tagline, or mascot. Most of these marks come out of the public domain or common language, even if the mark is made up, like *"Starbucks"* or *"McDonald's."* For instance, our band, Beatnik Turtle, is a combination of two well-known words: *"beatnik,"* which refers to the pre-hippies of the 1950s and early 1960s, and *"turtle,"* which is a reptile. It doesn't mean anything when put together, but over the course of twenty years, twenty albums, countless live shows, web and social presences, the book you're holding in your hand, and years of fan and media interaction, the two words have come to mean our band and particular brand of horn-powered geek rock.

There are six things you should know about trademark law:

1. Trademark is not copyright.
Unlike copyright law, which protects your copyright from falling into the public domain while you're alive, trademarks—even famous ones— can fall into the public domain quickly if they're not diligently protected.

After all, if you're taking a word or symbol out of the public domain but aren't actively using it to ensure it identifies your product or service, then someone else should be able to use it. This is why famous brands such as Coca-Cola, Budweiser, and McDonald's have to aggressively protect their trademarks from any use that might confuse and "dilute" the value they've built in their marks with the public. The law only allows companies to keep their marks if they actively use and maintain them.

2. The first person to use the mark usually gets the rights to it.

Under the law, the first person to publicly use a mark for a specific product or service in commerce automatically owns it. To claim a trademark, you need to be the first musician in the world to publicly use your name, logo, tagline, or mascot. Proof of your first public use can come from your domain name, your website, a newspaper ad, a poster announcing a live show, and so on.

3. The value of your trademark grows over time.

The more you repeatedly and consistently use your trademarks over time, the stronger your trademark rights become and the stronger the protection the law gives you.

4. You can end up sharing a similar mark with others as long as it's not in the same trade or service.

In general, you only have the rights to a mark for music purposes. So this means another company might be able to use the same marks for their product or service as long as it's not competing in your music space and causing confusion in the market. The problem is, with the world getting more and more connected, many names are global.

5. One exception about sharing a similar mark: famous brands.

If your mark is too similar to another famous mark outside of music, however, you'll likely be infringing and may be contacted to stop using it. For instance, if you name your band *Google*, it's likely that Google would successfully prevent you from operating under this name even though you're a band, not a search engine. This is true even if you named your band *the Google*, *G00gle*, *Gooooogle*, or even *Gue Gull*, since these are similar sounding or looking. Courts make these fact-based decisions, and there are always exceptions for attorneys to argue, but it's best to avoid any name or mark similar to ones already in use. If you're still stumped about what name or mark would be considered fair game, consult an attorney.

6. You need to protect your mark.

Once you have a mark, you need to protect it from dilution and confusion in the marketplace just as aggressively as the famous brands do. If another artist starts using your name or any other marks of yours, you have to prevent them from using it or risk losing yours. This means they need to change their name, even if the other band plays different music from yours. The public and your fans may become confused about which artist is who when it comes to shows, albums, and merchandise, and the longer you let the other artist use the name or mark, the more strength they'll have to defend it in court.

Unfortunately, enforcing your rights usually costs money. You'll want to hire an attorney to send a cease-and-desist letter to any infringing party and either stop them from using your name or mark or negotiate a compromise, such as allowing them to choose a different name while retaining some element of their former name. You'll also want to register your trademark so you have standing in court.

HOW TO TRADEMARK AND REGISTER YOUR NAME, LOGO, AND OTHER BRAND ELEMENTS

Like copyright, a trademark is automatically generated as long as it's distinctive and you use it, so you don't need to register with a country's trademark office. However, doing so will give you additional rights, including a public record that can act as a deterrent to other bands to use your name when they search for a name of their own.

As an independent musician, you sell products (trademark) and perform music (service mark), so there's plenty you may want to protect. Under the law, each country has designated classes of goods and services. These classes vary by country. Note that each trademark and class you register costs money. The top classes you may consider applying for a trademark for include:

- Entertainment services, including the use of your name in conjunction with performing as an artist (Class 41 in the U.S.).

- The sale of digital media (CDs, downloadable audio files, etc.) under your artist name (Class 9 in the U.S.).

- The use of your artist name in posters, pamphlets, newsletters, and other promotional materials (Class 16 in the U.S.).

- The use of your marks on T-shirts and other merchandise (Class 25 in the U.S.).

Trademark registration is more complicated than copyright registration, and although many online registration sites can walk you through the process, we recommend using an attorney. They can help determine if your application will succeed and if it's worth doing, since if your registration is rejected, you likely will lose the expensive application fee. Trademark offices employ examiners to review each application, perform their own trademark search, and request additional information if they find an issue with your application. Once your registration is approved, you can use the registration symbol, ®. Until then, you can use ™ or ℠.

Whether you choose to register your mark is typically a matter of cost. Unlike registering your copyrights, which is not necessarily cheap, registering a national mark is definitely expensive. This is because you might have to register in multiple classes and/or in multiple countries, and it always involves an attorney. One cheaper alternative in the U.S. is to register a mark in your home state which usually only charges a fraction of the cost of a federal registration. While this will only protect your mark within the state's boundary, it gets the mark into the public register and can establish the the fact you used it first.

RIGHT OF PUBLICITY

You have a right as a person to control your persona and identity in the public, especially for commercial purposes. The law treats your unique likeness, name, and public image as your exclusive property right to do with as you wish. This right of publicity exists for everyone, but it's only when a critical mass of the public knows who you are that this right can become important in creating revenue.

As an artist, your goal is to build an audience hungry for your music. As you build this following and grow name and brand recognition, others will be interested in you talking about or endorsing *their* products to *your* audience. And they'll pay you to do this, since, unless you sign your right away to someone else, the law prevents anyone from using your likeness or image to promote products, services, or causes without your permission.

Making money from licensing your likeness and fame to endorse, sponsor, or brand a product or service used to be only available for famous actors, athletes, musicians, or politicians. Today, with the rise of social media, anyone who can build a sizable audience can exploit this revenue stream. Depending on the number of followers you can acquire or the demographic of the audience, marketing departments may come calling with checks in hand.

The right of publicity generally arises out of common law or some statute enacted in your country or state. Like copyright, you can sell or license your likeness to be used by third parties. You can protect your right by carefully considering what products or services you endorse and working out a specific licensing agreement. Also, as you grow your name and brand recognition, you can trademark your name and likeness in those classes of products or services you're using it in. Since by definition your likeness is unique, it's likely you'd be able to trademark it as long as you meet the test of how it's associated with your brand of products or services.

Your right lasts not only during your life but also survives your death, so it's another thing to consider in your will so your children or estate can continue to exploit your likeness in the future—just like the estates of Marilyn Monroe, Elvis Presley, and John Lennon do today.

If you're a band, then you'll need to ensure everyone is in agreement on the use of everyone's likeness for commercial purposes, since you each have a right of publicity. This right of publicity should be documented in your band agreement (which we discuss in chapter 2, "Your Music Business"). This also means that if you ever use *someone else's* image to promote you, such as in a poster or a video you create, and you don't have a prior agreement with that person, you need to clear any identifiable person's likeness so you can use their likeness for your commercial purposes. This may require paying a license fee.

But your right of publicity isn't simply about making money by endorsing, advertising, or doing product placements for *other people's* products or services. Your right to publicity as an artist, when combined with your merchandising rights, can also drive up the value of your own products and merchandise. The more you can boost your fame and increase the number of followers you can reach, the more in demand your products and merchandise will be, and the more you'll be likely to charge.

MERCHANDISING RIGHTS

Merchandising is the business of using your persona and your right of publicity—your name, likeness, and brand elements—to sell products and services. It's made up of many rights we've talked about: copyright, trademark, and your likeness. When these elements are combined and applied to products and services, it can become a major part of your income. Merchandising usually involves:

- You as the artist and your likeness (the right of publicity).

- The trademark owner of your artist or band name.

- The copyright owner of your brand logo, images, graphics, photos, and text.

- The copyright owners of any song lyrics (the songwriter and publisher).

- The merchandising rights owner.

As we discuss in chapter 2, "Your Music Business," the ownership of these are spelled out in your band or business operating agreement. For instance, the agreement would outline who owns your band name, particular copyrights, trademarks, and your likeness. It should also outline who owns the merchandising rights. Merchandise rights refer to the right to sell products and services with your name, likeness, and copyrighted brand images and text. As an independent artist, you're likely the owner of these rights, but you can assign some or all of it to someone else, such as a company specializing in merchandising (handling everything from design to order fulfillment) or your merchandise manager (the person we discussed in chapter 4, "Your Team," who is responsible for designing, creating, distributing, and selling the artist's merchandise).

Because merchandise can be a lucrative income stream, music labels often negotiate a percentage of the merchandising rights as part of the record deal with an artist. Those artists who maintain their merchandising rights typically sell them for an advance (and possible royalties) to a merchandise company that handles everything from design to order fulfillment. While this may be an option, note that these one-stop merchandise shops usually only purchase the merchandising rights from national or major-label acts. These rights are yours when you are an independent musician, and creating and selling the merchandise yourself means all the profits will be yours as well.

PART 2
GETTING PAID AND MAKING MONEY

9

DISTRIBUTION AND STREAMING

Goal: To set up music and video distribution for streaming, sales, royalties, licensing, and promotion.

Team Roles and Responsibilities: Distributor, Web Designer/Webmaster, and Manager

WHAT YOU GET OUT OF THIS
By the end of this chapter, you will:

1. Understand how to choose the best digital distribution partners for your music and videos.

2. Apply income-boosting techniques to use on digital sales and streaming platforms.

3. Distribute your music on your own.

4. Know services that can distribute and sell your source tracks, stems, beats, loops, samples, and presets.

5. Understand how streaming platforms work, how to generate the most income from them, and how to effectively use the top streaming platforms.

6. Know eleven ways to make money from your distribution and streaming.

MONEY MAP

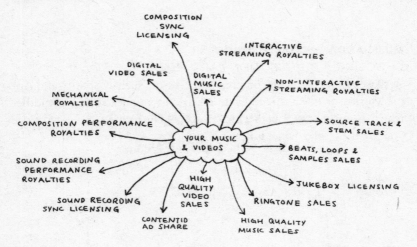

COMPOSITION
SYNC
LICENSING

INTERACTIVE
STREAMING ROYALTIES

DIGITAL
VIDEO SALES

DIGITAL
MUSIC
SALES

NON-INTERACTIVE
STREAMING ROYALTIES

MECHANICAL
ROYALTIES

COMPOSITION PERFORMANCE
ROYALTIES

SOURCE TRACK &
STEM SALES

YOUR MUSIC
& VIDEOS

BEATS, LOOPS &
SAMPLES SALES

SOUND RECORDING
PERFORMANCE
ROYALTIES

JUKEBOX LICENSING

HIGH
QUALITY
VIDEO
SALES

RINGTONE SALES

SOUND RECORDING
SYNC LICENSING

CONTENTID
AD SHARE

HIGH QUALITY
MUSIC SALES

INTRO

The most exciting part about today's music world is how you can become a global artist by just putting your music up with a single distribution partner. What used to take manufacturing plants, trucks, and distributors to get you into a handful of stores that may or may not want to stock your music can be done with a few clicks and gets your music directly to fans no matter where they are in the world.

But this world is changing quickly; music streaming is taking over, and music listeners increasingly are turning away from paying for individual albums or tracks to pay a monthly fee to listen to entire catalogs of music. This has changed the income profile for musicians as they see purchases of albums and singles turn into fraction-of-a-cent plays on streaming platforms. Because of this, distribution partners are expanding their services to include collecting and distributing royalty and licensing income on behalf of musicians. This also requires an entirely new strategy for engaging with fans, getting the most out of your artist page profiles, and optimizing your release strategy as fans increasingly listen to singles rather than albums.

Choosing your distribution partner is a critical choice, since they handle more than music sales and streaming. They have many income-generating and promotional services, but they're not all equal, and so this chapter will give you the criteria to make the best choice for your music business.

MUSIC AND VIDEO DISTRIBUTION
CHOOSING A DISTRIBUTION PARTNER

Because iTunes, Amazon, or streaming services such as Spotify and Apple Music won't deal directly with musicians, you need to use a middleman to get your music out there to your fans. The primary criteria to judge your distribution partner is their fee model:

- **Subscription by song/album.**

These services charge a fee per song or album. With these services, you (usually) keep the full profit of every sale but pay a yearly subscription (and sometimes an initiation fee). Some examples of the subscription services are TuneCore (tunecore.com) and ReverbNation (reverbnation .com). You keep the entire profit, but there are yearly fees, and you often have to pay more to get into more outlets.

- **Subscription by artist/account.**

Pay a yearly fee to submit songs and keep them active but submit as many songs or albums as you want to; you keep all the revenue. An example of this type is DistroKid (distrokid.com).

- **Percentage sales cut services.**

These services take a cut of every sale and may or may not have an initiation fee. A good example of the sales cut method is CD Baby (cdbaby .com). The upside of these is that they usually put your music in many outlets for a single fee. The downside is that they will keep taking a cut of every sale, and this can be a drag on your profit.

Note that the digital stores themselves, such as iTunes and Amazon, charge fees in addition to your distribution partner fees and any payment processor fees. These digital store fees vary from 30–55 percent from the gross amount paid by the customer. Also, just because a service charges a fee, that doesn't mean it's necessarily a bad option. You need to evaluate each one based on what you want out of your income and sales and what you think you can achieve.

Also, evaluate these secondary criteria:

- **Outlets.**

Each service has a different mix of digital stores they will distribute your music to. Although all of them include the most popular sites like Spotify, Apple Music, and Amazon, there are hundreds of additional places your music can be distributed to for sale or performances, such as jukebox services, other streaming services, and more. Some of the digital distributors require you to pay more to get into more outlets.

- **Revenue features.**

These are extra revenue features not directly related to music sales, often for royalties, licensing, and others. See the next section below for a full list.

- **Extra features.**

Distribution partners can give you ISRC codes and bar codes, provide sales reporting to charting authorities, auto-verify you with streaming services so you can control your presences there, and provide other features to help your music business. Some charge fees for these extra features, and others supply them for free.

- **Metrics and stats.**

Sales reports from distribution services show you exactly what people have bought or streamed and when. This can help you make decisions on your campaigns and determine if your efforts are successful and are a key part of your release strategy. You will want to make sure there are a full set of reports available.

THE TOP SEVEN ADDITIONAL REVENUE SERVICES YOUR DISTRIBUTION PARTNER MAY PROVIDE

Your distribution partner may also offer or work with additional services to provide you with services to handle licensing, PRO royalties, mechanical royalties, sync royalties, and more. Beyond comparing the fees they charge and outlets they provide, you'll want to evaluate the services that are available and use the distributor providing the right mix of services for you. Consider the following:

1. Administrative PRO royalties.
Your distribution partner can provide you with administrative PRO services to handle your songwriting and publishing royalties for a fee and/or a cut of the proceeds.

2. YouTube Content ID and video royalties.
Digital distributors can handle your video sync royalties and get a cut of the ad revenue generated by video plays.

3. Sync licensing.
Some offer to put your music into sync libraries to get your music licensed by TV shows, movies, and other video creators.

4. Mechanical royalties.
Although you can handle mechanical royalties yourself to get paid when someone covers your song, you can also use these services to team up with a partner to handle mechanical royalties for you.

5. ISRC codes for songs and bar codes for albums.
ISRC codes are used by SoundExchange to collect noninteractive streaming royalties for your songs, and bar codes are still used by some charting agencies to identify your album. Some digital distributors provide these for your music.

6. Embeddable stores.
You may want to include embeddable stores for selling music if they are available, and some distributors offer widgets and tools to help sell your music.

7. Video distribution.
Some digital distributors will provide video distribution for your music, including the option to automatically create YouTube videos with the song or album image or providing distribution for your music videos to networks like Vevo and others.

You can potentially get better cuts from services outside your distribution partner. We explain about PROs, licensing, performance royalties, mechanical royalties, SoundExchange, and more in chapter 12, "Licensing and Royalties."

HOW TO DISTRIBUTE AND SELL MUSIC TO GET HIGHER CUTS, INCLUDING SELLING HIGH-QUALITY (HQ) VERSIONS

Most people are more willing to buy your music through major digital stores like iTunes, Google Play, and Amazon because they already trust their credit card with them and their music libraries are tied to them. Because of this, you should make sure your music appears in these major outlets and link them from your online presences, but you can also offer your music through distribution options providing a higher cut.

Services like Bandcamp (bandcamp.com), CD Baby (cdbaby.com), or VibeDeck (vibedeck.com) offer higher cuts through their webstores. You can also sell directly from your website using tools like CASH Music (cashmusic.org) or through digital download e-commerce plug-ins on services like Squarespace (squarespace.com).

Note that these options also give you the opportunity to sell HQ versions of your songs as well, which is a good option to provide to fans who want higher-quality tracks. These are usually lossless formats, such as FLAC, or high-quality MP3s or WAVs, depending upon the version you wish to sell. This is yet another income stream you can create for the same songs you sell and stream on other platforms.

If you use these methods, make sure to use the same sales techniques in the "How to Use Digital Stores Effectively" section below.

HOW TO GET WORLDWIDE DIGITAL MUSIC DISTRIBUTION FOR $0

Some distribution partners have no initiation fee. This means you can distribute your music for no up-front costs on streaming services like Spotify, Apple Music, Google Play, as well as major digital stores, such as iTunes, and Amazon. For example, it's free to distribute your music through RouteNote (routenote.com) since they only take a percentage of any sale you make (on top of what the outlets keep). Even better, if your music starts getting consistent sales, RouteNote lets you switch to a subscription fee so you can increase your cut. This option allows you to find out which tracks, EPs, or albums have enough sales to justify the fee, and after that, you can collect a higher percentage.

HOW TO DISTRIBUTE AND SELL SOURCE TRACKS, BEATS, STEMS, SAMPLES, AND PRESETS

Musicians might want more than just your music; they may want access to the original sounds and tools you used to create it. If you feel comfortable providing these and licensing them to others to create their own music, consider selling them to musicians.

You can sell these through digital marketplaces like Splice (splice .com) or AudioJungle (audiojungle.net) or Beatport (beatport.com), but these stores often work with labels or have curation requirements and may not accept every artist. You can try stores that will accept all artists, such as Rightsify (rightsify.com/sell-your-sample-packs-loops-presets), or tools that allow you to sell digital tracks, such as Sellfy (sellfy.com), Gumroad (gumroad.com), or general download-sales sites like Shopify (shopify.com) or PayLoadz (payloadz.com). And if your website is based on WordPress, you can try to download stores available or themes like Music Maker (musicmakertheme.com).

THE TOP THING TO KNOW ABOUT PATRONAGE, MUSIC DISTRIBUTION, AND REWARDS AS A DISTRIBUTION CHANNEL

As we note in chapter 11, "Patronage, Crowdfunding, and Raising Money," you can use your patronage or crowdfunding platform to distribute MP3s, videos, pictures, liner notes, or other extras to your patrons as incentives for pledging and rewards. This is another distribution channel, but it is exclusive to your funders and patrons. Remember you can sell this content later to the public, since you've limited this exclusive distribution to your superfans.

HOW TO SELL RINGTONES OF YOUR MUSIC

Although ringtones used to be bigger business in the past than they are now, they are still a revenue stream. If you make good searchable titles for your ringtones, you have a chance of getting discovered by ringtone customers. Also, consider marketing the ringtones directly to your fans. To sell these, use services like SnipSell (snipsell.com).

UNDERSTANDING VIDEO DISTRIBUTORS

You can opt to use a video distributor to syndicate your videos across more platforms and outlets than YouTube. There are multiple aspects of video distribution to handle, including monetizing your videos, getting your videos into additional networks and channels, and selling high-quality copies of your videos to your fans, which creates a new income stream out of the video you've already made.

Besides your distribution partner, which might offer video distribution, you can explore services like Vydia (vydia.com) or Symphonic Distribution (symphonicdistribution.com) to get your videos into publishers like Vevo, YouTube, Facebook, Dailymotion, and stores like iTunes and Amazon. Some video distributors also provide the option to submit your videos to networks like BET, MTV, and Music Choice. However, they have no say in whether any of these channels will accept or use the music or video.

HOW TO USE DIGITAL STORES EFFECTIVELY

Once you decide which online stores to use, use the following techniques to maximize your music sales:

1. Make sure your info helps sell your music.

Most distribution partners will ask for key information about you as an artist and your tracks, since they syndicate this information to their sales and streaming partners. You should ensure the info and images help sell your music and are aligned to your brand. Note that some digital stores pick up your info from the music credit databases we recommend in chapter 5, "Your Music."

2. Mention bands that sound like yours in the description.

If the terms of use will allow you to, list major bands with a similar sound in the album description so that searches for the other bands will wind up on your page.

3. Add quotes from good reviews.

Potential customers want to know what people say about your music. Like a movie poster, add a short quote or two from any great reviews of your music. Also, make sure to include the quotes on your website and other places where you market your music.

4. Include cover songs.

Including well-known cover songs can help get your music picked up by search results within the music site, since music listeners are likely searching for artists and songs that they're already familiar with. This is why, if you're comfortable recording a well-known cover song, it can help boost sales and royalties by piggybacking on its popularity. Typically, music buyers will listen to the cover and, if they like it, check out the rest of the music the artist makes. Or if you want to harness the power of the music store search bar without doing a cover song, try giving songs similar titles to other well-known songs or common phrases. This works because song titles can't be copyrighted and you can legitimately use the same title as other popular songs (or else, there would only be one song called "I Love You"). The only exception is using trademarked words in your title.

5. Link from your site.
Put links to your music on all your web presences to make it as easy as possible for your visitors to stream or buy your music.

6. Link back to your site.
Link back to your own website from your storefronts so customers can find more information about you and your music.

7. Drive fan reviews of the music.
You should ask your fans to rate your music and leave reviews on sites that have those features for the music. These ratings are influential; many buyers take a look at what others said before buying.

STREAMING
UNDERSTANDING STREAMING
Streaming is one of the fastest-growing trends in music today. It's also a key component of the recent global growth of overall music revenue, and it's poised to increase with a worldwide user penetration of over 45 percent today and growing. Of all the streaming platforms, as of this book release date, Spotify leads the pack with over 40 percent of the total market and over double their closest competitor, Apple Music. This market is worth over $8 billion worldwide today and continues to increase.

Streaming has significantly changed how listeners experience music because of the large libraries available that were never available to them before. It has had a direct effect of decreasing download sales. But also, because of the popularity of playlists, more than two-thirds of all songs played are *singles*, not albums. And because fans can follow the artists they like, they get notified when there's a new release, and trying new music and adding it to their profiles is a single click away. This has changed release strategies for musicians because fans are looking for their artists to give them new experiences on a regular basis, and we cover how to take advantage of these differences in chapter 18, "Your Release Strategy."

Streaming royalties have also been at the center of a big dispute between musicians and the platforms, with musicians arguing that royalties are far too low. According to research done by Information is Beautiful (informationisbeautiful.net), it would take over 180,000 streams *per month* on Spotify to make minimum wage for the year. In contrast, if you sold 550 albums at shows or through digital downloads on iTunes, you could achieve minimum wage. With the tens of millions of users on these streaming platforms, there's a huge opportunity to get a lot of streams, but the fractional payment means you can't rely on streaming royalties to be a significant source of income at this time; you must supplement it with other revenue streams we cover throughout this book.

That said, the income you can make through streaming tends to be steady. It's passive income, with your released songs generating revenue for you as you work on growing other aspects of your business. Plus, as you keep releasing tracks on a regular schedule, you can grow the number of streams played, since your consistent releases act as a promotional reminder that you're making music and making it easy for old and new fans to discover and stream your back catalog.

Streaming is just one category of many to get your music heard and discovered. To ensure you get the most marketing, promotion, publicity, and revenue you can from this get-heard method, you should follow the prep steps we outlined in chapter 5, "Your Music," all the registration steps we outline in chapter 12, "Licensing and Royalties," and all the techniques on promoting yourself through playlists in chapter 17, "Get Heard and Seen."

HOW TO USE THE TOP FOUR STREAMING PLATFORMS EFFECTIVELY

Although the streaming landscape is changing over time, there are a few platforms that are worth your time and effort to promote your music specifically. For each, we'll discuss how to get your music on them, how to get paid, how to take control of your profile, and how to get stats.

1. Spotify.

You can get your music on Spotify through your distribution partner. Money made from interactive streaming services like Spotify is paid directly by your partner (after their cut). Your partner may also auto-verify you as the artist with Spotify, so you can automatically control your artist profile through Spotify's artist app features. If your distribution partner doesn't auto-verify you as the artist, which many do, you can control your artist profile by going to artists.spotify.com and applying for access. Controlling your profile is critical, since it allows you to change the artist image, edit the bio, assign your top song, create artist playlists, and more. The app also gives you stats, demographic info, location info, and a snapshot of other artists they listen to, and may allow you to plug shows. If you want your lyrics to appear on Spotify, make sure they are available on Genius (genius.com). The best way to promote your music on Spotify is by featuring it on playlists, whether your own or other people's. You can also embed your Spotify music playlists, follow buttons, and widgets on your web presences and social profiles.

2. Apple Music.

You can get your music on Apple Music through your distribution partner. Like Spotify, you get paid for interactive streams directly by your partner (after their cut). Apple currently lets you claim your artist profile via iTunes Connect (itunesconnect.apple.com). This allows you to put up an image, make posts, and share content, plus connect it to your social profiles. Your stats are also available through iTunes connect. The best way to promote yourself on Apple Music is also through playlists, both your own as well as others.

3. Pandora.

Pandora has three levels of service: Pandora Radio, a noninteractive streaming service similar to radio stations; Pandora Premium, an interactive streaming service like Spotify or Apple Music; and Pandora Plus, an enhanced version of their radio service that allows on-demand streaming. To get your music into the Pandora Radio, your distribution partner might include a submission option, or you can use their submission portal at submit.pandora.com. These submissions are all reviewed by musicologists, so it's a long process to get a submission reviewed, and they only accept a small percentage of music. The Premium and Plus options are available only through a digital distribution partner. You get paid via your digital distribution partner for the interactive streams, and by SoundExchange in the U.S. for the noninteractive streams.

Your Pandora artist biography is supplied by TiVo Music Metadata (business.tivo.com/products-solutions/data/music-metadata), which you can search and keep updated via AllMusic (allmusic.com). LyricFind (lyricfind.com) provides lyrics. You can take control of your profile through the Artists' Management Platform (amp.pandora.com), which allows you to record audio messages to your fans, set up featured tracks, and do campaign management. Stats are given via Next Big Sound (nextbigsound.com).

4. Deezer.

Deezer (deezer.com) provides interactive streaming similar to Spotify and Apple Music, and while it's worldwide, it currently has a larger European listener base. To get your music into Deezer, your distribution partner might include a submission option, and if so, you'll get paid for interactive streams directly by your partner (after their cut). Use their Deezer4Artists (deezer.com/en/company/label_artists) tool to customize your artist page, display a status, create playlists, and get stats. Their uploader tool allows you to send content to fans. LyricFind (lyricfind .com) provides lyrics to Deezer.

10

PRODUCTS AND MERCHANDISE

Goal: To create physical products and merchandise and set up sales distribution.

Team Roles and Responsibilities: Product and Merchandise Manager, Graphic Artist, Copywriter, Photographer, Video Producer, Web Designer/Webmaster, and Manager

WHAT YOU GET OUT OF THIS
By the end of this chapter, you will:

1. Understand what makes fans want to buy from you so you can create a mix of products and merchandise to maximize sales.

2. Have fifteen categories of merchandise concepts you can use to generate new products to sell.

3. Create physical products and merchandise from your persona, music, and videos.

4. Know how to use print-on-demand services to create, sell, and ship products and merchandise.

5. Know how to sell and ship products and merchandise on your own.

MONEY MAP

INTRO

Customers tend to value physical items over digital when it comes to spending money. This means you should create a mix of physical products to sell your fans. This includes both music-based products as well as merchandise because, after all, you can't hand people a download.

As we talked about in chapter 3, "Your Persona," the clothes people wear and merch they buy say something about their identity. Creating products and merch uses your creativity, and with today's options, making unique merchandise is easy, even making your own brand of wine. The most successful music businesses grow beyond the music and create lifestyle brands by selling things like perfume, clothing lines, and services.

With today's technology, you can offer products for sale for free just by uploading an image and making it available for sale. Your fans pay for the production of each item, allowing you to profit on every purchase. Each one can be an experiment to find out what people like, and if you find a winner, you can then invest money into making more of those products. Your goal is to create a lure for them and provide something they treasure while giving you sources of income for your music.

KEY CONCEPTS

UNDERSTANDING PRODUCTS AND MERCHANDISE

Each product you make is an expression of your persona. All the brand elements, including your fonts, colors, tone, and style, should help you design what your fans want to see and connect it to everything else you do. If you don't have those aspects of your persona nailed down before settling down to make merch, putting some time into getting that together will help both your products as well as your public identity.

In fact, your persona can be your most valuable aspect of your music business if you achieve a level of fame such that others want to license its use, including your likeness, name, and brand elements. The income from that is the best kind: passive. This means it pays you no matter what else you do with your time, as they pay you for each time they stamp your logo on something. This is why you also have a merchandise right. As stated in chapter 8, "Your Rights," you can contract that away for income if other people value it and you feel comfortable letting other people use it. This means that not only does your merchandise itself have value but so does your ability to make it in the future. And all of this can get established and objectively proven from the stream of income you make from your products and merch.

Lastly, as outlined in detail in chapter 18, "Your Release Strategy," your new merch items can be part of your release plan as well.

THE FOUR WAYS TO CREATE A MIX OF PRODUCTS AND MERCHANDISE TO MAXIMIZE SALES AND REVENUE

On the web, convenience, speed, and access is what your fans want. But when they're in person at your show, with you playing on the stage, it's actual physical product they value—something they can touch and feel and remember the experience. Because of this, you always want to have multiple things to sell your fans to meet each fan's needs. You also need enough products available to get as much out of your fans as they want to buy: if all you sell are T-shirts, it will limit what you can make.

Consider blending products and merchandise, which includes the following mixtures:

1. Physical music (CDs, DVDs, vinyl, USBs, download cards) and video content media merch.

You need to have a mix of music and video content products (CDs, DVDs, vinyl, USBs, download cards) for your fans to buy.

2. Mass-manufactured and exclusive/limited-availability merch.

Mix common items like T-shirts with limited-run or limited-availability items, including autographed items, one-of-a-kind souvenirs from shows, or art pieces.

3. Inexpensive, mid-priced, and high-end products and merchandise.

Some of your fans will only have a few dollars to spend but will be happy with a sticker or button. Others will want the $250 one-of-a-kind coat you are selling at the merch table. You need to have a diverse mix of different-priced products and merch to target your minnows, dolphins, and whales and meet each of their desires at their price levels.

4. Practical and impractical products and merchandise.

Some fans will be more convinced to buy your merch like clothing, bottle openers, cups, or food, since they have a purpose, but don't be afraid to include items that are just fun and whimsical, such as glowing bands, toys, or photobooks.

PHYSICAL MUSIC AND VIDEO PRODUCTS
THE TOP SIX WAYS TO CREATE DESIRABLE PHYSICAL MUSIC PRODUCTS

Physical music products are becoming more of a novelty item than they are a primary way you sell your music. That said, when you're at a live show, creating physical products for your music is the only way you can hand it to someone for money, and they are the perfect memento purchase and impulse buy. When creating physical products out of your music that fans want to buy, try one of these six options:

1. Manufacture CDs.

For information on how to make a full CD production run, see "How to Make and Sell CDs" below.

2. Customized CDs/cases.

Sometimes, all it takes to make a CD sale is to offer a distinctive case so that the item itself is unique, creating demand for your music when you make in-person appearances. Consider other CD options from services like Disc Makers (discmakers.com) or Triggerpack (triggerpack.com).

3. Vinyl.

Vinyl has become an increasingly popular option for fans, especially in certain EDM circles as well as some genres if the fans demand it. They are perfect limited-run items and can fetch a premium price. They do carry more risk because they can break easily, take longer to make, have more expensive shipping, and are pricier to produce. Because of this, you will want to make sure there is demand before doing a run of vinyl. You will want to work with an LP manufacturer like UR Pressing (urpressing.com), Rainbo Records (rainborecords.com/vinyl.htm), Furnace Record Pressing (furnacemfg.com), or QRATES (qrates.com).

Note that there are some extra options to consider with vinyl. First of all, you have the option of having art appear on the disc via etching (urpressing.com/etched-vinyl) which can make one side unplayable but gives you art to display. Or you can make a picture disc (furnacemfg.com /vinyl/picture-discs.html), which is a lower-fidelity disc but can show a full image underneath.

If you want to remove the risk of doing a production run without being sure of the demand, you can do a crowdfunding campaign, or just use sites like QRATES (qrates.com), which allow you to do a campaign around vinyl. You will only have to do the run if the campaign succeeds.

4. Cassette tapes.

Just like vinyl, some fans are getting nostalgic for obsolete formats, and cassettes are also making a comeback in some markets. Fortunately, there are a few manufacturing services that allow you to make them. Check out Rainbo Records (rainborecords.com/cass.htm), National Audio Company (nationalaudiocompany.com/Cassette-Duplication -C14001181.aspx), Cryptic Carousel (store.crypticcarousel.com /collections/cassette-manufacturing), or others and make good use of the packaging and liner note space.

5. USB drives.

USB drives come in a variety of custom shapes and sizes with even functional items like can openers, lighters, and pens. There are also playful options, such as Pez dispensers, transformer robots, and toy cars. These are more expensive per unit compared to CDs and download cards but are useful items for the buyer afterward because they can store data. You can get very creative with USB drives because you can put more than just music data on it, and you can also tie other things to it to make it more valuable. For example, the band Imagine Dragons created only one hundred "Lifetime Membership" USB drives, priced them at $100 each, and sold all of them ($10,000). Besides buying cheap USB drives yourself, you can also use services like Disc Makers (discmakers.com) to create them for you. There's a wide range of USB drives you can make because they are a promotional item for businesses. Sites like Alibaba (alibaba .com) (search for *USB drive*), Premium USB (premiumusb.com), or CustomUSB (customusb.com) have USB drives in all kinds of shapes and sizes. Set a premium price on a unique-shaped USB and you can improve your revenue.

6. Download cards.

Download cards contain a onetime code that allows music downloads, giving you another way to sell your music in person. They can be used for show sales or as business or promotional cards. Try Disc Makers (discmakers.com), Dropcards (dropcards.com), or Card Included (card included.com), or make your own with open-source software like CASH Music (cashmusic.org).

HOW TO MAKE AND SELL CDS

With new laptops and automobiles lacking CD drives, and most people getting their music through digital music stores or streaming it on their computers, phones, and tablets, the CD format is dying. However, this isn't true worldwide; there are some countries where fans still buy a lot of them. To make a run of CDs, use the following steps:

1. Determine how many you will make.

Add up the number you need for press, radio, promotional copies, free copies, and the amount you'll need to sell.

2. Choose a CD creation method.

For creating fifty discs or fewer, just use a CD burner and a Sharpie or use print-on-demand services like CreateSpace (createspace.com). It's free to set up an account and upload the art and music to make the CD available for sale. You can also make CDs for yourself at cost, even a single disc. This method is good for short-run promotion and giveaway needs. For creating between one hundred and five hundred discs, use CD duplication to create CD-Rs. Note that these don't last as long as replicated CDs. For creating over five hundred discs, use CD replication from a glass master CD to make the highest-quality product. Most CD houses don't even offer replication unless you're going to print five hundred CDs or more. Although this method has the highest up-front costs because of the volume required, it also has the lowest cost per CD with the best result.

3. Create your album art.

CDs have inserts with your album cover and room for liner notes, lyrics, and even QR codes of your music or web links.

4. Distribute and sell your CDs.

Use sites like CD Baby (cdbaby.com), Bandcamp (bandcamp.com), or others to sell your CDs to fans. Some of these have features such as name-your-price, and sites such as CD Baby have an inventory available with distributors or major stores like Best Buy or Walmart.

THE TOP FOUR WAYS TO CREATE PHYSICAL PRODUCTS OF YOUR VIDEOS TO SELL

Similar to CDs, you may want to create physical products of your videos to sell to your fans. If you want to make video products for your fans, try the following:

1. Print-on-demand DVDs.

If you just want to allow your fans to buy DVDs online, consider DVD print-on-demand services like CreateSpace (createspace.com). Note that Blu-ray on demand is not offered due to licensing fees. Similar to the CD option, this is a $0 up-front cost option. Also make sure to use affiliate links to the CD if you sell on platforms like Amazon. You can also use this option to print a small number of inventory items to sell at shows or events.

2. Blu-ray manufacturing.

Disc Makers (discmakers.com/products/bluray.asp) and Oasis (oasiscd .com/products/bluray.asp) as well as other stores have a range of options to manufacture discs for sale. When you make a physical product for your videos, make sure the outside packaging meets your marketing needs and makes it an attractive product to buy.

3. USB drives.

The same options for USBs in "The Top Six Ways to Create Desirable Physical Music Products" work great for videos as well. Plus, you can combine video, music, and other types of content together, giving you a better chance of selling the USB full of content.

4. Download cards.

Just like music, you can sell a download card for your videos. Try out options like Digi-cards (digi-cards.com) or Dropcards (dropcards.com) or do-it-yourself tools 'like CASH Music (cashmusic.org) which allows you to create download codes you can print on anything you want. For example, you could sell a bottle opener with a download code.

MERCHANDISE
UNDERSTANDING ON-DEMAND MERCHANDISE SALES SOLUTIONS

Whether you want to sell T-shirts, posters, stickers, or other merchandise like mugs, watches, or more, there are services that will handle all these merchandise options for you, often for free. Your print-on-demand merchandise manufacturers allow you to upload images and print them on any items they make. Sites like CafePress (cafepress.com), Spreadshirt (spreadshirt.com), Zazzle (zazzle.com), Printful (printful.com), and more can make many types of merchandise for $0 up front. You will be able to make money on every sale with no inventory required.

Here's what you should know about on-demand sales solutions:

1. Be aware of their payment terms and restrictions.

These solutions may cost you nothing to use, but they all have different terms. These are not agreements you should click through without reading. First of all, your marginal profits on these are very low compared to mass-manufactured merch. Second, many make a profit by overcharging for shipping, and although they push that cost to the fan, your fans may spend a lot on single merch items when their final bill comes in, which will hurt your sales overall. Also, their payments terms to you may be restrictive; sometimes they will not pay you until you meet a minimum profit amount, and if you don't earn enough within a specified time period, they will keep that profit as well.

2. Make merch for sale immediately and experiment.

Since this option costs nothing, you can have merch available for sale after you finish your first logo or image for your music, and you can try out many ideas and merchandise. You can also make one-off T-shirts or gear for events by buying them at cost.

3. Make special event items easily.

Because you can make one-off or small-run items very simply using this method, you can make gear for the performing artists or merch for the fans tailored to a special event by buying them at cost.

4. Use your online sales figures to see what works.

Once you get some sales info, you can make the decision on when to graduate your merch to make an inventory of them with a local merch dealer or sites like Merchly (merch.ly) or Bandwear (bandwear.com) or other services aimed at corporate clients such as Branders (branders .com) so you can make more units for a far lower cost to make a higher margin on the items you already know will sell well.

5. Use print-on-demand to cheaply test out live-event merch.

You can inexpensively discover which items sell at live events. Just make a handful of sample items (at cost) and sell them for either a small profit or at cost at shows to see which sell and which don't. You can make one or two of items very easily and put them up as limited-availability sales items.

THE TOP FIFTEEN MERCH IDEAS YOU CAN MAKE AND SELL

Because it's so easy to create nearly every type of merchandise today, use this master list to brainstorm what to offer your fans. Also remember you can make new versions of the merch that works for you each time you release a new project, since they will generate new imagery and angles to promote your work.

1. T-shirts.

This is the workhorse of the music merch business, and it is worth your time to experiment with designs on print-on-demand options until you find designs that work. Fortunately, there are multiple types of T-shirts, including silkscreen, three-color, and photo print, and each has different looks, pricing, and options. Just know each type can affect your price margins.

For the design, play with your logo, album/EP/single covers, lyrics, mascot, photos, and any other imagery you like. You can even slip in a QR code or Spotify code if you want a song to go along with the shirt.

Make sure to factor in how many units to make so you don't overspend on your inventory. Account for giveaways, promotional uses, rewards for fans, your crew, and of course the ones you'll need for sale in a good mix of T-shirt sizes.

Use a local T-shirt manufacturer if have one in your area. You'll save on shipping, plus those stores often have graphic designers on hand who will help you design the shirt and allow you to see physical proofs. The designers also tend to be in or know other bands, so they are good contacts to have. U.S.-based T-shirt services include Merchly (merch.ly), One Hour Tees (onehourtees.com), or Bandwear (bandwear.com).

2. Clothing.

From hoodies to hats, there is a long list of clothing items you can offer your fans. To get ideas, look at the options print-on-demand services offer.

3. Posters.

All your imagery is fair game to make posters. Remember, posters are something your fans use to decorate their home, so experiment to find designs that sell. Fortunately, commercial printers as well as print-on-demand sources make it possible to make high-quality posters even in very low quantities. This not only allows you to make many designs available to your fans on demand, you can also make one-off posters for your merch stores at gigs. The qualities of posters you will want to experiment with include size, finish, and paper (or "stock"). Depending on the vendor, the choices can range from low-end newsprint all the way up to canvas and fine art print papers.

4. Stickers.

Today, stickers are used on the backs of laptops more than nearly any other use. Plus, promotional stickers can have your website address, QR code, Spotify code, or social media codes on them. Those stickers also reinforce your brand and are great entry-level merchandise items for sale that are perfect giveaways as extras if they hit a certain price limit. Besides the print-on-demand items, services like Sticker Guy! (stickerguy .com) and Disc Makers (discmakers.com) handle sticker ordering.

5. Lifestyle merch.

From high-end perfume to clothing lines, this type of merchandise usually comes from a well-established persona and brand with a large fan base. But these are the types of items to eventually aim for as your career progresses. Your final goal would be to get these types of items in stores all over the world, from department stores to major retailers.

6. Participatory merch and live show items.

Try creating a part of your live show set where your fans can participate—for example, if they have a shaker, drumstick, or tambourine. This will make anyone who doesn't have the items feel left out unless they get one for themselves, which you will have available for sale at your merch table. Other types of related merch include glow sticks, lighted bracelets, and blinking necklaces. These look cool when people are dancing with them, and they attract fans to your merch table if you keep some of them lit and out for people to buy.

7. Persona-based merch, photographs, and autographed merch.

Once you have a name, people will want photos and other merch based on your persona and brand elements. And your autograph can enhance the value of nearly everything else you sell. This even includes your old gear, which can then be sold at a premium, or even broken gear, such as drumsticks, guitar strings, and guitar picks. Keep in mind, you can also put your name on new music gear. If you're a guitarist, you can brand guitar strings and sell them at your merch table. Even non-musicians sometimes want items like this.

8. Mascot products.

If you have a mascot (which we talk about in chapter 3, "Your Persona"), you can create stuffed animals, stickers, plastic figures, and posters using the design. Don't underestimate the power of a good mascot; The Grateful Dead's dancing skeletons and dancing bears represent a significant amount of merchandise sales.

9. Sponsored items.

As we will discuss in chapter 13, "Advanced Income Techniques," you can sell your sponsor's products, merch, or service coupons for them. You can work it to get an extra cut or get merchandise at cost. For example, if you have a beach party vibe, you can team up with a beach clothing vendor and sell them at your shows.

10. Food items.

There's a surprising number of options to let you slap your own logo on food items of all sorts and sell it as your own. For example, explore the options at sites like 4imprint (4imprint.com/sgroup/190/Food-and -Candy) or ePromos (epromos.com/promotional-candy-food-drink/_ /N-11125). You can even make candy hearts (like the kind sold on Valentine's Day) with your own messages written on them at services like My Custom Candy (mycustomcandy.com) or M&Ms (mymms.com). This includes even branded wine options at services like Personal Wine (personalwine.com/corporate-wine-gifts). But remember to follow the alcohol sales laws.

11. Books, photobooks, and ebooks.

Because self-publishing books is easy to do, you can make books as merch items. And with print-on-demand options available, you can make a few of them to sell at your shows and find out if more people want them. For instance, create a behind-the-scenes book about you and your music, a book of lyrics/album covers/info about the music, a photo book with pictures from your live events, or a collection of your thoughts like Henry Rollins. Ebook vendors like Lulu (lulu.com), CreateSpace (createspace.com), and Ingram (ingramcontent.com) make physical copies easy to come by online or as a handful of merch items. If you want help putting it together, BookBaby (bookbaby.com), which is a branch of the CD Baby family, also has services to help you deal with the production side of print on demand as well as ebook publishing.

12. Artwork.

If you also paint, sculpt, or create any other type of art, you can create and sell your own artwork to your fans. These can be one-of-a-kind items that demand a premium price. Additionally, you can sell others' artwork. This is especially powerful when the art you sell complements your persona, music, or the themes or lyrics you write. Keep in mind that if the art you create is imaged-based, you can create additional products using your artwork, such as adding it to a T-shirt, clothing, and other merch.

13. Cheap, high-margin toys and souvenirs.

Manufacturers like U.S. Toy (ustoy.com) have huge categories of items you can buy in bulk. Many of them are well under a U.S. dollar each, but at a merch table, you can sell items like these for a dollar or two, giving you a very high profit margin on each sale. Selling glow necklaces not only attracts people to your merch table, you can sell them for three times or more what you paid for them, and it's a low-priced item that can be bundled with other merch as an incentive.

14. Custom-designed merch.

With services like Alibaba (alibaba.com), you can get in touch with manufacturers of nearly any kind of item you can dream up. They will help you create designs, put together a mold to manufacture it, and, depending on the item, make it any color you desire. This would let you create something unique for your fans.

15. Grab bag mystery bundles.

Bundle leftover items that don't sell well into mystery bundles of merchandise. Include a few items they normally want with leftovers and you can reduce inventory and provide your fans with another item to buy at the merch table.

HOW TO SELL YOUR MERCHANDISE ONLINE

If you go with a volume manufacturer for your merchandise, you may also want to offer it to your fans online rather than just at shows. You can take orders yourself if you can set up an e-commerce website, or hire a fulfillment services to take orders, ship the products, and inform you when your inventory is low.

1. If you handle the shipping yourself, find a storefront vendor.

There's no end of businesses that handle transactions for you while you handle the shipping. Solutions include Limited Run (limitedrun.com), which takes only 5 percent of your sales, Gumroad (gumroad.com), Amazon Webstores (webstore.amazon.com), and Shopify (shopify.com).

2. If you want others to handle your shipping, use a fulfillment vendor.

Vendors that are geared toward musicians include Whiplash (getwhiplash.com); Limited Run (limitedrun.com), which teams with fulfillment vendors; and also Topspin (topspinmedia.com) and Bandcamp (band camp.com), which can handle inventory, shipping, and orders for you. For a business-focused solution, you can use Amazon Fulfillment Services (amazonservices.com/fulfillment), to stock your merchandise, take the orders, ship the items, and handle payment.

THE SECRET TO INCREASING YOUR REVENUE ON EVERYTHING YOU SELL

No matter where you sell your merchandise online, keep in mind that most stores have affiliate options to get a cut of the sale on the front end as well as the back end when you sell the merchandise. They don't care if you are sending people to your own items or to others on their site. Plus, nearly every print-on-demand service has affiliate options as well. This means you should be becoming an affiliate to every place that sells your merch and products and create and use affiliate links for all of them. For more information, see chapter 13, "Advanced Income Techniques."

11

PATRONAGE, CROWDFUNDING, AND RAISING MONEY

Goal: To maximize the amount of money you can raise for your music business through patronage, crowdfunding, and other fund-raising methods.

Team Roles and Responsibilities: Manager, Attorney, Accountant/ Bookkeeper, Business Banker, Publisher, Social Media Manager, Marketer, Publicist, Graphic Artist, Copywriter, Photographer, Video Producer, and Web Designer/Webmaster

WHAT YOU GET OUT OF THIS
By the end of this chapter, you will:

1. Know multiple methods to raise money by going directly to fans.

2. Be able to run a successful crowdfunding campaign from start to finish and maximize the number of pledges and amount of funding.

3. Create an ongoing patronage/fan club revenue stream for your music business and tie it directly into the activities of your music, live events, releases, promotion, and so on to boost the amount of revenue you can generate.

4. Create appropriate rewards to maximize the pledges and monthly income you can make.

5. Be able to take donations and tips directly from fans through your online presences.

MONEY MAP

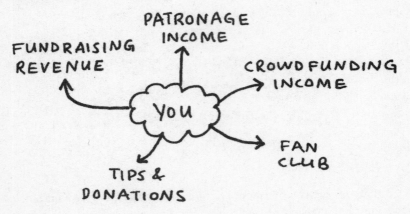

INTRO

As we mentioned in chapter 2, "Your Music Business," you can now start a music business for $0, since you can get worldwide music distribution, merchandise, promotion, and licensing for free. But what if you have a project in mind that needs funding?

One of the most popular ways for musicians to raise money for their projects is crowdfunding. Whether you need funds for the production of your next album or a tour, crowdfunding is a powerful presales mechanism that gets fans involved in your projects. When run successfully, a crowdfunding campaign captures your backers' enthusiasm and spreads the word to new fans. Also, crowdfunding allows you the chance of getting the support of larger backers, especially if you choose the right rewards.

If you want consistent support, patronage allows your fans to fund you on a monthly or even per-release basis. This can give you stable income streams from your fans and even gives you something you can grow as you build your fan base.

Note that each of these methods has downsides, since musicians who ask for support from their fans can be perceived as being a small-time artist or needy, and the choice of whether to do this or not depends on your genre or persona. Also, this can give fans a sense of ownership in what you create, which can cause them to make demands that you might not agree with. And the highest-end rewards often require you to give personal access, which can cut into the time you'd work on your music or other aspects of your music business.

That said, the advantages are that none of these methods stops you from tapping into every other source of income for your music, so it stacks very well on top of the rest of your music business. It also brings your fans closer to you and makes them into fan clubs who want to see you succeed and are willing to put their money behind you. To tap into these advantages, use the techniques below.

KEY CONCEPTS
WHY YOU NEED TO CATER TO THE HIGH ROLLERS: MINNOWS, DOLPHINS, AND WHALES

As we discussed in chapter 2, "Your Music Business," you should classify your fans between three spending levels: minnows, dolphins, and whales. Minnows spend the minimum amount of money, dolphins are your regular customers, and whales are superfans who have money, want to spend it, and love you and your music.

If you do a financial breakdown of your income, you will usually discover your whales contribute the most and are worth concentrating on.

This idea is used in this chapter as you create rewards aimed directly at each level. Minnows are an on-ramp. Dolphins will contribute a lot of your core income. But the mistake often made by musicians is not giving enough high-end rewards for your whales to support you. Why not have a $10,000 option for your crowdfunding campaign? Why not allow your whales to spend $100 month or more on your patronage? We'll talk about these reward levels below and how to accommodate each level, but these are highly based on knowing who your fans are, what they like, and what would cause someone to want to spend $100 a month to support you.

CROWDFUNDING
CHOOSING A CROWDFUNDING PARTNER

The most important crowdfunding choice you'll make is choosing your crowdfunding partner. Because your campaign is a huge investment in time and effort, you'll have to make sure it's worth your time to evaluate each potential partner, since it can make a huge difference in the success of your crowdfunding campaign.

The primary criteria to judge your crowdfunding partner is their funding model:

- **All-or-nothing funding.**

Services like Kickstarter (kickstarter.com) will only pay you if you raise more than your funding target. Otherwise, the money is not collected from your backers. This model can be an advantage, since you are not required to try to get your project done if you don't raise enough funds to succeed.

- **Flexible funding.**

Flexible funding services like Indiegogo (indiegogo.com) allow you to choose between all-or-nothing or partially funded campaigns. This allows you to collect money from a campaign that didn't reach its target, which might be appropriate for certain types of campaigns.

Also, evaluate the platforms on these secondary criteria:

- **Fees and platform costs.**

Each platform has their own fees and percentage cuts they take out of the campaigns. They also have different payment processors they can use, which could limit the campaign or your backers and also can affect how you can get your cut.

- **Campaign limitations and requirements.**

Not every platform will handle each type of crowdfunding campaign. For example, Kickstarter allows charitable companies to run a campaign, but not for their charity itself, which GoFundMe (gofundme.com) does allow.

- **Geographic limitations.**

Because each country has different rules on fund-raising, crowdfunding platforms might be limited by the geographic region they can operate within.

- **Campaign features.**

Each platform usually restricts options such as the length of campaign, how to contact your backers, and more. These are usually displayed in their help and are worth evaluating between platforms.

HOW TO RUN A CROWDFUNDING CAMPAIGN

The key to successful crowdfunding is organizing your campaign to maximize fund-raising. Musicians who dive straight in without following the few simple steps below miss out on providing the "social proof" people need to see in order to decide to back a project. Campaigns that use these techniques capture the momentum of successes to carry a campaign past the initial goal into higher, "stretch" goals to bring in more money.

To do this, follow the sequence below:

1. Choose the project.

Choose a compelling project your fans will want to be a part of. The more concrete you can make it, the better. Typical projects include albums and tours, but if you can be unique, concrete, and also give fans something that they would want to see or hear, you can stand out and possibly gain backers just for the novelty.

2. Choose a crowdfunding platform.

Follow the steps as outlined in the "Choosing a Crowdfunding Partner" section above to pick the best one for your needs.

3. Choose the funding goal and at least one stretch goal.

The first goal should be the lowest amount possible to fund your goal, but it must fully fund your project. Don't forget to add in the platform's cut, or you'll find yourself short. Also announce your stretch goal on day one, because that might encourage people to pledge beyond the minimum.

4. Shoot a video.

Videos go viral in a way that no other media can, so it's the most critical marketing component of a crowdfunding project.

5. Make a list of promoters.

Use the full list of channels we cover in chapter 14, "Marketing," plus any bloggers, friends, other musicians, and all others with an audience you can reach who can help you get the initial word out.

6. Plan your rewards.

Use the "How to Choose the Right Rewards" section below to plan out your rewards.

7. Get initial backers.

Make a list of initial backers of people you know will donate on day one. Get their promise to contribute before the project even starts. These initial backers will help you "seed the tip jar" and provide social proof that your project has supporters, has momentum, and is achievable. People like to join in on projects that they think are going to be successful. Your goal is to trigger this psychological reaction by using your initial backers effectively in the first days of your campaign.

If you can, try to get celebrity or high-profile backers. This can also help provide additional proof that your project deserves support. If you are not well known yet on your own, their names will help you establish credibility with your potential backers.

8. Choose the start and end date.

Studies show most funding occurs at the beginning and end of a campaign, and four-week campaigns tend to do best. The start date should be on a Monday or Tuesday. This allows a "soft launch" and provides a few days for your initial backers to pledge before you publicly announce the campaign. Also, plan your end date so it doesn't fall on a holiday or a time when people would be less likely to contribute.

9. Do a soft launch on a Monday or Tuesday.

On your launch day, ask your initial backers to contribute but hold off announcing it to your fans until Wednesday afternoon, the next step below. This initial backing provides social proof that you already have people who are willing to contribute money to your project. This is no different from dropping a twenty-dollar bill into your tip jar before playing at a venue. People are more willing to tip when they see someone has already done it. And if they see a bigger bill, they are more likely to tip with a bigger bill themselves.

10. Kick off the official launch on Wednesdays in the afternoon.
Research shows Wednesday afternoons are when people reshare the most on social media as they take a break from work or school and get on the internet. Your video is at the center of this, and it should be as shareable and viral as you can make it. To do this, share the video and announce it on all your media. Also ask any promoters, initial backers, and any media you know that has an audience to share it that same Wednesday.

11. Make announcements at appropriate points.
As the campaign progresses, you will want to keep your backers informed. These announcements can reach new backers but are also aimed at convincing existing backers to contribute more (for example, to help you make a stretch goal you are close to reaching).

Make announcements:

- At the beginning, middle, and end of the campaign. Also, perform weekly updates.

- When *close* to your main goal or any of your stretch goals to encourage new backers or more contributions from existing backers.

- When achieving a goal to celebrate the milestone and announce the next stretch goal.

- If you have gained a high-profile backer or notable media coverage.

- On the last few days, to encourage final contributions (remember, the beginning and end is when you'll get the most contributions).

- When the campaign has ended.

If you are getting a lot of activity, keep the announcements to no more than once every few days unless you have noteworthy news to share.

12. Close out the campaign and deliver.
Make the final announcements, and then, if you've achieved your funding goal, make sure to follow through! Each person who has backed you

now feels like they are a part owner of your project, and they will want to hear your progress and see the final result. Also, make sure to talk to your accountant. Crowdfunding campaigns are taxable income and are reported to the government.

HOW TO CHOOSE THE RIGHT REWARDS

Your rewards are very similar to your merch booth. You'll want low-end rewards to lure in your minnows and get people to participate, and you'll want to make sure to provide high-end rewards for $10,000 or $25,000 (USD) or more for your whales.

1. Set $1 rewards.

Always have a $1 reward to hook people that are only casually interested in your project. Once they become a backer, crowdfunding platforms allow you to message them, and with each update you send, you'll get more chances to upsell them to a higher reward or forward this campaign to their friends. This is why you'll send messages when you're close to achieving each goal. For a good low-barrier $1 reward, try choosing a single downloadable track.

2. Set $10 rewards.

A $10 reward is the perfect price point for a downloadable digital album. But don't just offer the exact same thing that they could buy at iTunes or other digital stores; add something extra so it becomes a true reward—for example, an additional song or a downloadable lyric sheet PDF.

3. Set $25 rewards.

Data shows that the $25 reward is the most common pledge, so offer a variety of rewards at this level to capture this special price point. This is also the first level where you can consider non-digital rewards. But if you do so, make sure to offer at least two $25 rewards—a physical reward that you can mail and a digital reward equivalent that you can dub the "save-the-earth" version. Push them toward the nonphysical rewards that you don't have to ship.

4. Setting rewards greater than $25.

Prepare a graduated set of rewards for levels greater than $25 all the way through $500 or so. For these levels, there's no end to the type of rewards you can create. Offer previous albums or rarities from your back cata-log. Create different packaged rewards—different CD cases, vinyl, USB drives, and so on. Offer a souvenir photo book of the "making of" your project. Offer to add their name to a "thank-you" page in the liner notes. You can also let fans buy some control. For example, let backers who pledge $100 or more have a chance to vote for the album art (from a pre-selection), create a set list for a tour to their city, backstage access, or a day with the band, house concert, or party. Also, don't overcommit yourself, but think big; someone might fund your $10,000 or $25,000 reward.

Before locking in your rewards, research other successful crowdfund-ing campaigns to get ideas on what worked for others, and note the re-wards they created. And don't limit yourself to just looking over other musicians; ideas can come from any campaign. Check to see which rewards were chosen and which were not. Finally, don't forget that giving clever names to each reward level can get people to commit to it.

PATRONAGE
UNDERSTANDING PATRONAGE

As we talked about in chapter 2, "Your Music Business," you need to blend in some stable sources of income along with the inconsistent sources, such as music sales or licensing. Fortunately, your fans want to support you directly, beyond just buying merch and music, and they are doing so more and more using patronage. Historically, artists were sup-ported by royalty, wealthy individuals, or large organizations. Today, there's an app to let fans give you support directly.

Modern patronage acts like a fan club, giving extra content, special ac-cess, special requests, and member-only perks to your supporters. They will do this if you structure your music and outreach around getting supporters using these steps:

1. Entertain your fans on a regular basis by putting out a regular stream of new releases using the techniques in chapter 18, "Your Release Strategy." These releases should be come with extras.

2. Maximize your reach to pull in as many new fans as possible by getting your music and videos out broadly, and cast a wide net using the forty-five categories of places to get your music heard as we cover in chapter 17, "Get Heard and Seen."

3. Turn listeners into supporters by marketing your patronage page using techniques covered in chapter 14, "Marketing."

4. Consider putting yourself out there as well. As Martin Atkins says, "People don't support artists because they love their music. They support artists because they love them." This is where the thirteen qualities any music business should have that we talk about in chapter 2 come into play, especially authenticity and your story.

5. Make the patronage as attractive as possible, offering good rewards, extras, and perks they can't get anywhere else. See suggestions for this below.

Once you put together a good patronage platform, you can let your fans fund you on a monthly basis or give you a fixed amount per thing you release. This can give you consistent, parallel, passive income, giving you a stable stream to base your revenue while you give them regular entertainment and the extras that make your fans want to be a part of your club. The best part is that all the other sources of income, including video income, music licensing, and more, are still available to you as your fans support you.

CHOOSING A PATRONAGE PARTNER

Patronage is starting to pick up steam and thus has a few sites and platforms that allow you to do it. The most well-known platform is Patreon (patreon .com), which spearheaded this movement and has a lot of name recognition with your potential supporters. They may already be using it to support other creators, and thus adding you is an easy thing for them to do. New platforms are appearing to step into this space, including Drip from Kickstarter (d.rip), and you'll want to compare their features using the criteria below:

- **Fees, platform costs, and payment options.**
  Each platform has their own fees and percentage cuts that they take out of the patronage, including what they charge your patrons.

- **Platform limitations and requirements.**
  Patronage platforms are starting to limit the kinds of creators they will allow, sometimes blocking certain types such as ones based on

overtly sexual themes. Choose a platform that can support your type of art.

- **Reward delivery features and engagement tools.**
You'll want the platform to be able to deliver video, digital assets, and specialized messages per user group so you can more easily deliver custom rewards, early access content, and messaging and blogging.

HOW TO CHOOSE THE RIGHT REWARDS

Your patronage rewards will have similar minnow, dolphin, and whale tiers to your crowdfunding, but they will have different rewards. Similar to crowdfunding, we will give ideas (in USD) to try out in each tier you can riff off for your own music business.

1. Entry level $1 or $2 rewards.
Always have a low-end reward to hook your minnows who want an option to give you some support. Once they become subscribers, you can keep messaging them to convince them to increase their rewards. Good things to offer in this tier include alternative versions of your songs, images, or downloads of extras.

2. Most common supporters at $5 rewards.
The $5 reward is one of the most common for patronage platforms, aimed at your dolphins, and should start giving fans early access to releases and more extras the low-end reward tier doesn't see.

3. Prerelease and limited access options at $10 rewards.
This is $120 a year, and—depending on the size of your fan base—could be when to give them access to the streams of your live shows (which you can still charge everyone else to access), prerelease tickets, or access to your music-writing streams if you want provide it. You could also provide the ability to buy limited access merch at these levels and above that are not available at lower levels.

4. Custom request $15 or more rewards.
At this level, you can start offering the types of rewards that require you to occasionally talk directly with the fans, such as Google Hangouts or

Skype sessions with them every three months, or mini concerts for people at this level along with all the lower-level rewards.

5. Personal access between $15 and $100.

At these levels, you can offer more customized items, such as a custom-written song based on request or occasional personal access to you via electronic methods. Keep in mind you can limit the number of people that can sign up for each reward, so you don't have to provide too many fans this kind of access if you don't wish to.

6. Very high-end, $100-or-more-a-month rewards.

You should always offer $100 or more rewards for your whales, but you can be creative about what your fans would want for $1,200 a year or more. This could include guest-list access to your shows with backstage privileges and more.

Don't forget you can offer multiple rewards at the same level, meaning you could have a $15-per-month reward for live show access and a $15-per-month reward for your fans all over the world who can't come to shows.

Before locking in your rewards, research other patronage profiles. Similar to crowdfunding, don't limit yourself to just looking over other musicians, since ideas can come from any campaign. Finally, just like crowdfunding, don't forget that giving clever names to each reward level can get people to commit to it.

Finally, once you have a patronage platform, you'll want to constantly plug in everything you do, and your rewards should help with this. You can also give special items at your merch table at your shows that are only available if they sign up for your patronage on the spot. Don't just think digital; use your real-world events to get fans to support you every month instead.

FAN CLUBS AND OTHER FUND-RAISING OPTIONS
HOW TO CREATE A FAN CLUB AND MOTIVATE FANS TO JOIN
Your biggest fans deserve something special from you on a regular basis, but they also deserve to have a better method to support you beyond simply buying your music or merchandise. Subscription-based fan clubs are one way to do this, giving your fans benefits that they want, while giving you a mailing list of dedicated fans with another income stream in return.

In many ways, patronage platforms are modern-day fan clubs. Rather than start your own fan club from scratch, you should use these platforms, especially since they come with easy-to-use communication and engagement features. However, if you reach a certain level of popularity, you may wish to manage your fan base completely or set up a special club in addition to your patronage service. This can give you more control over membership pricing and the rewards you provide your fans, and, by cutting out the middleman, increase the amount of money you can make.

Of course, taking this step will require you to handle much of what the platforms do for you on your own. Managing a fan club includes many administrative tasks. That's on top of determining what exclusives and rewards to provide to motivate them to join your club and keep them engaged. Another method is to use a direct-to-fan sales-and-marketing platform, such as Topspin (topspinmedia.com) or GigRev (gigrev.com), to help handle the pieces. Such a service focuses on providing solutions for creatives with large fan bases to promote and sell music, films, products, merchandise, tickets, and more directly to their fans.

Some ways to motivate fans to join could be to create exclusive short-run items only available for purchase or giveaway to fan club members or to give fan club members access to prerelease tickets for live events.

Whether you choose to DIY your fan club or use a direct-to-fans platform, be sure to use the patronage and crowdfunding reward level techniques discussed above. Doing so will entice your most diehard fans to contribute and support you more.

HOW TO TASTEFULLY TAKE DONATIONS AND TIPS FROM YOUR WEB PRESENCES

As discussed in chapter 8, "Your Rights," you must be able to take all forms of payments. Once set up, there's nothing stopping you from having fans tip or donate money to you directly—whether online or in person. Whether you do so is a matter of whether it aligns to your persona and personal preference. Here's how to integrate this into your web presences and angle it so it doesn't appear like you're begging:

1. Choose your platform.

Payment platforms like PayPal.Me (paypal.me), Square (square.com), and other online platforms make it easy for fans to send you tips and donations online. These can also be used to take tips live and in person, but you can also use devices like DipJar (dipjar.com), mobile apps such as BuSK (busk.co), or any other credit card platform.

2. Use buttons, widgets, or apps from the donation site, and embed them in your web presences.
Make it as easy as possible for fans to see you take donations and the buttons to use on your web presences.

3. Frame your message so it's about supporting you as an artist.
Avoid the phrases *"tip"* and *"donate money to me"* and instead ask for their *"support."* Remind them that any money received goes to helping you continue to bring music into the world.

4. Consider giving each donor a thank-you gift.
As discussed above, consider incentivizing donations by creating "suggested support amounts" that unlock a thank-you gift, such as links to digital downloads. Services such as BuSK (BuSK.co) have built-in features to distribute digital tracks. At a minimum, always send a thank-you.

THE TOP EIGHT ADDITIONAL WAYS MUSICIANS CAN RAISE CAPITAL
Not everyone can fund their music project on $0. Some projects are just too large or require personnel or equipment or tours, videos, or albums. Fortunately, there are many methods to get funding. Some take more time or work than others, but all are ones you can take advantage of right now.

1. Day job.
Let's face it: shows are usually played at night, and you can record music anytime. There's your "night gig," and then there's your "day gig," and they can live together in harmony. Take advantage of the steady income and benefits of a day job until your music business "tells you" it's time to quit by giving you enough income to live on.

2. Friends and family.
Of course, the time-honored way to get started is to turn to people that you already know to get that initial stake. Considering the low-cost options we discuss above, you might need less than you think, and a few hundred dollars might be enough to get you going.

3. Advances.

As we discuss in chapter 13, "Advanced Income Techniques," there are many types of advances available to musicians based on their future income streams, including tour, royalty, publishing, and label advances.

4. Sponsorships and endorsements.

Companies love associating their product with cool music. Companies like Adidas, Taco Bell, Hype Hotel, Red Bull, Southwest Airlines, and more all work with musicians to capture the right vibe for their message. We'll talk about this in more detail in chapter 13, "Advanced Income Techniques."

5. Grants.

Grants are money given to artists or organizations to support an artist or a project, and we talk about how to tap them in chapter 13, "Advanced Income Techniques."

6. Bank loans.

Music businesses can qualify for bank loans, especially if they keep good accounting books, have a business plan, can prove they have a solid income history, and have good prospects for future income. You can work with your business banker to see if your own bank would give loans to your business. Another option is to work with a company that understands advances to get a loan, such as Lyric Financial (lyricfinancial.com) and Sound Royalties (soundroyalties.com).

7. Credit cards.

The high interest rates on credit cards make them a poor choice to raise money, but, since many people use them as a source for short-term funds, we've added it for completeness. Just keep in mind the interest adds up if you don't pay off the balance and it can affect your credit rating.

8. Sign to a label.

As we discuss in chapter 13, "Advanced Income Techniques," a label will help you raise the money needed for recording an album and give you an advance to cover your own finances. They also can provide tour support if they get a cut of the tour proceeds. However, they will take copyrights to your music as well as a percentage of other income sources in return.

Many of these options don't require you to give up your copyrights to raise this money, and as long as you take advantage of all the other sources of income, once you get your business started and pay off the loans, you can directly benefit from owning the rights to all your music and use that to continue to make your music.

12

LICENSING AND ROYALTIES

Goal: To license your music and collect all the royalties and ad share revenue you're owed worldwide.

Team Roles and Responsibilities: Attorney, Publisher, Accountant/Bookkeeper, Songwriter(s), Musicians, Recording Producer, and Manager

WHAT YOU GET OUT OF THIS
By the end of this chapter, you will:

1. Understand all the royalties your compositions and sound recordings can generate worldwide.

2. Register all your compositions and sound recordings so you can get all the royalties you are owed.

3. Know additional royalty revenue streams that may be available to you.

4. Understand what licensing is and how it works, and know the most important license agreement terms.

5. Understand the role of music supervisors and how to pitch your music to them for licensing in film, TV, advertising, and movie trailers.

6. Know the services that can help you license your music and get it in front of music supervisors and other creatives who are looking for music.

7. Understand what music publishers do so you can decide whether to do it yourself, have someone on your team handle it, or sign with a professional.

MONEY MAP

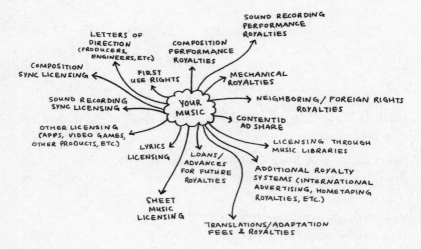

INTRO

The song "Over the Rainbow" from the film *The Wizard of Oz* has generated over $1 billion in royalties. While this is one of the most popular films of all time, its success demonstrates the income potential music licensing has for musicians. In a world with declining music sales, musicians are licensing their music for films, TV shows, movie trailers, and commercials to create performance royalties and licensing income.

Unfortunately, royalties are often considered some of the most confusing parts of the music business, and most musicians don't participate in it or only sign up for a few of the royalty income streams, but this chapter will bring these within your reach. With just a little bit of prep work, you can get all the royalties you are owed for your music for your entire lifetime. Plus, all the successes of your get-heard-and-seen campaigns will generate more royalties as a side effect to all your hard work.

Meanwhile, if you spend just a bit of time understanding music supervisors—the people who choose and license music for TV shows, movies, trailers, and ads—you can make your music friendly for licensing and add another income stream. This is covered below, and if you can perform these steps, perhaps your song can be the next "Over the Rainbow."

KEY CONCEPTS
WHAT COPYRIGHT LAW GIVES YOU OWNERSHIP OF AND WHAT YOU CAN EARN FROM YOUR MUSIC

If you want to make money with music today as an independent musician, you need to understand you play many roles: songwriter, artist, publisher, label, and producer. Each one of these jobs creates income streams you can tap. Unfortunately, most musicians today don't realize how to turn these into income streams. This is because in the past, these roles were performed by separate people or, in some cases, organizations (such as a music label). But since so many artists are independent today, these income streams can all be yours!

We will tell you how to register to get each of these sources of income in the rest of the chapter, but in this section, we're going to outline the income streams and what they're based on. Below is a list of each role you'll play and the money you'll be making based on each one.

1. You as the songwriter.
The law automatically gives the songwriter of an original song ownership of the copyright. This gets you:

- **First use rights.**
  Copyright law gives you the right to decide who will be the first licensee of your composition. Typically, the label would pay you a fee to get this exclusive first use right (and often would cap the fee), but if you're acting as your own label, you can skip the fee. Once you've released the song, it's "published," and the law gives others the ability to cover, broadcast, or stream your composition without your permission via a compulsory mechanical license; in return, it generates royalties for you.

- **Composition mechanical royalties.**
  Anytime your song is copied onto physical products like CDs, vinyl records, USB drives, digital download cards, or cassette tapes,

sold as a digital download, sampled, or streamed through interactive streaming services like Spotify, Apple Music, Amazon Prime Music, Google Play, Deezer, or others, you're entitled to make money.

For physical products and digital downloads, this royalty was normally paid to you by the label creating these products. If you're on someone else's label, your agreement with them should outline how royalties are handled. If you're a songwriter who is also your own label, then you don't need to pay yourself, but you may need to pay other cowriters or make an agreement with them to waive the royalties. For interactive streaming services, the royalty is paid by the streaming service to a mechanical rights collection organization (MRCO) such as Harry Fox (harryfox.com) or Music Reports (musicreports.com) in the U.S. Outside the U.S., the local PRO may handle mechanical royalties like they do performance royalties, such as in the UK, with PRS (prsformusic .com). You need to be a member of your country's MRCO and have your composition registered so they know who to pay. And anytime your composition is covered by *other* artists, they need to pay you or your publisher for making the cover while the mechanicals they generate over time can be collected and handled by your MRCO or PRO as stated above.

• **Composition performance royalties.**

Anytime your composition is performed live in public (by you or other musicians) or the sound recording of your composition is played or broadcasted in any way (radio, TV, movie theaters, music venue performances, background music in restaurants, company offices, played on hold, in other establishments, etc.) or interactively and noninteractively streamed through any streaming service, including video services such as Netflix, Hulu, YouTube, Facebook Video, and others, you can make money.

This is collected and paid to you by your performance rights organization (PRO) partner, which collects money from these music users and tracks plays of all music through sampling surveys, cue sheet records, submitted set lists, and other data and reports collected from broadcasters, streaming services, and others. In the

U.S., this could be ASCAP, BMI, or SESAC. Outside the U.S., this would be your country's PRO, such as SOCAN (Canada), PRS (UK), IMRO (Ireland), APRA/AMCOS (Australia/New Zealand), and so on. You need to be a member of your country's PRO and have your composition registered, with you listed as the "songwriter" so they know who to pay. PROs split these royalties fifty-fifty between you and your publisher (discussed below).

- **Print and publication royalties.**

Anytime your composition is made into sheet music or your lyrics are printed (such as in liner notes or on the back of an album), you can make money. This is usually paid by the company who's creating copies of your song (either online or on paper) or the label who's reprinting your lyrics as liner notes. These royalties are usually paid to your publisher, who then pays you your share.

- **Composition synchronization fees.**

Anytime your composition is used in any audiovisual work, such as a film, TV show, advertisement, or movie trailer, you can make money. This also includes when it's for DVD, Blu-ray, or an interactive video-streaming service, such as Netflix, Hulu, or others. This is true whether they use the sound recording of your composition or if they have someone else record it and use that cover version instead. This synchronization fee is usually paid to you by whoever licenses your composition for the audiovisual work they're creating. These royalties are usually negotiated and paid to your publisher, who then pays you your share.

- **Composition transcription fee.**

Anytime your song is used in a terrestrial radio commercial or advertisement, you are owed money. This is usually paid to you by whoever is producing the commercial. This fee is usually paid to your publisher, who then pays you your share.

- **Other uses.**

Anytime someone wants to use your composition for some other use not listed above, such as in a greeting card, a toy, an app, or some novelty such as a singing fish, you can make money. This is paid to you by the company or manufacturer of the product using your composition. This fee is usually negotiated and paid to your publisher, who then pays you your share.

2. You as the recording or performing artist.

As the artist who records the song as a sound recording, you get:

• Sound-recording performance royalties.

Every time the song you performed on is played on noninteractive streaming or digital radio services, you make money. This is paid to you in the U.S. by a special PRO called SoundExchange (SoundExchange.com)—but only if you're a member—the song is registered and lists you as the performer or "featured artist." Outside of the U.S., this is handled by the country's PRO, such as SOCAN in Canada or PRS in the UK. Since music is played across borders, technically, songwriters should get the royalties paid out across the globe. This is handled by designating a sub-publisher in each country to collect royalties there and share half with you. Often, the subpublishers you'll be partnering with are services through your digital distributor or PRO.

• Fees for playing live or recording.

Though these are *not* revenue streams generated from copyright, they illustrate how copyright law and all the money you can make from it goes to those who create original music, not simply perform it. Any-time you perform live or record in the studio, you should make money, but this is usually based on your time and skill, not any intel-lectual property rights. When playing live, the money you may make is usually paid to you by the venue at which you're performing, through ticket sales or at the door. You need to work out a deal or writ-ten agreement with the venue, booker, or venue each time you play out. When recording in the studio, typically it's the label who pays an advance to the artist so the artist can afford to create sound record-ings. If you're both the artist and your own label, then this doesn't make much sense. However, you may want a certain performer or guest musician to record and appear on your sound recording. That performer may want to be paid for their time (work-for-hire) or share in the songwriting credit and percentage of the royalties created. If you add the artist to the song or sound-recording split agreement as a cowriter, then the artist or performer becomes a songwriter.

3. You as the publisher.

Unless you've entered into an agreement with a third-party music publisher, you are responsible for registering your compositions to get all the royalties owed to you no matter where your music is played or how. This includes domestic royalties and foreign or neighboring royalties being generated all over the world. Your job as the publisher also includes convincing music supervisors and potential licensees to license your songs, including getting it into film, TV, advertising, movie trailers, video games, and any other media. Being the publisher for the songwriter and song gets you:

- **Composition performance royalties.**

Anytime you get a song is played on TV, film, advertising, or movie trailers, you can make money. This is paid to you by your PRO—but only if you're a member and you've registered yourself as the "publisher" for the composition, and only if they pick up plays of your composition in their surveys and reports. If you're both the songwriter and the publisher, you'll receive two payments for the same performance of your song, since you're fulfilling both roles. Of course, if you skip this registration, you'll leave half the money on the table.

- **Composition synchronization royalties.**

Anytime you license the song for use in any audiovisual work, such as in a film, TV show, advertisement, or movie trailer, you can make money. This is usually paid to you by whoever licenses your song for the audiovisual work they're creating. Again, as an independent artist, if you're both the songwriter and the publisher, you are owed money twice! Note that once your composition is out there being performed in the audiovisual work, it also generates composition performance royalties, which you share in as the publisher.

- **Composition transcription fee.**

Anytime your songwriter's song is used in a terrestrial radio commercial or advertisement, you are owed money. This is usually paid to you by whoever is producing the commercial. Again, if you're both the songwriter and the publisher, you are owed money twice!

4. You as the label and sound recording owner.

Unless you signed away your rights to a third party or music label, you're the sound recording owner. You own the master recordings of your songs, and the law gives you a master use right. This is a separate copyright from the one you own as the songwriter, so this generates more revenue streams to tap. Being the owner of the sound recording gets you:

- **Sales revenue from master use rights.**
Anytime you sell a copy of your sound recording as a physical product like a CD, vinyl record, USB drive, digital download card, or cassette tape or through a digital download, you make money because you own the master right to sell the copies to the public. This right grants you a monopoly to sell your sound recording to the world. This is generally how labels made most of their money with music in the past. With the decline in both physical and digital download sales and the rise of streaming, most of the money a label can make with music is through streaming royalties as well as by tapping into many of the other income streams we outline throughout this book—revenue sources typically reserved in the past for songwriters, artists, publishers, and more.

- **Interactive streaming royalties.**
Anytime your sound recording is streamed on interactive streaming services, it generates revenue for the sound recording owner. This is usually paid directly to the sound recording owner by these services through your digital distributor.

- **Sound recording performance royalties (noninteractive streaming royalties).**
Anytime your sound recording is streamed on noninteractive streaming or digital radio services, such as Pandora Radio, Spotify Radio, and Live365, you can make money. This is paid in the U.S. by SoundExchange, which is a sound recording PRO, but only if you're a member and the sound recording is registered with you listed as the "sound recording owner." Outside the U.S., this is handled by the country's PRO.

- **Sound recording synchronization fees.**
Anytime your sound recording is used in TV, film, advertising, or movie trailers, you make money. This is usually paid to you by

whoever licenses your sound recording for the audiovisual work they're creating.

• **Sampling fee.**

Anytime someone wants to use a sample of your sound recording for their song or in a mash-up, you can make money. This is paid to you by the label or musician using your sound recording.

• **Other uses.**

Anytime someone wants to use your sound recording for some other use not listed above, such as in a greeting card, a toy, an app, or some novelty such as a singing fish, you can make money. This is paid to you by the company or manufacturer of the product using your composition. This fee is usually negotiated and paid to your publisher, who then pays you your share.

5. You as the producer.

As the producer of the sound recording for the artist, you may get:

• **Fees for producing.**

Anytime you produce sound recordings for an artist, you may make money. As a producer, you may want to be paid for your time (work-for-hire) or percentage of the music sales. If so, these have nothing to do with copyright. However, you can negotiate a share in the songwriting credit, which would make you a songwriter and give you the same rights as songwriters get. This would be worked out in a written agreement between you as the producer and the artist and/or songwriter(s). Note that if you act as a producer for artists who are just starting out or have small followings, you may want to charge a flat fee rather than try to collect money from them later based on music sales, since it's an uncertain bet they'll make money, and they may not be organized enough to pay the royalties even if it is successful.

• **Sound recording performance royalties (U.S.).**

In the U.S., producers can get sound recording performance royalties if the artist designates a *"letter of direction"* (LOD) specifying you as the producer of the track and gives payment details. This means anytime the sound recording you produced is streamed on a noninteractive streaming service, you can make money. This is paid to you as the producer in the U.S. by SoundExchange, but only if the LOD is submitted. Note that you can also create letters of direction for engineers, mixers, or other music production roles.

All these income streams can come to you if they are set up properly. Note that this can get complicated if you're in a band or group, since you'll need to clarify who receives these income streams or the percentages. You also need to determine who will administer and handle these royalties so everyone can get paid, which can take a lot of work and effort. And if no one takes on the proactive part of the publisher role, your music probably won't get placed on TV, film, advertising, or movie trailers and generate income from licenses or royalties.

UNDERSTANDING THE DIFFERENCE BETWEEN LICENSING AND ROYALTIES

Copyright law creates many different revenue-generating opportunities that all stem from the two copyrights you always have with music—the composition and the sound recording—and the fact you can license their use and charge fees. Once your music is released, each performance generates *royalties* if you've registered your compositions and sound recordings properly. If other people want to use your composition or sound recording in their work or product, then you can charge a fee for people to *license* it from you. Once licensed, your music may also generate *royalties* when it's performed depending on how it's used. Here's what musicians should know about each:

- **Royalties.**
Many performances and streams of your music generate automatic royalties either by law, such as compulsory licenses we discussed in chapter 8, "Your Rights," or the way the music industry evolved. Each time your released music is broadcasted, performed, streamed, or covered by someone else, a fee for its use is generated. These fees are typically collected by authorized organizations in your country, which are allowed by law to charge users for the use of music in their catalog and pass them onto their registered songwriters, publishers, and sound recording owners.
    The only way to get these royalties is by signing up with the right organizations or services so they can identify your music in the world, track how many times it's played, and know who to cut the check to. These

organizations collect large amounts of money from broadcasters, streaming services, establishments (music venues, restaurants, and other users of music who are open to the public), and many other music users both within and outside of their country so they can distribute it as royalties to their members. Of course, if you don't sign up with these organizations, then you won't get a cut of the income they're collecting *even if you are technically owed a royalty payment*. You need to participate to get paid, but once you do, you'll successfully get a passive income stream for your music business.

• Licensing.

If other people want to use your composition or sound recording in their work or product, then they need to ask for your permission and negotiate a license for its use from you. This can be the label that pays you for your composition's first use rights (see chapter 8, "Your Rights," for more details) but more commonly refers to licensing your music for film, TV, commercials, movie trailers, and video games. For example, if a director of a TV show wants to use your copyrighted song off your latest album in her show, she would need a license granting her permission to include it within her work (or infringe on your copyright, for which you can sue). This means she needs to negotiate how she can use your music and how much money it will cost. It's entirely up to you (and the market) on what type of deal you can negotiate. By the way, in this example, the director would have to license both the composition and your sound recording, since she wants to use your version from your album. This results in two separate licenses, and that means you can collect *two* separate fees. Assuming you agree, the use is memorialized in a contract known as a *license agreement*. The agreement would specify the basic terms, such as the fee, the area of distribution, exclusivity, payment method, and so on. Once licensed for inclusion in her work, your music may also generate additional royalties when the show airs on TV or is streamed.

Keep in mind, as we discussed in chapter 3, "Your Team," it's your publisher who ensures all your compositions are registered, handles the publishing administration (including the collection of any money earned), and is tasked with exploiting your song catalog to generate more royalties and licensing income for you. Of course, if you don't have an agreement with an outside publisher, this is your job, but you also keep all the money.

You can improve your chances of creating these licensing and royalty opportunities by releasing music throughout the year, getting it heard and seen, performing marketing, promoting your music, getting publicity, playing gigs, and touring. These will all help boost the royalties and increase the chances others will want to license your music. Equally important is understanding the multiple ways you can license your compositions and sound recordings so you know where you can focus your efforts and the type of money you can make.

UNDERSTANDING ROYALTIES AND ROYALTY COLLECTION PARTNERS

UNDERSTANDING THE THREE MAIN TYPES OF ROYALTY INCOME STREAMS

Collecting your royalties boils down to two simple things: knowing the three "automatic" main royalty income streams, and registering with the key organizations to get all the money owed to you worldwide.

In short, your composition generates two royalties: *mechanical royalties* for each copy created, and *performance royalties* for each public performance. Your sound recording only generates *performance royalties* for each public performance. We'll discuss all three of these in detail in the next section, but here are a few key implications:

- **You must sign up with multiple partners to get all you're owed.**

Beyond your distribution partner, which will pass on sales and mechanical royalties created from streaming services, to collect all the money owed you within your country, you need to sign up with three royalty collection partners: mechanical partners to collect the royalties your compositions generate and two performance ones—one to collect the composition royalties and one to collect the sound recording royalties.

- **You need to collect these royalties worldwide.**

All the above royalties are collected in each country separately. To capture all the money owed to you outside your home country, you need to either grant your home country's collection organization the rights to collect your royalties being generated in other countries or sign up with a publishing administrator who can collect it for you.

- **You need to qualify to sign up.**

Each of these collection partners have membership criteria, but in general, you need to have a composition and/or a sound recording available for sale or published. With the internet and distribution partners, this bar is easier to cross. They won't let you join if you don't have any songwriting credits or own any sound recordings, or if you're a DJ who doesn't produce original tracks and instead arranges existing pieces of music that aren't yours.

- **When your music is licensed for use in any video, you generate all these royalties and more.**

When your music is licensed to be used in video, whether recorded or as a live feed, you've hit the jackpot because you can collect both licensing and royalties for it. You can get a license fee by the film, TV, advertising, or movie trailer studio so they can legitimately use your music in their work, and it will generate mechanical and composition performance royalties. If they decide to use your sound recording as well, you can additionally collect sound recording licensing and performance royalties. All these residual royalties are collected from your mechanical and performance collection partners. Plus, if the video work is worldwide, you will get those as well, which is why it's even more important to make sure you've set up your mechanical and performance royalty partners to collect global royalties.

- **There's no mechanical royalty for the sound recording owner, only for the songwriter.**

You may have noticed one gap in the pattern: Where's the mechanical royalty for your sound recording? This doesn't exist. The sound recording owned by the label (which, again, may be you) doesn't generate any type of mechanical royalties like the composition does. Mechanicals are only collected by songwriters. In fact, the sound recording copyright a label has is known as a *"master."* Under copyright law, having the "masters" gives the sound recording owner a monopoly to sell the specific sound recording it owns to anyone in the world, and anyone who doesn't ask for permission to use the sound recording is *"pirating,"* such as when people post copies of the sound recording online or through a peer-to-peer network. Revenue generated from this right comes from sales. Of course, this doesn't stop licensing the sound recording for synchronization or other uses, such as sampling, ringtones, or more. It also doesn't stop it from generating sound recording performance royalties (mostly outside the U.S. as noted above).

• **Beware of how many middlemen you cut into your rights.**
In the licensing and royalty world, there are plenty of services that are willing to do the administrative work needed to register your music in exchange for a cut, but the more middlemen you cut into your rights, the less money you'll make. Also, these extra cuts lower how much money you can raise if you choose to auction a percentage of your current and future mechanical, performance, and other revenue streams your rights create for you (as discussed in chapter 11, "Patronage, Crowdfunding, and Raising Money"). If you expect to make significant income from this, you can make more and keep more control by spending the time to do the administration yourself or through a trusted team member.

• **You have other income streams beyond these three.**
As discussed at the start of the chapter, your composition and sound recordings can generate other licensing fees or royalties beyond these mechanical and performance royalties. For example, this includes printing and publication fees (for your lyrics), composition and sound recording transcription fees, sound recording sampling fees, and other novel uses that can generate money for you.

UNDERSTANDING MECHANICAL ROYALTIES

In general, under the law, you're entitled to royalties when people make any copy of your composition and bring it into the world in any way. This includes audio recordings, video recordings, sheet music, and more. This is known as a *"mechanical royalty."*

• **How you make money.**
To generate this mechanical royalty, your label (which can be you) pays you to record your unpublished composition, lets the sound recording get sampled by other musicians or sold as a ringtone, and makes it available for interactive streaming services, including video-streaming services such as Netflix, Hulu, YouTube, Facebook Video, and more. It also is generated through online stores when you click to sample the sound

recording to see if you want to purchase it. Meanwhile, your publisher (which can be you) tries to get your composition covered or interpolated by other musicians.

• **How much you can make.**

These royalties are usually set by the law though the rate varies on the length of the song, how it's used (for example, a ringtone generates a higher royalty), and the length of the play (for example, when it comes to streaming or sampling the song on iTunes). Mechanicals are usually paid to you as the songwriter but split with your publisher as per whatever agreement you may have. If you're both, you'd collect all the money.

• **Who helps you collect within your country.**

A mechanical rights collection organization (MRCO) is empowered by law to collect composition mechanical royalties for its members. In the U.S., this is Harry Fox (harryfox.com) and Music Reports (musicreports .com). Outside the U.S., this can be your PRO (such as PRS For Music Limited in the UK, which combined with the Mechanical Copyright Protection Society, a previously separate MRCO) or a stand-alone MRCO. Note that each MRCO takes a cut of the royalties you receive.

• **Who helps you collect in other countries.**

Your MRCO has reciprocal agreements with equivalent MRCOs around the world. If you agree to have the MRCO act as your subpublisher, it can register your composition with these neighboring MRCO databases and collect the mechanical royalties your composition generates in each of those countries. Most MRCOs won't automatically do this and require a form directing them to do so. For example, Harry Fox requires you to fill out a "notification of foreign activity" form for each song or album to direct them to collect on your behalf. More likely, you'll partner with a publishing administration service to go directly to neighboring MRCOs instead. Services offering publishing administration include distributor partners, such as CD Baby (members.cdbaby.com/publishing), TuneCore (tunecore.com/music-publishing-administration), or Songtrust (songtrust .com). Note that these administration services will also take a cut of your royalty revenue and may differ from your local MRCO's cut.

UNDERSTANDING COMPOSITION PERFORMANCE ROYALTIES

In general, under the law, every time your composition is performed publicly in any way, all the money you make is known as a *"performance royalty."*

- **How you make money.**

To collect this composition performance royalty, your composition needs to be either performed live in public (by you or other musicians) or the sound recording of your composition needs to be played or broadcasted in any way (radio, TV, movie theaters, music venue performances, background music in restaurants, company offices, other establishments, and so on) or interactively and noninteractively streamed through any streaming service, including video services like Netflix, Hulu, YouTube, Facebook Video, and more. Keep in mind your compositions may have multiple sound recordings—the original version, an acoustic version, a cover version by another musician, multiple live recordings, and so on. Each of these versions generates performance royalties for your composition if played. Note also that in the U.S., movie theaters don't pay for composition performances, though they do outside the U.S. This means your composition, if used in a film, may generate more performance royalties outside the U.S.

- **How much you can make.**

These royalties are usually negotiated on by PROs on behalf of their members. They charge license fees to those performing or playing the compositions in ways listed above. This creates the large pool of money they then distribute to their members (after taking out administration costs). How much you make depends on how many performances of your music were caught in their sampling surveys, cue sheet records, submitted set lists, and other data and reports collected from broadcasters, streaming services, and others. Who gets paid is set by law; royalties are paid fifty-fifty to the songwriter and publisher team. If you're both, you'll collect all the money.

- **Who helps you collect.**

A performance rights organization (PRO) is empowered by law to collect composition performance royalties for its members. In the U.S., the major PROs include ASCAP, BMI, or SESAC. Outside the U.S., this is your local PRO (such as PRS in the UK).

- **Who helps you collect in other countries.**

Your PRO should have reciprocal agreements with equivalent PROs around the world. If you agree to have the PRO act as your subpublisher, it can register your composition with these neighboring PRO databases and collect the performance royalties your composition generates in each of those countries. Some PROs won't automatically do this and require you to fill out a form or check a box directing them to do so. Alternatively, you can partner with a publishing administrator to go directly to neighboring PROs instead. Services offering publishing administration services include distribution partners, such as CD Baby (members.cdbaby.com /publishing), TuneCore (tunecore.com/music-publishing-administration), or Songtrust (songtrust.com). Note that these services will also take a cut of your royalty revenue, which may differ from your local PRO's cut.

UNDERSTANDING SOUND RECORDING PERFORMANCE ROYALTIES

In general, under the law, every time your sound recording is performed publicly in any way, all the money you make is also known as a *"performance royalty."*

- **How you make money.**

In the U.S., sound recording royalties are limited. The only way to collect this sound recording performance royalty is for your sound recording to be interactively and noninteractively streamed through a streaming service. Outside the U.S., your sound recording not only generates performance royalties from streaming but also whenever it's played or broadcasted to the public in any way. This is because currently, under U.S. copyright law, there are *no* performance royalties generated within the U.S. when sound recordings are broadcasted such as on terrestrial radio, TV, or via other methods. This means your sound recording may generate more performance royalties outside the U.S.

- **How much you can make.**

These royalties are usually negotiated by PROs on behalf of their members. They charge license fees to those performing or playing the sound recordings in ways listed above. This creates the large pool of money they then distribute to their members (after taking out administration costs). In the U.S., how much you make depends on the number of streams your music generated and is paid to the sound recording owner and may be split with featured artists and producers (through an LOD). Outside the U.S., this also includes how many performances of your sound recording were caught in their sampling surveys, cue sheet records, and other data and reports collected from broadcasters, streaming services, and more. This is paid to the sound recording owner.

• Who helps you collect.
A performance rights organization (PRO) is empowered by law to collect sound recording performance royalties for its members. In the U.S., this PRO is SoundExchange. Outside the U.S., this is your local PRO (such as PRS for Music Limited in the UK).

• Who helps you collect in other countries.
Your PRO has reciprocal agreements with equivalent PROs around the world. If you agree to have the PRO act as your subpublisher, it can register your sound recording with these neighboring PRO databases and collect the performance royalties your sound recording generates in each of those countries. Most, like SoundExchange, require you to fill out an international mandate form directing them to collect on your behalf. Alternatively, you can partner with a publishing administrator to go directly to neighboring PROs. The same services listed for composition performance royalties above applies here.

THE NUMBER-ONE ADDITIONAL REVENUE STREAM YOU SHOULD TURN ON FOR YOUR MUSIC

While YouTube Content ID isn't a royalty partner, registering your music with it can produce additional passive income based on ad revenue. Also, they'll report any video views using your music on YouTube to your mechanical and performance royalty partners. This increases the chances you'll receive more of the money your music is generating.

Since technology has made it so easy to create and distribute videos worldwide, there are people all around the world—students, kids, amateur filmmakers, and more—who may be posting videos on YouTube with your music who don't know about clearing music rights or simply don't care. You could go after each infringer separately, but the best way to handle these uses is to monetize it by using the tools YouTube provides.

Content ID allows you to upload all your sound recordings and video content to their backend system. Doing so doesn't make it available to the public. Instead, it creates a "digital fingerprint" that scans all the videos on YouTube to see if any use it. If there's a match, the system gives you three choices: you can block the whole video from being viewed, track the video's statistics, or monetize the video by running ads against it and either keeping the money or sharing it with the uploader. And any of these options can be country-specific—monetized in one country but tracked or blocked in others. Unless you're under a business obligation to take your material down (for example, an exclusivity agreement with a label), getting a cut of the advertising is a good option.

To get the most out of this revenue stream, upload your entire music catalog to monetize it. Also, whenever you release something new, you'll have to add it so you don't miss out on revenue. Of course, when videos use your music (including your own), be sure to help promote them, since you'll be helping to generate ad share revenue for yourself in the process.

Lastly, keep in mind Content ID is limited because it can only catch exact matches for the recording and is limited only to YouTube. For instance, any covers of your song won't be picked up unless they used samples from your original recording. This means you'll miss out on both the ad share and the mechanical royalties these views are generating. To help capture these instances, services such as Audiam (audiam.com) and Rumblefish (rumblefish.com) will track down these uses Content ID can't catch for a fee. These services also go beyond YouTube, reviewing and monitoring uses on Facebook, Vimeo, and more.

REGISTERING YOUR MUSIC TO ENSURE YOU CAN MAKE ROYALTIES
UNDERSTANDING WHY YOU NEED TO REGISTER YOUR MUSIC

Most musicians don't register to collect their royalties for two reasons: they either don't know how or they don't want to take the time. But if you're going to treat music as a business, you should register to get royalty income as soon as you can because, except for one royalty organization that holds it for just a few years (SoundExchange), there are no retroactive payments waiting for you once you get around to it. The longer you wait, the more you're missing out. Fortunately, this can be simplified down to a basic checklist. Plus, once the prep steps are done, you can register your music in large batches all at once.

Keep in mind that you only need to register each song once and then it will pay you royalties for *your entire life*. Besides, if you're going to go through all the trouble to get your music heard, played, streamed, and bought by fans, you should collect all the royalties it generates. If any of your songs make it big, the checks will automatically come to you.

There's one more benefit to following this checklist: once you've grown your royalty income streams, you'll be able to raise more money by convincing publishers, labels, and even the public to give you advances based on the future income streams. This can open up new ways to fund your music business, tour, or next project. We talk about how to do this in chapter 13, "Advanced Income Techniques," but all of this starts by following the recipes in the next two sections for all your music.

Lastly, know that the world of royalty collection is changing. As Jon Bahr, VP of music publishing and rights management at CD Baby, says, "The royalty landscape is developing and growing rapidly as streaming becomes prevalent, so there will be new opportunities for musicians to earn money in the future." This means the amount of money you can make from royalties will grow over time, but it also means the services and organizations that collect your royalties will merge, change, and hopefully simplify. But until the day where you only need to register with one collection agency, follow the prep steps and checklist below to ensure you're paid all the royalties you're owed worldwide.

THE TWELVE PREP STEPS BEFORE YOU REGISTER YOUR COMPOSITIONS AND SOUND RECORDINGS

Before you can register your compositions and sound recordings, you need to sign up with multiple organizations so you can get paid. You need to register with many different organizations because of the complicated nature of copyright. Some of these organizations will cost money to join, but considering your music can generate revenue for you for your entire life (and then some), it's worth it. We're assuming you're doing all of this for yourself, so we'll assume you're responsible for all twelve of these prep steps, but if you are represented by a publisher or label, some of them might be done by whoever is representing you.

Also, always keep up with the latest royalty opportunities and adjust this list as needed. For example, at the time of this writing, legislation in the U.S. might establish a new rights organization called the Mechanical Licensing Collective. If it does, add a step to sign up with makingmoney-withmusic.com/resources. Plus, we will keep you up to date with new royalty opportunities at the Making Money with Music newsletter (makingmoneywithmusic.com/newsletter).

Fortunately, you'll only have to do these steps once. After you're a member, you shouldn't need to register again. To do this, follow these prep steps:

1. Create a copyright office account (U.S. and Canada only).

If you're in the U.S. or Canada, you *may* want to register your composition and sound recording copyrights with the appropriate copyright office. This doesn't generate royalties, but it's the basis of why your music makes money for you and gives you extra protections in case someone infringes. To do this, you need to create an account. We outlined these steps in chapter 8, "Your Rights."

2. Choose a distribution partner to release your music.

To get your music in distribution sites, digital stores, streaming sites, and more so you can make sales and streaming income, choose a distribution partner to release your music. We discussed how to do this in chapter 9, "Distribution and Streaming."

3. Choose a method to create ISRC codes.

As discussed in chapter 5, "Your Music," the International Standard Recording Code (ISRC) is an international standard that uniquely identifies sound recordings. It's the code that allows you to collect royalties for streaming, so you'll need one for each sound recording you release. Most distribution partners will generate them for you, which is the easiest method to get them and the way most musicians do this, but you can also create your own ISRCs yourself. Since every sound recording requires an ISRC, this can be a useful option if you act as a label for multiple artists, release a lot of music, or release many different versions of a composition, such as remixes, demos, live versions, or more. To do this, you need to apply to become an ISRC registrant at ISRC (usisrc.org), meet their criteria, and pay a onetime fee (about $100). Doing this will allow you to assign up to one hundred thousand ISRCs per year, and this registrant code is yours for life. You'll need to track your codes on a spreadsheet and what sound recordings you've assigned them to, and when you send your music to a distribution partner, you'll need to inform them of the ISRC.

4. Choose a composition PRO.

When your composition is performed, such as onstage or on terrestrial, satellite, or digital radio, you're entitled to a royalty. PROs track your performances and pay you, but only if you're a member and only if you register your compositions. Each country has one or more PROs to choose from. For instance, in the U.S., there are three major ones—ASCAP (ascap .com), BMI (bmi.com), and SESAC (sesac.com), which is invite-only, whereas in Canada there is only SOCAN (socan.ca). Note that you do not have to join a major PRO if you can find one that meets your needs. For example, Global Music Rights (GMR) (globalmusicrights.com) is invite-only for major artists but might have more exclusive benefits, and if you create Christian music, you can join specialized PROs like CCLI (ccli.co .uk). Since each PRO is authorized to collect all performance royalties for any given song, this means you can only be a songwriter member of one PRO at a time. However, this restriction doesn't exist for publishers, since publishers can represent many different songwriters. If you do it all— you're your own songwriter and publisher—then pick the same one for both. Either way, choose one and proceed to steps 5, 6, and 7.

5. Register as a "songwriter" with the composition PRO.

As discussed in chapter 8, "Your Rights," when a PRO pays out royalties, its generally split in half: 50 percent for the songwriter and 50 percent for the publisher. To create a *songwriter* account, follow the PRO's registration steps. This will involve a fee, may require you prove your identification and provide banking and tax details (so they know how to pay you and what to withhold for taxes), and can take a week or more to process. Once done, you'll have a songwriter account. When you end up registering your compositions in their system, you'll be able to associate those compositions you wrote with your account to ensure you're paid the songwriter half of the royalties generated.

6. Register as a "publisher" with the composition PRO.

To get the other 50 percent of the royalties your music generates, you'll need to also create a *publisher* account. If you don't have an agreement with a third-party music publisher (a publisher usually does all these registration steps for you and your music), you are the publisher, and you deserve this cut for the work you're doing to register and promote your own songs. Some PROs, such as BMI, will automatically send the publisher share to the songwriter if there is no publisher registered for the song, but most don't pay out the publisher share if you're not registered, so it's a good idea to register it. This process should be similar to step 5. It may take a week or more to process, so if you're registering as a songwriter, do both at the same time. Once completed, you'll have a publisher account. This means when you end up registering your compositions in their system, you'll be able to associate those compositions you're the publisher on with your account to ensure you're paid your 50 percent of the royalties.

7. For U.S. musicians, register as a *"both"* account with a sound recording PRO.

Outside of the U.S., sound recording performances are usually handled by your country's PRO, so you can skip this step and proceed to step 9. However, if you're a musician based in the U.S., you'll need to register with SoundExchange, since it's the one U.S. PRO that can collect these royalties. It's free to join SoundExchange, and you can do so online. Like other PROs, they'll need identification information so they'll know who to pay. You can sign up as a sound recording owner, a featured performer, or both. You should register as a *"both"* account for the greatest flexibility. Also know when registering that it's possible SoundExchange already has royalties waiting for you. This may happen if they've captured your sound recordings in their surveys. You can search their unclaimed royalty database at soundexchange.com/artist-copyright-owner/does -soundexchange-have-royalties-for-you/search-for-artist and get paid if there are any available once you register.

8. For U.S. musicians, complete an international mandate at SoundExchange to ensure you receive foreign sound recording performance royalties.

You can give SoundExchange the foreign collection rights, since they have nearly fifty international performance rights agreements around the world. Although there are no sound recording royalties generated within the U.S. for terrestrial radio and public performance royalties, these are generated outside the U.S., and SoundExchange can collect them with any countries they work with. To grant them this collection right, you need to complete an "international mandate" form, which allows Sound-Exchange to register your sound recordings with their partners. They will then pass these royalties on to you for no additional administration fee. For musicians outside the U.S., sound recording performances are also handled by your country's PRO, so you can skip this step.

9. Register with your mechanical rights collection organization (MRCO) or go through a publishing administration partner.

To ensure you receive all the mechanical royalties owed to you, you need to register with your country's MRCO. In most countries outside the U.S., this is likely handled by your PRO or a corresponding MRCO. However, in the U.S., there are two MRCOs you'll need to collect from to get all the royalties. These are Harry Fox (harryfox.com) and Music Reports (musicreports.com). For example, Harry Fox includes mechanical royalties from Spotify, while Music Reports includes Amazon Unlimited. To collect royalties from Harry Fox, you can sign up directly with them if you've released music through a U.S.-based third party, such as a music label, within the last twelve months (self-releasing music through distribution partners does *not* count). Otherwise, you can use the user-generated content management service Rumblefish (rumblefish .com) or go through a partner that registers this for you, some of which are listed below. Music Reports requires you to go through partners to collect their royalties, all of which also collect from Harry Fox. Partners that can do this include distributor partners like CD Baby (members. cdbaby.com/publishing), TuneCore (tunecore.com/music-publishing -administration), or other publishing administration services such as Songtrust (songtrust.com) and TuneRegistry (tuneregistry.com). For non-U.S. musicians, this may be handled by your country's MRCO or, in some cases, your PRO, such as the UK's PRS, which handles both.

10. Verify that your PRO and MRCO collect foreign performance royalties or choose a foreign rights collection service partner.

Check the policies of your PRO and MRCO to see if they collect foreign performance royalties, and research how promptly they return your royalties to you because some payments can be delayed by up to two years as the collection works its way through the system. An alternative is to collect these royalties through a publishing administration service, such as CD Baby's Publishing Administration (members.cdbaby.com /publishing), TuneCore (tunecore.com/music-publishing-administration), or Songtrust (songtrust.com). These services will take a cut of your royalties but may pay you more quickly, so you will want to carefully compare each to make sure you get the most revenue and best payment options for your music.

11. Sign up with a YouTube Content ID partner.

As discussed in the section above, to collect advertising share revenue generated by videos using your music on YouTube, you'll need to sign up for Content ID. You can do this by applying at YouTube directly, but know YouTube tends to only work directly with musicians whose content is frequently uploaded and who they deem "need the tools" because they are selective about who they work with. Because of this, most musicians sign up with a YouTube Content ID partner such as Audiam (audiam.com), Ad-Rev (adrev.net), Songtrust (songtrust.com), Rumblefish (rumblefish.com), or an add-on publishing administration service that their distribution partner—such as CD Baby or TuneCore—provides. Each of these services can get your music into Content ID, and most charge only a percentage of the ad share revenue generated (around 15–30 percent). Another benefit is most of these partners will report plays of your music in videos to your MRCO and PRO that you registered with in the steps above (which most musicians miss out on!). Note that since these services only make money when your content is used, they may not offer you all the choices YouTube provides copyright owners, including the ability to take down a video.

12. Set up a tracking system for registrations.

In chapter 5, "Your Music," we suggested you document songwriter ownership (split sheets) and credit information for each composition and sound recording you create. You should augment this spreadsheet to include columns for each MRCO, PRO, or service you join, so you can track whether you registered each song and sound recording with them and the date you uploaded the info into their databases. If you want more advanced tools, you might consider services like TuneRegistry (tuneregistry.com) or Jammber (jammber.com).

THE FOURTEEN REGISTRATIONS YOU SHOULD DO FOR EVERY COMPOSITION AND SOUND RECORDING TO ENSURE YOU'RE PAID WHAT YOU'RE OWED

Now that you're registered with the necessary organizations and services, the next step is registering your compositions and sound recordings with their databases so they can start collecting royalties and paying you.

Note these registrations change as the rights landscape changes. As of this writing, there is a proposed rights organization in the U.S., the Mechanical Licensing Collective. If it does, add registering each song with this new organization to the list. Remember, we will keep this list up to date for you at makingmoneywithmusic.com/resources

To simplify this section, the checklist will assume you own all the rights. If that's not the case, you'll adjust the steps based on your situation. Follow this checklist:

1. Register your composition copyrights (optional for U.S. and Canada only).
We outline these steps in chapter 8, "Your Rights."

2. Register your sound recording copyrights (optional for U.S. and Canada only).
We outline these steps in chapter 8, "Your Rights."

3. Register each composition at your PRO as a "songwriter" for domestic performance royalties.
Use your PRO's system to register as the songwriter for each composition. You'll likely need to log in with your *songwriter account* to do this. Registering your composition will ensure you receive the songwriter half of any royalties generated. When entering the name of the composition, be sure to list any alternate titles or misspellings. And, if you cowrote the composition, be sure to list all the other writers and corresponding publishers with the correct share of ownership as documented in your split sheet agreement. Each PRO's system is different, so follow the instructions carefully and enter in all the data they request.

4. Register each composition at your PRO as a "publisher" for domestic performance royalties.
If you're your own publisher, then use your PRO's system to register as the publisher for each composition. You'll likely need to log in with your *publisher account* to do this. Registering your composition will ensure you receive the publisher half of the royalties generated. Each PRO's system is different, so follow the instructions carefully and enter in all the data they request.

5. Verify you will collect foreign performance royalties for each composition.

As discussed above, your PRO or your foreign rights collection service partner will collect foreign royalties for the composition. If not, register the song with the service you use so you can collect these royalties.

6. Upload your sound recordings with your distribution partner and schedule your release.

Upload your sound recording to your distribution partner. Register all the information about your song and sound recording in their database, since this information is used by many streaming services and stores. Your distribution partner will collect mechanical royalties from the services they distribute to—namely, royalties generated by sales and streams. This could include some foreign mechanical royalties from stores and streaming services outside of your country that they distribute to. Schedule the release date based on your release schedule (see chapter 18, "Your Release Strategy"). Be sure your release is for a date after you've completed the rest of the checklist.

7. Generate ISRCs for each sound recording.

If you can create your own ISRC codes, be sure to enter this into the distribution partner's database after uploading the songs rather than letting them generate a new one. Otherwise, get the ISRC from your distribution partner for the next registrations.

8. For U.S. musicians, register the sound recording as a "sound recording owner"; for non-U.S. musicians, register with your PRO.

Register your sound recording information with SoundExchange under your *"sound recording owner"* account, including the ISRC. If you're a musician outside the U.S., your sound recording performance royalties should be collected by your PRO. Verify they track and collect this royalty and how to ensure it is registered properly.

9. For U.S. musicians, register the sound recording as a "featured artist"; for non-U.S. musicians, register with your PRO.

Register the artist information for your sound recording with SoundExchange under your *"featured artist"* account. You may also register an

LOD for the producer, engineer, or other music production roles, if applicable. If you're a musician outside the U.S., these royalties should be collected by your PRO. Verify how featured artists are compensated and how to ensure it is registered properly.

10. Verify you will collect foreign performance royalties for each sound recording.

As discussed above, your sound recording PRO or your foreign rights collection service partner will collect foreign royalties for the composition. If not, register the song with the service you use so you can collect these royalties.

11. Register each composition at your MRCO for domestic mechanical royalties.

Register your composition with your MRCO so you can collect mechanical royalties when your song is covered by other artists, whether through sales or streaming services or played on video-streaming platforms. Keep in mind some of your mechanical royalties will come from your distribution partner for sales and streams to those services they distribute to.

12. Register each composition at your MRCO for foreign mechanical royalties.

For U.S. musicians, if you're affiliated with Harry Fox, to ensure you receive mechanical royalties generated from plays of your music in foreign countries, complete a "notification of foreign activity (secure.harryfox .com/public/ForeignActivityNotification.jsp). However, if you're not affiliated, then you can still collect mechanical royalties by registering your composition with the publishing administration service(s) you choose in step 10 of "The Twelve Prep Steps Before You Register Your Compositions and Sound Recordings" above, such as CD Baby, TuneCore, or Songtrust. (And keep track of whether your service can handle all the royalties. For example, at the time of this book's publication, TuneRegistry doesn't collect foreign mechanicals outside the U.S.) For non-U.S. musicians, these royalties may be handled by your MRCO or, in many cases, your PRO. Contact them and verify if they collect foreign mechanicals and how to ensure your composition is registered correctly with them so they can track.

13. Upload each sound recording Content ID digital rights service partner and register the composition and sound recording information.

Once you register, your partner will require you to upload your sound recording into their system and fill out legal and registration information. Follow their instructions. If this is the first time you're registering your composition and sound recording, take the time to register your entire back catalog. You can, and should, also register your video content.

14. Register each song in the credits databases.

We outline these steps in chapter 5, "Your Music."

Once you've finished all these registrations, update your tracking system. This information is especially important when you're responsible for registering information on someone else's behalf.

THE TOP THREE WAYS TO HELP WITH YOUR TWELVE PREP AND FOURTEEN REGISTRATION STEPS

While you can be your own publisher and do all of the registrations and administration of your compositions and sound recordings on your own, you may want to focus on the music, and offload these tasks to a person or service that can help you get it done. Below are three ways to handle this, and each comes with its own pros and cons:

1. Your team.

You can assign these tasks to the appropriate member of your team. For example, as discussed in chapter 3, "Your Team," it's your team member in the publisher role who's responsible for registering and ensuring both of you, the songwriter and publisher, collect all the royalties your composition generates. For the sound recording, this is the responsibility of the sound recording owner, which typically is the label. If you're your own label, then this work can also be assigned to your publisher, though a more traditional role would be whoever is managing your label, usually your manager.

2. Sign with a music publisher.

Music publishers make a living registering music and getting them licensed. They usually have deep connections within the music and media world and actively lobby music supervisors, television and film production companies, and other commercial music users to license your music. These publishers are essentially agents for your music and spend their entire day promoting, marketing, and pitching the songs in their catalog to others in the hopes of generating license opportunities. Typically, music publishers work song by song, although some may want to publish your entire music catalog. Since their job is to match existing music to the needs of their customers—the music users—a lot depends on your style, genre, lyrics, the quality of the sound recording, and, of course, luck. Music publishers will ensure the songs or catalog they're pitching are registered with every service to ensure you get the royalties you and the publisher are owed. Traditionally, music publishers focus on the composition and not sound recordings, since that was the domain of the label.

3. Contract with a publishing administration service.

Publishing administration services are a one-stop shop where you register your payment details, your composition, and sound recording information with them, and they'll handle the rest for a setup fee and/or cut of the royalties (anywhere from 15–30 percent of what you earn). These include CD Baby (members.cdbaby.com/publishing), TuneCore (tunecore.com/music-publishing-administration), or other publishing administration services like Songtrust (songtrust.com) and TuneRegistry (tuneregistry.com). These services will do many (but not all) of these steps for you. They require you to upload your composition and sound recording information to their databases and fill out the details, and they'll do all the work of registering across the different organizations (and may include registering with foreign PROs and MRCOs).

You can avoid the steps above by using these publishing administration services, plus simplify your accounting by receiving one overall royalty check. They may also be able to remit your royalties faster because they collect them directly through deals with royalty collection partners. Keep in mind they don't actively promote licensing opportunities like music publishers do, and they perform the administration of your composition and sound recording royalties for a share of the revenue. Also, note that some of these services collect synchronization royalties beyond YouTube monetization that you could collect on your own and keep more of the income (we discuss synchronization licensing in the next section). Lastly, since you can get advances based on these royalty streams, these middlemen may lower the amount of money you collect and therefore lower the amount of money you can raise (see chapter 13, "Advanced Income Techniques," for more details).

THE TOP EIGHT ADDITIONAL ROYALTY REVENUES STREAMS YOU MAY BE ELIGIBLE TO TAP

There are some other revenue streams that you may be able to collect if you meet the criteria.

1. Supplemental performance royalty award programs.

Some PROs have created supplemental programs so songwriters and publishers can generate royalties for songs that didn't get caught in their surveys. For instance, the ASCAP Plus (ascap.com/music-creators /ascaplus) program allows songwriters and publishers to submit proof of where and when their registered music was played. This is reviewed by an ASCAP panel who decides how much royalties to award. Some of the songwriters in our band did this on a few occasions and were rewarded checks for a few hundred dollars.

2. Local or international live performance royalties.

If you perform your music live at PRO-licensed venues within the U.S., you should submit your set list and the venue at which you played so your PRO has a record of the songs you performed, like ASCAP OnStage (ascap.com/music-creators/ascap-onstage) or BMI Live (bmi.com/faq /category/bmi_live). Each has their own submission requirements, including a deadline for submitting, so register soon after each performance and follow the instructions they provide. Also, note that most PROs will want to ensure the venue is licensed with them. You can also do this if you perform outside your home country, but because this involves neighboring royalties, the submission requirements may be different or require additional proof of where you performed. Note also that if you write concert or classical music, the submission method may be different.

3. Local or international television, film, movie trailer, and video game performance royalties.

If you get your music placed in a TV show, film, movie trailer, or video game, you may generate performance royalties or neighboring royalties if you notify your PRO, usually by getting the production studio to submit a "cue sheet" on your behalf logging its use within their work. We discuss cue sheets below in the licensing section.

4. International advertising and commercial performance royalties.

When your composition is used in an advertisement or commercial that is broadcasted internationally, you may need to notify your PRO. For instance, ASCAP requires an "advertisement claim form" and an MP3 of music used. Each PRO has its own submission requirements, so follow your PRO's instructions.

5. The Sound Recording Special Payments Fund (SRSPF).

The SRSPF (sound-recording.org) are funds set aside for session musicians who work under the Sound Recording Labor Agreement (SRLA) to get a royalty for recordings they have played on, primarily members of the American Federation of Musicians (afm.org). See the website for this fund to find out how this royalty is calculated and how to become eligible.

6. AFM and SAG-AFTRA Intellectual Property Rights Distribution Fund.

The AFM and SAG-AFTRA Intellectual Property Rights Distribution Fund (afmsagaftrafund.org) generates royalties for musicians and singers who do session work or TV, film, or theatrical performances. Although the fund was created by the American Federation of Musicians (afm.org) and SAG-AFTRA (sagaftra.org), it's an independent fund that collects money from sources all over the world, and you do not need to be a union member to collect it, although that's the easiest way to become eligible.

7. Digital audio recording technology, home taping, and private copy royalties.

If you have significant sales as shown by major reporting agencies like Nielsen's SoundScan, you can collect blank media and rental royalties set aside by laws such as the Audio Home Recording Act in the U.S. and others around the world. The money is paid by manufacturers of media into two funds—a musical works fund (composition) and a sound recording fund.

Note that 4 percent of these funds are not routed to AADC and are reserved for non-featured artists, such as session players, background vocalists, symphony, opera, ballet musicians, and vocalists, and this royalty is managed by the AFM SAG-AFTRA fund (afmsagaftrafund .org) mentioned above.

8. Translation/adaptation performance royalties.

If you speak multiple languages, subpublishers may hire you to translate or adapt popular songs to your local language. As a result, you can get paid for the work and are entitled to a cut of the performance and mechanical royalties generated in your territory.

LICENSING
UNDERSTANDING MUSIC LICENSING

If other people want to use your composition or sound recording in their original work or product, then they need to ask for your permission and negotiate a license for its use from you. One of the most popular licensing opportunities is getting your music used in video—television, film, advertising, movie trailers, and video games. These are known as *synchronization (sync) licenses.*

Unlike some of the other royalties, there's no statutory or compulsory license for sync, so you can charge whatever you want for the license and even refuse to let them license it. What you decide to charge is entirely decided by what you can get them to pay. The sync fee for the composition is paid to the songwriter and publisher team while the sync fee for the sound recording is paid to the sound recording owner. And, if you own both, you get paid twice. Once licensed, your music may also generate royalties depending on how it's used, as we discussed above. This is on top of what you make with your synchronization license(s)!

For example, when our band, Beatnik Turtle, licensed one of our songs to ABC Family–Disney for use in a nationwide television advertising campaign, we negotiated two licenses: one for the right to sync our composition to video images in the advertisement and another for the right to use our master. Since we owned all the rights and acted as our own publisher and label, we ended up receiving all the money.

LICENSING YOUR MUSIC THROUGH MUSIC SUPERVISORS
UNDERSTANDING THE FOUR TYPES OF MUSIC SUPERVISORS

When it comes to getting your music in television, film, advertising, and movie trailers, you need to understand music supervisors, who are the people responsible for finding the perfect song for the scene or story being told and licensing the music. It's a job requiring equal amounts of artistry, love of music, technical skill, and knowledge of the legal world.

Music supervisors live and breathe music. They're constantly discovering new music by searching streaming services, frequenting MP3 blogs, listening to music podcasts, and keeping up on music news and websites, so you will want to make sure your music is found there. Their deep knowledge of music is critical to help directors elicit a particular emotion or mood or to build pacing within a scene. As a result, they have huge catalogs of music and stems expertly cataloged so they can find the perfect piece of music when they need it most. But they also have musicians they've met at the ready who have proven they can create music on demand that meets their needs within tight deadlines (often over a weekend). These musicians thrive in creating music at a moment's notice and can sign over the rights quickly.

Music supervisors deal with demanding clients, directors, editors, musicians, and publishers who give them vague descriptions like "I want a song that's *blue*." And they do this within extremely tight schedules, such as within a weekend, a day, or even a few hours. Once the ideal music is found, they need to immediately negotiate a licensing deal to secure the rights. But despite their expertise, even if they find what they think is the perfect track, anyone on the production team can veto their choice, including the director, editor, producers, or even the actors. In the case of advertising, the client always has the final say on what's used. Because of this, music supervisors need to have multiple music options at the ready.

Most music supervisors specialize in one of four areas: television, film, commercials and advertising, or movie trailers. Each medium has different needs you should understand if you want to improve the chance of licensing and placing your music.

1. Television music supervisors.

There's more TV being made now than ever, with broadcast, cable, streaming, and innumerable other delivery methods available today.

Like trailers, television requires quick turnaround times. Shows can be filmed within a week. This not only keeps television music supervisors busy, it also opens up a lot of opportunities for musicians. That said, compared to films, music budgets are smaller. As a result, music supervisors live in a fast-paced world, and musicians that work with them need to be responsive.

Television show music requirements depend on the style, its setting and time period, and what the scene calls for. Similar to movies, some studios commission scores, but there are plenty of scenes where existing songs set the right mood. Although having your stems available is a good idea, they'll be more likely to just use the finished tracks.

2. Film music supervisors.

Films have historically been popular targets for musicians, since getting placed in a film can be extremely lucrative, especially from a performance royalty perspective. Films take longer to make than other media. This allows music supervisors more time to find and clear the rights of music—although if you're contacted to license your music for a film, make sure to respond promptly.

Perhaps the biggest difference today is the number of independent films being made, since production capabilities are now in the hands of more people than ever. Major film studios have a music budget and a process to license the music. Independent films may lack both. Instead, they may offer a step-deal paying out license fees based on the box office receipts. Of course, independent studios may lack the bookkeeping capabilities and staff to pay your royalties even if they're owed.

Studios typically commission a score for the film, but they may license existing songs for scenes depending on the director's needs. For example, "Stuck in the Middle" in the film *Reservoir Dogs* or "Starman" in *The Martian*. Instrumental versions of your songs are just as useful as the vocal versions, since directors and music supervisors sometimes need background music during scenes.

3. Movie trailer music supervisors.

In the past, movie trailers were only seen before movies or in television commercials, but today, trailers are available on demand. As Danny Exum, a movie trailer music supervisor, said, "Trailers are big business, getting as much as one hundred million views online, and there's never enough fresh songs out there to use." Since trailers usually don't use the film soundtrack, this makes it another licensing opportunity for you to target. You don't have to get your song placed in the film in order to be in the trailer.

Trailers need to generate the right emotions in a short amount of time. To do this, music supervisors need snippets of music to create impactful moments. As Exum explained, "Trailers follow a three-act structure: an opening, a middle, and then a big payoff at the end. Each act needs different music." To do this, supervisors want your song stems, as well as the final track. That way they can blend and slice the music around the needs of the trailer.

4. Commercial and advertising music supervisors.

Historically, many musicians felt uncomfortable licensing their music for advertising, but today, these are usually seen as great opportunities for exposure as well as income. For instance, Tim Quirk from the band Too Much Joy related in a panel at SXSW that he was hesitant at first to license his band's music to a beer company, but the rest of the band overruled him. Afterward he realized that, unlike a music label, the beer company didn't ask for the rights to their music. They were happy to license the music to have their product "bask in the glow" of the band's image, with no commitments afterward. In fact, some brands, such as Red Bull and Nike, have become well known for promoting and breaking up-and-coming artists.

Advertising music supervisors who work with independent musicians usually do so to target demographics, such as age. They hope to associate their product with the same vibe that energizes the artist's audience. Being new on the scene can be helpful, since the buzz you're already trying to generate for your music is exactly what they're looking for to promote their brand to fresh audiences.

Commercials, like trailers, have precise timing requirements. For this reason, many music supervisors turn to trusted music production houses to compose custom music. If they do use an existing song, they'll want both the instrumental version as well as the stems. This allows them to maneuver around the lyrics, since a lyric sung at the wrong time might conflict with a voice-over (VO). Or they may want to cut out certain instruments and bring the lyrics down during the VO and then up again at the end.

One thing that's common to all four types: if they take a pass on your music, *it is not a criticism*. It just means the song didn't fit their needs for that project. Understanding this can help you avoid taking any rejection personally. But if they do place your music, be sure to thank the music supervisor and stay in touch. Building that relationship is one of the most likely ways to get your next licensing deal.

GETTING YOUR MUSIC IN FRONT OF MUSIC SUPERVISORS

Music publishing has always been a relationship industry. If you can get to know music supervisors or directors directly, you can start pitching songs to them or become a trusted resource. This is especially true if you are known to be great at a particular genre of music. In fact, this industry is usually split up between people who make music, people who have the relationships, and the music supervisors who choose the music. The relationships take so much time to build that they're a specialty.

1. Check the credits of your favorite show.

If you see a TV show and have music that fits its style, check the credits to learn who the music supervisor is and search the web. The same technique works for movie trailer production houses. They often highlight their latest trailers and list the staff or have a contact page. Reach out directly.

2. Attend music industry conferences.

Music supervisors can be found at music industry conferences like South by Southwest (sxsw.com), the National Association of Record Industry Professionals (narip.com), and the Association of Music Producers (ampnow.com). If you contact a music supervisor directly, keep in mind their mailbox probably has hundreds of unread emails from musicians. To cut through the crowd, make your message short, and make it easy to click a link to get a high-quality download of the song. It should be a download because they will want to put the song into the video editing software to see if your song works for them.

3. Get your music in services music supervisors use.

Most music supervisors have a short list of trusted partners who supply music, including music production houses that specialize in creating pre-cleared music libraries tailored for music supervisors as well as various curated and non-curated music matching services. Getting your music into these resources can get you into the ears of music supervisors. We discuss these in the next section below.

4. Get your music out there.

One of the easiest ways to increase the chances of music supervisors finding you is simply by getting your music out in the world as we discuss in the entire next section of the book, "Releasing Your Music and Getting Noticed." This means creating and releasing a steady stream of music; promoting it effectively; getting it heard and seen; and generating publicity and media coverage. In short, it is what this entire book is all about. The more you grow your music business or conquer particular niches, the more likely licensing opportunities will come to you.

HOW TO PREPARE YOUR MUSIC FOR MUSIC SUPERVISORS

Most music supervisors are wary about working with independent artists because nearly all of them have been burned by musicians who didn't have their legal rights in order. Many have war stories of negotiating a deal with an artist only to find the song contained samples that weren't cleared. Because of this, many supervisors demand "no samples" policies or exclusively deal with large publishers, use precleared music libraries, or license only from agents they trust.

If you want to improve your chances, this means you need to have both your music and business in order. Here are some tips before you reach out to any music supervisors:

• Be easy to contact.

You never know when a music supervisor may reach out to you. Have a contact page on your website, monitor your social presences for direct messages or public questions, and be ready to respond at any time. This includes turning around licensing contracts on short notice.

• Have your tracks at the ready.

Many times, music supervisors will want a high-quality download of the track you've released. If you followed the recommendations in chapter 5, "Your Music," you'll have these on hand, in various formats, properly named, with the correct ID3 information. However, some may request stems or instrumental versions. This is especially true for film and movie trailer music supervisors. If you don't have mastered stem or instrumental versions ready, given the deadlines they usually face, you may have to drop everything and go back to the masters to create what they're looking for. Not only are the stems licensable, sometimes they're needed so they can remix your music, take just a small piece, or cut out the vocals to better fit their video. As music supervisor Toddrick Spalding explained, "A track might be perfect except for that one harp part. If you have the stems, you can easily take that part out and instantly have the right track."

• Send only mastered tracks.

Given how hectic their jobs are, only send professionally mastered tracks. These are not demos; songs prepared for licensing must be ready to go into a feature film or advertisement *tomorrow*. Preparing your music in this way will make it easy for music supervisors to drop your music in their demo reels, try it out, and find you if they decide to use it.

• Own all the rights.

The number-one thing that will kill a sync license deal is if you can't prove you own the rights to the music they want to license. Fortunately, independent artists usually own both the composition and sound recording copyrights, making negotiation and licensing a lot simpler. To prep your music, make sure you own all the rights to the composition and sound recording. This also means you need to have used precleared samples, loops, or beats or have gotten permission to use them in your sound recording. If your music is used and licensed, and you're a U.S. or Canadian musician, this use also justifies registering your composition and sound recording with the copyright office.

• Know everywhere else you've licensed your tracks.

If you're lucky enough to have licensed the same song and gotten it placed previously, the music supervisor will want to know. Whether you've licensed it elsewhere for some other product, film, TV show, or trailer doesn't necessarily rule out your song's use (unless you've given up exclusive rights—which we discuss below), but it could affect its use in advertising, since your song could be associated with a competing brand for a different commercial they weren't aware of. Music supervisors appreciate artists being up front at the outset, which builds trust, increasing the odds of future licensing deals.

THE TOP SEVEN LICENSE TERMS

Once a music supervisor has chosen your music, they'll typically supply you with the sync license agreement they want you to sign for the compositions and sound recordings they decide to use. Note that if your fee is too high or they want a different version of your song, they can have someone else record a cover version. While they won't need to license your sound recording, they will still need to negotiate a sync license for your composition so they can use it in their work. And, you'll still be entitled to the mechanical and performance royalties generated by their cover of your composition.

If you get a deal, you'll want to have an attorney help negotiate the terms of the deal (and the fee!) and explain what rights you're giving up and keeping. With sync licenses, every term is negotiable. For example, if the film studio wants worldwide rights rather than just your home country, you should charge more for the larger geography you're giving them.

Below are some of the most frequently used terms found in licensing agreements, so it's a good idea to become familiar with them. As you review the terms, keep these points in mind so you can structure the most beneficial deal for yourself:

1. Worldwide versus region versus country.
The larger the territory a licensee wants the license to cover, the more the fee should be. Worldwide rights should earn a higher fee than rights in one region or territory.

2. General versus specific use.
The more general and vague the license, the more the fee should be. Don't grant more rights or uses than the licensee wants at the moment. That way, the licensee has to come back for additional licenses and pay you another fee should they ever need to use the song in different ways in the future. For example, if a filmmaker wants to license your music for a film intended to only be seen at a film festival, limit the license for that specific use so they will have to come back to you to negotiate another license for broader distribution if the film becomes successful.

3. Any technology known now or forever versus specific technology known.
Related to the above, most licensees want the license to cover all technology uses known now and any that may be developed in the future. Since

technology changes rapidly, if you agree to this term, you may cut off future lucrative revenue streams. Instead, you should limit the license to specific, known technologies. That way you reserve the rights you have in your music so if a new technology comes along, the licensee will need to come back to you to make a new deal (and pay you another fee).

4. Perpetuity versus limited duration.

The longer the time they want to license your music, the more money they should be willing to pay. In general, you should avoid granting a license "*in perpetuity*," which would allow the licensee to use your music as defined in the agreement forever.

5. Exclusivity versus nonexclusivity.

You'll usually want to enter into a nonexclusive license so you can continue to license the composition or sound recording to others at any time without any restrictions. This is usually tied and limited to one of the other terms above, such as exclusive rights within a particular territory or specific use. While the user may not necessarily want exclusive rights to *your music*, they may want to have exclusivity of *your track* to limit you from licensing it to competitors, other studios, products, or brands. Depending on the length or coverage of the exclusivity they want for your music, they should be willing to pay a higher fee, since they're asking you to limit or restrict future possible licensing deals. Note, you can only grant an exclusive license if all of the owners of the work agree.

6. Assignment of copyright.

The purpose of negotiating a license is so you *don't* give up or restrict your copyright in the music. If your license agreement includes terms about assigning all your copyright interests or creating a "work-for-hire," it's not a license agreement (and your attorney should flag this). If you agree to any terms like this, you'll lose your copyright interest and cut off any revenue streams your music is creating for you. In fact, by assigning it, they get the copyright and income it produces.

7. Creative Commons.

Some musicians and sites use Creative Commons licenses (creativecom mons.org) to allow the music to be shared freely. Creative Commons is a nonprofit organization that provides free tools to help authors, musicians, and other artists create simple licenses that change copyright terms from "All Rights Reserved" to "Some Rights Reserved" and spells out what can be done with the music in plain language. The organization has drafted a number of premade and linkable licenses that are free to use and customize depending on your needs. Depending on the Creative Commons license you choose to use, the license does not preclude you from licensing your music for money elsewhere, especially if you don't allow commercial use, although it may allow fans to freely share your music without compensating you. Note that these licenses are perpetual, meaning they cannot be revoked once you grant them.

SUBMITTING CUE SHEETS TO PROS AND GENERATING ROYALTIES FOR PLACEMENTS

If your music is licensed for use in a television show, film, commercial, movie trailer, or any other similar visual medium, you should work with the licensee to submit a "cue sheet" to your PRO. Each PRO uses their own format, but in general, cue sheets list the name of the song, the artist, the publisher, where exactly it was used in the work (including the start time and duration), and other related information.

Submitting it significantly increases your chances of getting performance royalties for the music you licensed by notifying the PRO exactly where your music was used. That way, they can track it in their surveys or work with other countries' PROs to track and collect royalties owed to you. Depending on the TV show or film your music is used in, the boost to your performance royalties can be significant. And, if you're a U.S. musician and the film or TV show is aired in Europe, the foreign performance royalties your PRO may receive for you can be even greater. One simple form can end up creating additional passive "mailbox money" for yourself, so it's well worth your time to get this process right.

Since the PROs pay out for the performances of the music when the films or TV shows are shown, broadcasted, or streamed, this doesn't affect the studio's pocketbook, so asking the studio for assistance in filling out your PRO's cue sheet forms shouldn't be an issue. That said, some independent or smaller studios may not know to do so, so you may need to assist them. Make sure the information in the cue sheet is accurate. Check the spelling and make sure the composer (songwriter) and publisher names are listed correctly.

One more note: as discussed above under the royalties section, if your music is being used in a commercial that will be aired internationally, your PRO may require additional paperwork other than a cue sheet so it can track performances. Be sure to check with your PRO to make sure you file the right forms.

OTHER LICENSING OPPORTUNITIES
THE TWO TYPES OF SERVICES THAT CAN HELP GET YOUR MUSIC DISCOVERED AND LICENSED

Many music supervisors, production studios, advertising companies, and independent filmmakers rely on music services to help them find the right music. There are many services you can use to increase your chances of getting your music licensed. In short, there are three main types of services:

1. Music matching and licensing services.

These services are aimed at making it easy for music supervisors to license music for their media projects. Most of them have a submission process that includes evaluating your music to determine if it matches their needs. There are two types: curated and non-curated.

Curated services include Jingle Punks (jinglepunks.com), Audio-Sparx (audiosparx.com), Getty Images Music (musicfaq.gettyimages.com/category/submitting-music), APM (apmmusic.com), Audiosocket (audiosocket.com), and more. Some specialize in particular uses, such as SongLily (songlily.com), which focuses on licensing music for games and apps, and Motion Array (motionarray.com), which is focused on video. Another example is Taxi (taxi.com), which requires an annual fee to join. Taxi aggregates "wanted" listings from media companies for their musician members. Submitting a song for consideration costs an additional fee. Taxi's staff then reviews each submitted song and decides which ones to send on. If the music user chooses your song, Taxi puts them in touch with you to work out a licensing deal. But note there are hundreds of these services, and it's worth investigating the market to find the best one for you.

Non-curated matching platforms allow anyone to upload music to their music library if you agree with their sync licensing terms (which may ask for exclusivity). Examples include platforms like Songtradr (songtradr.com) or self-service platforms like and Synchtank (synchtank.com) and MDIIO (mdiio.com). Also, your distribution partners may offer this publishing administration service as well—for instance, CD Baby and TuneCore, which offer a sync split fee option to list your song in its catalog for music supervisors and other media users to license. Note that all the considerations we outlined above for curated music matching services apply to non-curated.

You should carefully compare each service's features, payments, and terms and conditions. Make sure to consider the percentage of the sync license fees they'll pay you. Although some services may take a higher percentage of your sync license, they may have closer relationships with music supervisors or media users and therefore be more successful in licensing music. As a result, the percentage of the fee may not necessarily be your deciding factor. The most important term is whether they want exclusive rights to get paid no matter who finds the licensing opportunities and to limit your ability to license to other competitors. When in doubt, talk to your attorney before making a decision to submit.

2. Music production houses and licensing services.

Music production houses specialize in licensing music for their music supervisor and media clients by hiring musicians to create original music for their libraries. Many of these production houses focus on specific genres, styles, or moods, and they often have musicians create different versions of each song, chopping them into fifteen- and thirty-second clips and making instrumental versions. Depending on the music production house, the music is either licensed per use, covered by a yearly subscription arrangement, or sold royalty-free.

Unlike the curated and non-curated options, to get your music considered for inclusion, you need to contact and build a relationship with these houses. They want proof you can create and produce quality music. Many want a work-for-hire arrangement, exclusive rights to the music, or part or all the publisher share of the composition rights. Again, you will want to become very familiar with their terms and may want to discuss with your attorney before signing any deal.

HOW TO GET YOUR MUSIC LICENSED FOR VIDEO GAMES, APPS, AUGMENTED AND VIRTUAL REALITY GAMES, AND OTHER INTERACTIVE AUDIO NEEDS

With technology creating new applications every year, there's more need for interactive sound design and music than ever before. This is especially true for video games, which require sound effects, sound design, theme music, background, and cut-scene music and ambient sounds. Music and sound are a huge part of the overall game experience. Although the video game industry is exploding with the creation of mobile game apps, augmented and virtual reality games, and other platforms, the industry is relationship-based.

Most companies use the same musicians they've worked with in creating the music and audio design for their games. This makes it hard to break into the business. That said, there's a lot of video game development going on, including a vibrant independent game industry, and all of them need music. As George Sanger (fatman.com), one of the most legendary interactive music and sound designers in the business, said, "Repetition is a big problem in game audio," since video games today are designed for upward of six to eight hours of gameplay.

Unlike TV, film, commercials, or movie trailers, when it comes to music for video games or other products like casino slot machines, theme park rides, and mounted fish that sing when you clap, it's mostly about work-for-hire. Most companies want music royalty-free so they can pay once and not have to worry about it afterward. The standard way to charge for this industry is per minute of music. The hard part is determining how many minutes are actually required, since many games require layers of music, multiple cut scenes, theme songs, and more.

Other tips include:

1. Network with video game designers.

Connecting directly with the company heads, product managers, and developers and building a relationship is the key to breaking into this part of the music industry. Besides going to conventions like the Game Developers Conference (gdconf.com) or GameSoundCon (gamesoundcon .com), you can use game developer resource sites like GameDev (gamedev .net), or Indie Game Music (indiegamemusic.com) to reach out and connect with developers looking for music.

2. Use SongLily.

You can submit your music to the curated music matching licensing service SongLily (songlily.com), which specializes in licensing music for games and apps.

3. Negotiate your agreement.

Negotiating points include additional terms that may not be found in a typical license agreement. For example, a video game license should include how much money per minute of music delivered, whether you make money on royalties based on sales, and whether the music rights revert back to you after a number of years. See the "The Top Seven License Terms" above for more to consider.

4. Promote your work to generate future deals.

If you negotiate a deal and it's work-for-hire, include terms that allow you to use the music you create for your portfolio and as a promotion. To connect it to the game, you should also ask for a license to use their marketing materials and images from the game so you can use them to snowball more jobs in this industry. Otherwise, you'll have a harder time creating promotional materials for your website and leveraging your previous work.

HIRING A MUSIC PUBLISHER

Another way to get your music out there is to negotiate a deal with a professional music publisher that acts as an agent for your compositions. They actively promote and lobby music supervisors, media companies, and others to license your music.

Typically, music publishers work song by song, although some may want to publish your entire music catalog. Since their job is to match existing music to the needs of their customers, their success depends on your style, genre, lyrics, the quality of the sound recording, and, of course, luck.

When you negotiate a deal with a music publisher, you will want to be aware of the rights and provisions the publisher wants for promoting your music. The following provisions might be part of the deal:

- Granting them all or part of the publisher's share of the music.

- Granting them all or part of the songwriter's share of the music.

- Asking for administrative fees for every deal they negotiate.

- Requiring that the musicians pay a monthly or yearly fee to keep promoting the music.

- Asking for exclusive rights to the music.

If you want to engage a music publisher, your goal is to grant as little as possible so you can make as much as possible off the royalties. Note that if a publisher asks for monthly or yearly fees to promote the music, be wary, since music publishers can't guarantee results (they aren't the ones making the licensing decisions; they only pitch it). In general, successful and respected publishers are selective as to which artists they take on, since they have a reputation of providing good music for licensing. You should be wary of any that charge fees because it might be the fees they make money on, not the royalties. You should research any publisher you consider signing up with, including searching them on your favorite search engine (usually adding the word *"scam"* by their name) and asking their current and former clients about them.

Another option for music licensing is to use a music administrator. Unlike a music publisher, music administrators do not actively try to get a song licensed; they simply handle the business side of things should you make a licensing deal happen on your own. You pay them fees in exchange for handling this work rather than a cut of royalties.

UNDERSTANDING THE ENDLESS NUMBER OF LICENSING OPPORTUNITIES FOR YOUR MUSIC

There are many other uses for music beyond the ones we've discussed in this chapter. For instance, there are musical greeting cards, e-cards, toys, ringtones, apps, sheet music, and other products requiring sound design and music, such as that dusty singing plastic fish on the wall of your grandfather's den. Plus, new uses for music seem to be invented every day. Some of these require work-for-hire arrangements, but many can be licenses depending on your relationship and negotiation skills. And since these uses are not compulsory, they should be similar to sync licenses in that it's up to you as to how much to charge.

13

ADVANCED INCOME TECHNIQUES

Goal: To apply advanced revenue-generating techniques to boost the amount of money you can make for your music business.

Team Roles and Responsibilities: Manager, Attorney, Social Media Manager, Product and Merchandise Manager, Live Event/Tour Manager, Graphic Artist, Photographer, Video Producer, Web Designer/Webmaster, and Musician

WHAT YOU GET OUT OF THIS
By the end of this chapter, you will:

1. Know how to get sponsorships, endorsements, product placements, paid appearances, and more.

2. Understand how to make advertising revenue from your website.

3. Generate an additional cut on everything you sell through affiliate sales income for your music, products, and merchandise.

4. Be able to tap numerous sources for advances for your royalties, sales, streaming, or merchandise income streams.

5. Have eleven advanced ways to generate revenue from your fan base.

6. Know how to get grants for your music projects.

7. Know how to get scholarships and fellowships if you're a music student.

8. Know dozens of ways to make money off your skills as a musician, plus be able to apply your music business skills in other industries or careers.

MONEY MAP

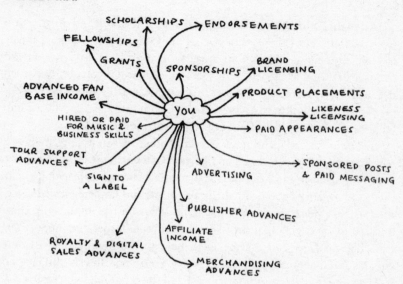

INTRO

The previous chapters covering digital distribution, products, merchandise, licensing, and royalties outlined the foundational income sources musicians should build for their music business. The advanced techniques in this chapter represent additional income streams that you can layer on top of what you've already created to boost revenue.

These are called *"advanced"* for four reasons. First, you should tackle the previous income sources before these because, in many cases, they "unlock" these additional sources of income and make them possible. Second, some techniques like endorsements, sponsorships, and appearance fees are only available to you after you've achieved a certain level of fame, fans, and followers (which we'll discuss in the entire next section of the book, "Releasing Your Music and Getting Noticed"). Third, it usually takes some creativity to decide how to use these for your music—they're not as automatic as the others we've discussed in other chapters. And fourth, many of these are not as straightforward to tackle as signing up online and clicking on a service to make it happen. Some of these techniques require you or a team member to build business relationships, negotiate deals, and execute agreements. They take more time, energy, and attention to implement and aren't the best thing to focus on when you're getting started.

All of that said, some of these are fairly easy to set up and do once you have the foundational pieces in place. For example, once you have music for sale, you can easily sign up to get special affiliate links so you can make an extra cut when people buy your music. And if you play live, even if you're only playing to rooms of fifty people, getting sponsored or advertising is still within reach, since local businesses may pay you a small fee to get their logo on the banner you use for your stage.

These advanced techniques are yet another reason it helps to have a trusted team member focused on figuring out ways to tastefully monetize your shows, music, fan base, and social media. Having a team member take on this manager role so he or she brainstorms and implements things on the business side can allow the artist to focus on the music side, since music is a key engine that drives its own revenue-generating opportunities. The manager can use the ideas here to build additional income streams as momentum builds for the artist. And since these are all layered income sources that don't interfere with all the other ones you've already built, you can start phasing them in as soon as possible to create extra income. The best part is all these techniques grow as your music business grows. For example, once you've gotten one sponsorship deal, others will follow because you're proven.

KEY CONCEPTS
UNDERSTAND HOW TO MAKE MONEY FROM FAME
(YOUR FAN BASE AND PERSONA)

Every business out there—from corporate behemoths to your local mom-and-pop shop—is looking for the same thing: opportunities to get exposure to new customers so they can grow their business. As a musician, you have two things they want: access to your fan base (and the demographic they represent) and association of their brand with your persona. The bigger your fan base and the more defined your persona, the more likely you can turn on these advanced income streams.

In an increasingly more democratized media world, *you are a channel* they can pay to get access to your audience. This is where your live events and, increasingly more importantly, your web, social, and mobile presences come in. Each of these presences are also communication channels you control. Each one is a possible revenue source you can unlock, since brands will pay you to get their message—their product or service—to your audience. All you need to do is work out an arrangement that benefits both sides.

PAID ADVERTISING AND PROMOTION INCOME STREAMS
THE TOP SIX PAID ADVERTISING AND PROMOTION INCOME STREAMS

There are many ways for businesses to advertise their products and services. They can do so on their own, but more frequently, they work with or through other people, businesses, or media, such as through:

1. Sponsorships.

This refers to a business "sponsoring" you to do something specific, such as help paying for your live event or tour in exchange for giving them advertising and exposure. For example, you could get a local business to sponsor your live event in exchange for placing an advertising banner onstage.

2. Endorsements.

An endorsement is when you publicly show your support for a business by stating you use its products and services. In return, you might get endorsement fees, free products, discounts, and more. This could be music-related companies, such as Gibson guitars, Ableton Live, or Ludwig drums, or other companies like those selling cars, soda, video games, sporting goods, or others.

3. Product placement.

Product placement is a subtle type of advertising in which companies that produce products or services pay to get their goods to appear in movies, television, or other media. Product placement has expanded to You-

Tube, Instagram, Twitch, Twitter, and social media, with celebrities such as Kim Kardashian making $75,000 or more to post pictures of themselves wearing a certain brand of clothing or drinking a certain product on their social media. If you are getting paid to place a product in your social media, it's important to disclose that fact, as laws often require this.

4. Likeness licensing.

This is when a business licenses your likeness to use in advertising or placement on their products or merchandise. They're required to get a license from you if they want to use it due to the right of publicity and possibly merchandising rights as discussed in chapter 8, "Your Rights." For example, when Apple added the Beatles' music catalog to iTunes, Apple had to license the likenesses of the Fab Four to include their pictures in iTunes advertising.

5. Brand licensing.

This is when a business uses your brand imagery, such as your logo, in its advertising or places it on their products or merchandise. In the Beatles and iTunes example above, Apple needed to negotiate the use of the Beatles' logo, album art, and other images for their advertising.

6. Paid appearances.

Another method is for a business to pay you to appear on TV, at one of its events, or at their place of business to give them content or publicity. While this requires you to take the time to do the appearance, it might be relatively easy compared to putting on a show.

Each one of these can be a great revenue source. Plus, they're stackable (you can have many, and they don't interfere with each other) and they provide passive income (you'll get paid no matter what else you're working on). Unfortunately, however, there's no one formula for success you can use to make this happen for yourself, although some businesses like Red Bull (redbullmusicacademy.com) are known as musician-friendly and create events and opportunities for musicians to work with them.

While many will want to work with established artists who are known commodities and have large audiences, to aid your chances of making a deal, you'll want to make sure your music and persona are aligned with any business you want to work with. If your brand is detrimental to their message, you're working with a competitor, or there's a significant risk in associating with you, it's not likely they'll work with you. For instance, if you're an anti-capitalist anarchist with music about blowing up the established monetary system, it's unlikely Chase Bank will want to be associated with you, regardless of how large your audience may be. In addition, you'll need to have data and evidence of the size of the audience they can reach through you. For example, show off your social media followers, patrons, mailing list/newsletter subscribers, live draw, and press clippings. Also let them know of any other deals you've done with other companies, since this shows you're a known commodity.

If you build your business to tap these advanced paid advertising and promotion income streams, you'll want to have an attorney assisting you in the contracts and potentially use an agent to help you get and negotiate deals. They can help you specify how your persona and brand can be used (you might not want them to put your face on a sex toy, for example) and clearly define how you can terminate the agreement. Doing so can protect your business in case they misuse your persona or decrease its value.

Lastly, tapping into these types of income streams is not for every artist. Some artists reject these streams, since they feel it damages their music or persona or gives the perception of "selling out." Others don't want to risk turning off their fan base if they start promoting products. These are all personal values every musician needs to consider before tapping these advanced income streams.

THE THREE WAYS TO GET PAID FOR PROMOTING OR INCLUDING MESSAGES IN YOUR CHANNELS

Celebrities with hundreds of thousands or millions of followers can make tens of thousands of dollars for a single social media post promoting a product or service, but you don't need to have the same level of followers to begin using this method. Typically, it becomes achievable once you hit ten thousand followers or more, or if you have a niche demographic certain businesses want to reach.

Once you achieve a certain number of followers, the following paid advertising and promotion techniques may unlock for your social media channels:

1. Getting paid to "like," post a sponsored message, or post links on social media.

Businesses may pay you directly to highlight their work online. For instance, they may pay you to like their Facebook pages or Instagram photos, give their videos or YouTube channels a thumbs-up, or share links to their websites or product pages.

2. Getting paid to include products or services in your posts.

If you have a visual channel like YouTube or Instagram, businesses will pay you to include their products or services in your content. This method might be a better choice if you're concerned a promoted post may turn some of your fans off, since having a company's product in the background of a video might make sense in the context of your video or the photo you post. Or use services like desirelist (desirelist.com) to connect you to those services and organize your payments.

3. Getting paid to include native advertising.

With native advertising, companies pay you to include their content in your channels to appear as if you posted it. This is usually a technique for blogs, but it can include tweets and other social media. For instance, a guitar company could contact you to include a blog post about how much they enjoy their latest product. Since this is content written by another source, but under your name, it can put your own persona and brand at risk, since it may look fake to your fans.

You can try to negotiate each of these on your own with businesses directly, which would involve you or a team member negotiating terms and signing a contract. Or you can use services like SharePop (sharepop.com) or Sni.ps (sni.ps), which help connect people with ten thousand or more followers with major brands by paying you to post sponsored content, products, or messages. Such services make turning on this income stream easier than contracting with these businesses directly. Be sure to read these service agreements carefully, since they usually include nonnegotiable blanket or boilerplate conditions you may have negotiated differently if you had worked a deal with the business directly.

Of course, for all these paid advertising methods, you'll want to make sure you're comfortable with the companies you work with and ensure their products or services match your persona and won't damage your relationship with your fans and followers.

DIRECT ADVERTISING
HOW TO MAKE MONEY BY PLACING ADS ON YOUR WEB PRESENCES

While advertising may not be for everyone, it can generate extra income based on your web traffic. Since the web is an advertising machine, there are many services designed to help you tap into this revenue stream. To do this:

1. Use pay-per-click (PPC) ad sources for your pages.

While the most popular source for PPC advertising is Google AdSense (google.com/adsense/start), there are others, including Chitika (chitika .com) and Taboola (taboola.com). These services pay you when visitors click on the ads.

2. Explore affiliate-based ads for your pages.

Affiliate ads, which we discuss in detail in the next section, only pay if the visitor clicks on the ad and makes a purchase. The amount you can make from this type of advertising is much higher than a PPC ad. For example, if you have a page that talks about your music gear, you may want to create an affiliate search block from eBay embedded in the page that includes active auctions for that piece of gear. If they click and purchase the gear, you'll make a percentage. Also, if you use affiliate ads, you'll have banners and ad image assets you can display on your site.

3. Sell advertising on your site directly to businesses.

An advanced form of advertising, once you have significant web traffic, is offering space on your site to businesses directly, handling the transactions and displaying the ad assets into your site. Alternatively, you can use services like BuySellAds (buysellads.com) to allow businesses to buy ad space on your site through their tool and let it handle things for you.

If you decide to do this, you will need to design space for the ads on your web pages. These ads may be text, images, banners, or videos. Each of these ad sources will give you the dimensions of the ad space required.

AFFILIATE SALES

Affiliate sales represent one of the most surprisingly simple income sources for musicians. It can give you an extra percentage off every piece of music and merch you sell and can even give you income from just talking about products and services. It comes from business relationships online stores make available to try to get people with an audience to send them business, giving them a cut of the business as a result. Although they do pay for ads, it's more effective for them to work with people like musicians, bloggers, YouTubers, podcasters, and others who know their audience well and can influence them and give them a cut. This can be as low as a few percent or as much as 15 percent of a sale; but even 5 percent of a computer purchase can be a significant amount of money.

To do this, you'll make a business relationship with these online sites. From there, you simply make special links to products or services for sale on their sites, which have a special code identifying who you are. These codes let the vendors know who to pay for sending business to their sites. These codes usually let you get paid for as much as a week after you sent them the business. So if your fan browses today, comes back in five days, and finally buys something, you'll still get paid.

As a musician, you have a perfectly good reason to send your fans to vendor websites: you need to send links to your fans so they can buy your music. You will still get your cut from your digital aggregator, but if you send customers there with an affiliate link, you will get another few percent off the front end of the sale as well as the money you will make from the sale on the back end. It doesn't matter to the vendor that you're getting something on the back end or that you have a stake in that particular product. In fact, they probably don't even know you're the same person. But that's only the start; you can also send links to whatever they sell if you can find a way to genuinely talk about it. We cover how to do this in the sections below.

Here's the best news: you actually get a cut of everything in the fan's shopping cart if they decide to buy other things, not just your music. You were the one that sent the vendor the business, after all! Follow the instructions below to make extra income from affiliate sales.

HOW TO SIGN UP TO BECOME AN AFFILIATE PUBLISHER

Becoming an affiliate publisher is *free*, so you will want to sign up for as many affiliate sites as possible to maximize your options. Use the following instructions to sign up to become an affiliate publisher:

1. Build your web, social, and mobile presences first.

Affiliate marketing companies will require you to enter your websites, social media, and name into their system to verify if you are a legitimate affiliate publisher. Although you can have an early version of your website if you are starting out, it should be a complete website and not just an "Under Construction" page, or they may reject you. They will not check to see if you have a huge following, but you must appear as a legitimate artist.

2. Decide which business entity gets paid and have your business name and tax ID ready to go.

The affiliate programs write checks and report to the tax authority, so you will want to have that ready when you sign up for the programs. If you try to start without this, they will hold your checks until you give them a legitimate name and tax ID or block you from signing up altogether. We talk about how to establish a business entity in chapter 2, "Your Music Business."

3. Sign up for the most likely places to sell your music.

You will want to sign up for the places where you will be selling your music. This should include at least iTunes (apple.com/itunes/affiliates) and Amazon (affiliate-program.amazon.com). Note that you can also talk about other albums or media to sell on iTunes and can link to just about anything sold on the planet via Amazon, so these are very useful affiliate programs for more than just your own music.

4. Sign up for the two largest affiliate networks.

An affiliate network groups together major brands and retailers under a service that takes care of their affiliate programs for them. You'll have to sign up on the networks first, and once accepted, you can search for retailers that fit you and your music and apply to each one through the network application system. Once you are accepted by a retailer, search the retailers' catalogs of products and create affiliate links.

The world's most well-known brands are found within CJ Affiliate (cj.com) and Rakuten Marketing (rakutenmarketing.com/affiliate.html). They include sites like Music123, Guitar Center, and more, which are worth applying to once you become a member of the affiliate network because you may want to talk about music gear.

5. Sign up for eBay Partner Network.

If you become an affiliate partner for eBay (partnernetwork.ebay.com), you can link to a search box of recent auctions for any search term. You can even embed them on your web presences. This allows you to make affiliate links for items that are no longer available via retail outlets. You also make an extra bounty if a person signs up for eBay for the first time as well as if they purchase something.

6. Sign up for any print-on-demand retailers and merch outlets you use.

The major print-on-demand retailers like CafePress (cafepress.com /content/cp-partners), Zazzle (zazzle.com/sell/affiliates), Spreadshirt (help.spreadshirt.com/hc/en-us/articles/207233389-Affiliate-Comm ission), and others have affiliate programs, and you should use them to create links for everything you do.

7. Sign up for affiliate programs on any retailers you use often.

Check to see if there are affiliate programs on any retailers you use often, as you may want to create affiliate links to them.

8. Learn how to make affiliate links and deal with special deals on their system.

Each one will have their own method to create affiliate links, and you'll want to become familiar with them when you sign up. Amazon's is one of the easiest to use; you will get a special bar at the top of the site. You can browse to any page and can make an affiliate link with a click. Others require you to use a special back end. Also, many of these affiliate programs will have special sales events and may give you images and links.

9. Use their reporting systems.

Affiliate sites have detailed reporting providing info where the clicks came from and which clicks resulted in a sale. You can use these to tune your marketing campaigns. This extra reporting is yet another reason to use your affiliate links for your music and merch sales.

HOW TO MAKE AN EXTRA CUT ON YOUR MUSIC AND MERCH SALES

Once you've become an affiliate publisher, you can create affiliate links to all your music and merchandise to start getting an extra cut. Here's how to do this effectively:

1. Choose a link shortener tool to use for your affiliate links.

Link shorteners like Bitly (bitly.com) or Ow.ly (ow.ly) are almost a necessity for affiliate links for two reasons. First of all, affiliate links are very long and are hard to copy and paste; a shortened link is much easier to deal with. Secondly, some unscrupulous sites will recognize affiliate links and overwrite your affiliate code with their own unless it's hidden in a link shortener.

2. Make an affiliate link for everything.

After using their affiliate link creation system and shortening your links, keeping them all in a shared spreadsheet like Google Docs is the easiest way to deal with the huge volume of links you'll be copying and pasting often. You will need to paste these into your online presences.

3. Replace all your non-affiliate links with affiliate links, and put the affiliate links *everywhere*.

Every single place you link to or talk about your music or merch should have affiliate links instead of plain ones, which don't give you a cut. Don't forget your YouTube descriptions, email signatures, social media profiles, and your website.

4. Follow the terms of service.

The terms and laws regarding affiliate sales can limit how you use them and may require you to tell people you get a financial benefit from the links. These terms matter because they can remove you from the affiliate program if you don't follow them.

THE TOP THREE AFFILIATE INCOME METHODS

You are not limited to affiliate sales for your music and merch; you can create an affiliate link to anything for sale on their sites, and if you get creative, you can come up with a long list of opportunities to make affiliate sales. This is not to say you should be just turning into a sales machine and selling everything you can think of; this is where the persona you've developed can guide you to let you know which are authentic conversations.

1. Talk about the products you bought or want to buy for yourself.

Your fans are naturally curious about you, and if you are used to talking about your personal life on your social media or blog, you can provide affiliate links to things you have just bought or want to buy.

2. Provide info about your gear with affiliate links on where to buy them.

Your musician fans want to know how you make your music and the gear you use to make it. You can both satisfy their curiosity and make something from this by providing affiliate links for them. Try making a page on your website that lists all the instruments, gear, plug-ins, and software you use and providing affiliate links for each one. Even your older instruments that are not available new can be listed by using the eBay affiliate program. The best thing about this is most music gear consists of larger-ticket items, so this is often worth the time due to the income you can make.

3. Give affiliate links that fit the lifestyle of your fans.

If you get to know your fans well, you'll get a better idea of what kinds of things they want to buy and what they'd be interested in hearing about. By talking about these kinds of life-enhancing items, you're providing them with useful info while giving yourself a cut of their purchases. These can often come out of the things you use in your own life.

SIGN TO A LABEL
UNDERSTANDING THE DECISION TO SIGN TO A LABEL

Labels can be thought of as business partners that give you funding and music business services, handling many of the tasks we've covered here in the book. Labels are one of the ways to raise money for your music as well as to get your music business off the ground because they not only provide you with an advance, they also provide the initial outlay of money for recording an album and give you a network of talent to tap to make your project successful. Because they are a business partner, they promote you as well as get you started. In return, you will be giving up some of your copyrights, plus giving up a cut of many of your revenue streams.

Here are high-level facts you should know before signing to a label:

1. Work with A&R.

The scouts for labels are called artist and repertoire (A&R) people and can be found listed in directories like the Indie Bible (indiebible.com) or sites like Music Business Registry (musicregistry.com), Music Xray (musicxray.com), or Submithub (submithub.com). They will look for proof you've got potential, so everything covered in this book to promote your music, grow your fan base, get you income, and get you noticed will also help you get signed.

2. Make sure it's a good deal for you.

Most labels offer only 360 deals, which means they will tap into your merch, publishing, touring, sponsorships and endorsements, and other income. They will also require you to assign them the copyright to your masters and all the income streams that come with it. Finally, you will be under other contractual provisions as to what you can and cannot do with your music and your public persona. We've interviewed well-known independent artists who evaluated their deals and asked the very pointed question: "What are you giving me in return for taking two-thirds of my income?" The label told them a list of things they were already doing or could do themselves, and they refused the offer.

3. Use an entertainment attorney to evaluate and negotiate the deal.

There's no such thing as a "standard agreement everyone signs." You deserve a skilled entertainment attorney working on your behalf to negotiate the deal.

4. You will still need to keep finding ways to make money with music.

Besides the advance, most musicians find their label royalties don't provide steady sources of income. The income sources covered here in this book are used by signed artists as well as unsigned.

ADVANCES

Once you've established yourself as an artist and have shown your music business can consistently produce income, you have the opportunity to get advances, or lump-sum payments, based on your future income. This allows you to raise funds now rather than wait for the income to come in over time. You do this by assigning all or some of the rights to your future revenue to a third party, and they pay you an advance in exchange.

Advances are not free money; they act like loans against your future income and work by assigning your future revenue streams to someone else. Depending on your deal, you might get your income stream back after you've paid them back, with interest, but some are permanent assignments, so you should understand the deal.

Because advances involve many of the rights we discussed in chapter 8, "Your Rights," all these transactions involve specific legal terms and terminology and result in a signed contract. Advance agreements vary greatly depending on the type and contain negotiable terms, including which income streams are being assigned, the length of the agreement, the territory of coverage, whether the assignment can be reverted back to the artist, and more, so you'll want to work with an attorney. And since advances generate taxable income, you may also want to consult your accountant.

To get these advances, you'll need solid proof of the revenue streams you're willing to assign to them. This means you need to have achieved a certain level of success and have the income results to prove it. Some of the more common advances include:

1. Publisher advance.

If you're working with a publisher, they may offer advances based on the royalties your music may produce in the future. In exchange, the publisher receives your share of the royalty income.

2. Royalty and digital sales advances from exchanges.

Once you've established consistent sales and royalty income streams that we discussed in chapter 12, "Licensing and Royalties," you can go to the open market and sell some or all of these for an advance. While you can reach out to music organizations or individual investors to make these arrangements on your own, you can also auction them off using innovative services like Royalty Exchange (royaltyexchange.com).

Royalty Exchange assists qualifying musicians by auctioning off some or all their future digital sales and royalties for a lump-sum payment. For a cut, the service analyzes the income streams and helps musicians decide which digital sales and royalty streams to include, which to exclude, and the percentage to go to market with, as well as organizing the auction. Since the term of this type of transaction is based on copyright, this can be your entire lifetime plus seventy years. This means you can potentially earn more than your entire lifetime's income from the percentage of royalties you auction off. If you decide to participate in this type of financial transaction, be aware of how Royalty Exchange's auctions work, the options available (such as setting a reserve or minimum), the bidding process, and the best ways to promote your auction.

For those musicians with consistent royalty revenue streams, these deals can be quite lucrative. For instance, Michael Skaggs and his band, Outline in Color, were able to generate over $40,000 by auctioning off 50 percent of their future digital sales, mechanical royalties, and YouTube synchronization and ad share revenue on their first two albums. This allowed them to pay off some debt the business accumulated, provided needed cash flow, and helped to fund other projects.

Two more options are Songvest (songvest.com) and Royalty Flow (royaltyexchange.com/royalty-ipo/royalty-flow), which gives artists the equivalent of an initial public offering (IPO) based on your royalties.

3. Merchandising advance.

If you're working with labels or merchandising companies who understand the merchandising space, your merchandise sales are another revenue stream you can tap. In exchange for the right to collect some or all the merchandising proceeds, the label or merchandising company may pay you an advance.

4. Label advance.

If you sign with a label, you'll usually negotiate to receive an advance to record an album. You end up paying back the label through your album sales and streaming royalties. An album that has managed to pay back the advance is called a *"recouped"* album. When this happens, it starts generating royalty payments to the artist.

5. Tour support advance.

Tours are usually expensive operations, requiring up-front capital for the lighting, sets, transportation, lodging, and other expenses. Labels or live touring companies might provide an advance to help fund the tour. You pay back the label or touring company by giving them the right to collect the ticket sales and other touring income.

GRANTS, FELLOWSHIPS, AND SCHOLARSHIPS
UNDERSTANDING GRANTS FOR MUSIC AND THE ARTS

Grants are money given to artists or organizations to support an artist or a project. The types include government grants, private companies, trusts, charities, and nonprofits, and even individuals offer money to musicians too.

Grant associations establish criteria and rules you must meet to get the funds. For instance, some grants are only available to nonprofits, so if you don't qualify, you'll need to get sponsored by a nonprofit. Services like Fractured Atlas (fracturedatlas.org) specialize in this. Additionally, applying for grants requires a lot of paperwork, so be sure to follow all the submission instructions carefully and make timely filings. And if you are awarded a grant, make sure you follow all the reporting requirements afterward. Grant associations will often want an accounting of how the project they funded went and what they got for their money. And, as with all income streams, grant funding is taxable income, so you may also want to consult your accountant.

The key to increasing the odds that you'll get grant funding is to apply for ones with mission statements and goals matching your project and music. For ideas, check the Savvy Musician's funding page (savvymusi cian.com/index.php?page=funding) and National Assembly of State Arts Agencies (nasaa-arts.org/state-arts-agencies/saa-directory) for a list of U.S. state agencies providing grants for music and the arts.

Not all grants are complicated. For example, the Awesome Foundation (awesomefoundation.org) gives away $1,000 to any project they deem "awesome"—no strings attached! Awesome Foundation chapters exist in major cities all over the world and meet regularly to review projects and determine who gets the grant. If you think you can prove your next music project is awesome, it's worth reaching out to them.

Finally, some grant organizations use more modern techniques which match today's music world rather than the grants given to classical music of the past. For example, Black Fret is a membership-based organization where a limited number of funders pay a membership fee, and attend concerts throughout the year by the applicants. They choose the musicians they want to fund by voting on them after seeing the shows, and the funders get entertainment throughout the year plus the satisfaction of helping musicians. The musicians get mentoring on top of the grant money.

UNDERSTANDING EDUCATIONAL GRANTS, FELLOWSHIPS, AND SCHOLARSHIPS

Educational grants, fellowships, and scholarships are funding that need not to be paid back but come with qualifying criteria and rules. In addition, these are specifically focused on you as an individual and your education.

- **Scholarships.**

Scholarships provide funding for students to pay tuition for music school and are not limited to colleges or universities, since there are other institutions catering to music education that offer their own scholarships. These are often competitive and may require an audition as well as a detailed application. There are many sources for music scholarships, and the best place to start is the school the student is attending or about to attend. There are also directories to look through, such as Majoring in Music (majoringinmusic.com/scholarships-for-music-majors), Scholarships.com (scholarships.com/financial-aid/college-scholarships/scholarships-by -major/music-scholarships), Unigo (unigo.com/scholarships/by-major /music-scholarships), and many others.

- **Educational grants and fellowships.**

Educational grants and fellowships award students or recent graduates funding for research, travel, teaching opportunities, internships, or other activities. They're often given to music students, masters, or Ph.D.s later in their academic careers and occasionally are also granted to recent music graduates to get them started in their new careers. Similar to scholarships, these are usually tied to schools and universities. You can also find some listings of these types of grants at the American Musicological Society (ams-net.org/grants.php).

ADVANCED FAN BASE INCOME
THE TOP ELEVEN WAYS TO GENERATE REVENUE
BY HANGING OUT WITH YOUR FANS

In today's world, people increasingly pay for experiences as much as they pay for merch. You can open up new income by giving your fan base access to the kinds of experiences they'll remember and enjoy. Plus, your fans want a deeper connection with you. With technology, you have the opportunity to do both with fans all over the world, not just the ones within reach.

These ideas don't just bring you closer to your fans; they represent new income streams because some of your superfans are willing to pay to have more access to you. In fact, many of these are mentioned in other chapters, but they get amped up when they become more advanced income streams as you become more popular, because access to you becomes a premium people will pay money to get. Remember, you will want to give certain rewards to your whales and dolphins that are not available to your minnows. This is a great way to do it. In fact, they can be something you charge for, or they could be fan club perks, crowdfunding/patronage rewards, or special ticketing options for your shows.

Consider the following ideas, and use them to come up with your own:

1. Create a backstage or sound check pass, and/or VIP seating.

We discuss these tickets in the chapter 16, "Get Gigs and Play Live." Remember: even attending a sound check can be a unique experience for a fan. Give some fans access behind the scenes as you're setting up, invite them to your sound check, or reserve a section of the audience for them. You can create special tickets for a select few of your superfans so they can join you. And by restricting these experiences to only a few fans, you make it all the more special. Set it up ahead of time via your social media presence and create a special ticket for them to print out and gain access. Always reserve time to talk and engage with them. Of course, don't let their access mess up your preshow prep and sound check. Also, if the venue is large enough, you also have the possibility of giving them VIP seating areas. This is perfect for high rollers or premium fan club members.

2. Hold a preshow dinner/postshow hangout.

Similar to giving fans access behind the scenes of your live show, you can also give them access to a preshow dinner or postshow hangout.

3. Perform a house concert.

Offer a house concert for your fans to give them a personal experience. We discuss these in chapter 16, "Get Gigs and Play Live."

4. Stream your performances online.

The streaming performances we discuss in chapter 16, "Get Gigs and Play Live," can become an income stream or reward perk. Also, some of the musicians who have done a great job developing fans just stream and talk with their fans as they drive around or do other things throughout their day.

5. Party bus.

Some people just want to party with you before and after a show, even if there's no show! For instance, some musicians have had success with renting a bus or van, getting some booze and snacks, and throwing a mobile party across town with a designated bus driver.

6. Stream while you're writing, recording, or mixing the music.

While we discussed this briefly in other chapters, streaming while you work can be something you allow your fans to see to build your fan base. But if you restrict the feed, it can be an income source or a reward.

7. Hold a private listening party.

Whether you're releasing a single, EP, or full album, consider making an event out of it by throwing a listening party for your superfans. If you play live, this can be *in addition to* your album release show. These can be big events held at a live venue, bar, coffeehouse, restaurant, or some other space where you can control the audio. Or, to make it really special, it can be at your studio, rehearsal space, or home. And don't simply let the music play; make it interactive and give them an experience they'll remember. Share stories on how you created the songs in between the tracks. Or share the meaning behind the lyrics and what inspired you.

Keep in mind you can have multiple listening parties—ones for different sets of your audience. For instance, you can restrict the first listening party to just your superfans or highest-paying patronage or crowdfunding supporters. Then you can throw a second listening party that's open to everyone. These events can also be streamed like we suggest in #6 above, or you can keep them private and local.

8. Stream and play video games with your fans.

If you're a video gamer, you can stream your game-playing online with your fans. Watching others play video games is big business. In fact, the streaming site Twitch generates one hundred million page views per month, with millions of video gamers broadcasting their games. Visitors show up to watch, chat online, and even participate and play along. Twitch shares ad revenue your channel creates with you, but also allows you to charge your audience and channel subscribers for access (usually through PayPal).

9. Travel with your superfans.

Your travel event could be day trips around the city or multiday travel events. If you plan the event right, you not only create a special experience for your fans, you can also work it so your trip is free. Ideally, your event would be connected to your music, but it doesn't have to be. For instance, back in 2007, the Brobdingnagian Bards, who are a Celtic/Irish music duo, planned out a weeklong trip to Ireland and invited their fan base to join them. They worked out the flights, hotels, itinerary, and transportation all in advance, and they included time for concerts. In the end, they created a single fee for the entire package and ensured it was enough to cover their costs. Of course, you don't have to set up a weeklong Ireland trip; you can create half-day, full-day, or overnight events that are local or in your area. Perhaps it's something related to your music, but it doesn't have to be. In our talks with musicians, just mentioning this as a possibility to some had their minds reeling on the possibilities—camping concerts, group outings to catch a mainstream musician who inspired you, a restaurant series in their town, and more.

10. Boat cruise with your superfans.

Similar to #9 above, setting up a boat cruise with your fans has become a concept that blends music with a vacation. One of the advantages of a cruise is that it's a multiday getaway where the hotel, transportation, and often food costs are already bundled. Work this out with the right cruise line and you can get a bunch of cabins set aside for your fans, as well as stages to play on. Your fans (and you!) get to take a full vacation while you give your fans some quality hangout time with you.

11. Provide premium updates or social media feeds.

Some fans will pay for the opportunity to read premium social media updates and info. One way to do this is to use Patreon (patreon.com) and limit the audience of some of your posts to particular reward levels. Another is to use services like Premo (premosocial.com) to charge fans access to social feeds.

SKILLS AS A MUSICIAN
HOW TO MAKE MONEY WRITING AND LICENSING SONGS FOR OTHERS

Rather than exploit your existing songs, you can always take commissions for writing songs. Music made to order for television shows, films, commercials, the theater, and video games is big business, with professional songwriters usually creating such music under work-for-hire agreements. While writing themes for television shows and films may seem out of your reach, you can still write music for podcasters, YouTubers, theater groups, indie and student filmmakers, web comics, businesses, and more. Often, these music users just use whatever music is handy, infringing on copyrights simply because they don't know the law or where to find the right music to fit their needs. As a musician, you not only can help improve their production values but also keep them out of legal trouble. At the same time, you'll be getting your music heard while promoting you and your music.

If you want to write songs for others, here are some of the top things to keep in mind:

1. Advertise that you will write songs on commission.

Create a page on your website offering to write songs for others. Advertise it to your fans and team through your blog, social networks, and newsletters. Also, use sites like Fiverr (fiverr.com) or Upwork (upwork.com), which have all types of creatives, or try sites that specialize in music, such as SoundBetter (soundbetter.com) to get work from all over the world. Or consider sites like Downwrite (downwrite.com) where you can compose music for special occasions. Note that there are many roles you can play in the commissioned song space, including being a lyricist, scoring music, composing soundtracks, writing custom music for weddings or celebrations, and more.

2. Determine what rights you (and they) want to license.

Typically, you will want to keep the rights to the composition and sound recording and give them a license to just the rights they need in exchange for payment. We cover music licensing in detail in chapter 12, "Licensing and Royalties." If your client asks for a work-for-hire agreement, make sure to charge a much higher fee for these rights. Of course, if you've chosen to write the music for free, make sure to only license the rights they need to produce their work (nonexclusive) and require attribution (a credit in the film, a mention on the podcast, a link back to your website, and links to where people can buy your music).

3. When you get a request, detail the working relationship in writing before you do anything.

For minor deals, a simple agreement in an exchange of emails might be fine for licensing your music. For more complicated deals, especially financial agreements or work-for-hires, you should have a signed contract that covers the rights more explicitly, since you don't know how the composition or sound recording might be exploited and used in the future. And, of course, for large deals, it's likely worth the financial cost to bring in a lawyer.

TEN CATEGORIES OF INCOME SOURCES FROM MUSIC-RELATED SKILLS

Once you've gained the skills to record, master, promote, market, and license your own music, you can use these skills to help other musicians or professionals in the industry. You can simply hire yourself out using sites like Fiverr (fiverr.com) or Upwork (upwork.com), or when you meet with musicians in your area.

Of course, there's no end to services you can provide, but consider the following areas of skills to give you ideas:

1. Audio engineering and studio skills.

These skills include recording engineering; mixing; mastering; producing; being a session musician; sound design; creating loops, samples, and plug-ins.

2. Live music skills.

Besides playing as a gigging player, you can be a live sound engineer, lighting engineer, booker, producer, DJ, or even a roadie.

3. Licensing and royalty skills.

Once you understand how it works, you can become a publisher for other musicians and help them with royalties and licensing.

4. Promotion skills.

After you get the skills for yourself, you can promote others by being a music publicist, radio promoter/plugger, marketer, or brand manager.

5. Video, photography, or theatrical skills.

Once you have the capability to do this for yourself, you can produce, edit, and record videos for other musicians, or make commercials or videos for businesses. There is also always a need for photographers for musicians. If you feel comfortable performing onstage or in front of the camera, you can appear in films/theater productions as a live musician or be behind the scenes as a music director/music supervisor, or score music for video.

6. Music business skills.

There is always need of music managers, accountants, bookkeepers, music agents, and all the other business activities related to music.

7. Teaching.

Teaching is within reach of nearly every musician for all the roles talked about above, and with the web, you're not limited to the classroom. Record yourself teaching lessons and upload them to sites like Udemy (udemy.com) and you can take your classes to the world. Also, if you are a good speaker, you can speak and earn honoraria or speaking fees.

8. Instrument repair or studio design skills.

There's always a need for instrument repair. Also, some folks want experienced people to design and build their studios.

9. Fine arts, therapy, and music hosting skills.

The fine arts have many positions specific to the space, including being a conductor, arts administrator, and accompanist. The medical community has music therapy needs, and musicians can hire out as a karaoke host.

10. Music writer and reviewer.

There are a number of music-focused outlets that have both staff and free-lance writing opportunities. You can also become a music reviewer.

HOW TO USE YOUR MUSIC EXPERIENCE TO ENHANCE YOUR RÉSUMÉ AND HIREABILITY

Although this is a book about music, it bears mentioning everything you learn and are doing in the music business is applicable to any job or career. The creativity, scrappiness, skills, and your ability to get things done can make you an attractive hire in any industry if you paint it the right way. After all, we musicians have to learn how to work with different personalities, learn business and financial acumen, and even demonstrate showmanship and engagement. These are all skills in demand everywhere.

In fact, if you work on your résumé, try adding the following phrases to your skill sets and background if you've done them:

- Business management

- Marketing and promotion

- Publicity

- Event planning and management

- Project management

- Communications, writing, and public speaking

- Social media engagement and management

- Customer service and engagement

- Research and analysis

- Graphic design

- Web design

- Sales

- Bookkeeping and accounting

Note that these are only a starting point, and you may come up with more if you review your chronicle, which we talked about in chapter 3, "Your Persona." (We keep ours up to date and turn to them if we ever have to talk about our own experience.)

PART 3

RELEASING YOUR MUSIC AND GETTING NOTICED

14

MARKETING

Goal: To create a marketing strategy for your music business to grow your fan base, increase sales, and promote everything you do.

Team Roles and Responsibilities: Marketer, Web Designer/Webmaster, and Manager

WHAT YOU GET OUT OF THIS

By the end of this chapter, you will:

1. Have a framework outlining how to define who your audience is, their demographics, and how to target and reach them.

2. Know the top seven musician marketing goals you can implement and examples of conversion tools to use.

3. Understand the four types of media methods you can use to reach your target audience and promote and publicize yourself.

4. Create effective marketing messages that get your targeted audience to promote you and increase your revenue.

5. Understand fourteen $0 marketing strategies you can implement for your music business.

INTRO

In today's world, the means of making and recording music is in any musician's hands. And with the internet, you can find nearly any piece of recorded music ever made anywhere in the world and download it within moments. So the question is: How do you market yourself when you are competing against every musician in the world?

This seems even harder if you're just starting out, since marketing yourself from nothing seems like a difficult mountain to climb. But when you're new, you do have something on your side: you can be fresh and exciting, and there are many $0 marketing techniques we'll cover in this chapter.

Marketing only makes sense when you have two things ready to go. First, make sure your music is ready to release. Second, make a solid persona. As Jed Carlson at ReverbNation (reverbnation.com) says, "Marketing can't fix a broken brand." To be specific, do you have your genre, music description, and bands you sound like handy? Are your bio, press kits, fact sheets, and chronicle up to date and ready? All these can form part of your marketing messages, and you may end up adjusting these depending on what you're marketing. (See chapter 3, "Your Persona," to develop this). If this prep work isn't ready to go, get that done before marketing yourself.

But once the minimal prep is ready to go, get out there. As Jim DeRogatis, music editor for *The Chicago Sun-Times* and cohost of National Public Radio's *Sound Opinions*, told us, "There's this perception that there's some mystery button that gets pushed, and buzz starts. It's this magic, elusive thing that every group is trying to get. But buzz just means that people are excited about the band and are talking about it." And people only talk about you if you're out there doing something worth talking about. The good news for independent artists is you can build this momentum with little budget. It simply takes creativity, a willingness to try out lots of ideas, some luck, and most of all, time to snowball.

KEY CONCEPTS

UNDERSTANDING MARKETING

The goal to marketing is to get your audience to make you money with music, not just get them to listen to your music. If you're not purposely getting your audience to open their wallets to support you, then you are simply entertaining them for free. This is fine if music is a hobby, but if it's a business, your marketing goal is to make a profit. To do this, follow these four steps:

1. **Know your target audience:** Understand who they are, where they pay attention, and how best to engage them.

2. **Structure your communication channels:** Organize your communication channels to deliver your message to the right audiences.

3. **Make marketing goals and prepare your conversion tools:** Decide the action you want your audience to take—for example, buy something, come to a show, or join your mailing list. Then include the related conversion tools in your marketing messages (we talk about conversion tools in chapter 7, "Your Online Presences").

4. **Create and broadcast your message:** This has two parts. First, create a message and broadcast it to your target audience using every communication channel you control. Second, use publicity (which we talk about in the next chapter) to get other people to cover your message to reach your audience.

The rest of the chapter will give you techniques to do each of these four steps effectively.

KNOWING YOUR TARGET AUDIENCE
THE TOP QUESTIONS YOU SHOULD BE ABLE TO ANSWER ABOUT YOUR AUDIENCE

Below are good questions to answer about each audience you have. The better you know them, the more effective you can use marketing, PR, and get-heard techniques to grow your audience.

If you are just starting out, your fans are probably just like you, and you should answer these questions as if you were the audience. You will improve your answers as you gain your fan base. But once you have some followers, you can use your current metrics sources and profile of your listeners and concertgoers to get a picture of the below.

- How old are they?

- What mix of genders and gender identites?

- Where do they live?

- What artists do they listen to?

- What do they do for a living? Where do they go to school?

- What words do they identify with? Do they have a name they call themselves or group they already identify with (for example, Juggalos, geeks, freethinkers, soccer fans, bikers, bronies, and so on)?

- Where do they hang out online?

- How do they like to receive communications (for example: message/discussion boards, Facebook groups, subreddits, websites, YouTube channels, and so on)?

- What influencers do they respect and listen to?

- What politics or causes do they relate to?

- What TV shows, movies, or other media do they watch or listen to? What part of the culture do they participate in?

- What are their aspirations? Expectations? Fears? Biases?

These questions are just a starting point. The goal is to understand your target audience so you can craft your messages and target the people most likely to enjoy your persona and your music.

HOW TO FIND OUT WHO YOUR FANS ARE, WHAT THEY LISTEN TO, AND WHERE THEY LIVE

One of the paradoxes of marketing is that in order to grow your audience, *you need to narrow it*. So instead of throwing your message "out there" like a grenade, you should target specific audiences. As Bob Baker (bob-baker.com), one of the premier music marketing gurus, says, "If you want to punch through a wall, you would use an awl, not a board. The sharper your message, the better chance you have of punching through." Once you focus your marketing, you can create targeted messages tuned to your audiences and deliver it to where your audience is hanging out.

In this world of social media when people are volunteering all kinds of information about themselves, it turns out there are actually quite a few resources within your reach to give you this information about your fans. Some are free, and others, for a fee, will give you deeper sets of info.

1. Use Facebook stats.

Go to the insights link and take a look at what it provides. You will get your fans' ages, sexes, how many talk about you in comments, and a lot of other useful information. If you end up friending your Facebook fans, you can see even more information.

2. Try Twitter stats.

Most Twitter users put in their location, so it's easy to use applications like Tweepsmap (tweepsmap.com) to show you the locations of your Twitter followers merged with maps you can glance at. This can help your marketing, as well as touring.

2. Look up your listeners on Last.fm.

Last.fm (last.fm) has locations, sexes, and listening habits of people who are listening to your music. Last.fm is also absolutely the best place to find out what other bands your fans really listen to.

3. Use ReverbNation stats.

ReverbNation (reverbnation.com) will pull information from multiple sources and give you good demographic information based on everything that it can collect.

4. For touring, try looking at the location of your fans.

Tools like Eventful (eventful.com) will let fans demand that you play in their area, and you can find the location of your Twitter followers using tools like Tweepsmap (tweepsmap.com). This allows you to potentially plan tour locations based on where your fans are located.

5. For videos, use YouTube stats.

Your creator studio has stats on all your videos, giving you demographic info out of this to help you find out the locations of your viewers and find out what other views are referring viewers to see you.

6. Ask them. (Surveys.)

There are more ways than ever of asking your fans questions directly. Try using a Facebook fan page questions or a form in Google Docs (docs.google .com), Twitter polls, or Free Online Surveys (freeonlinesurveys.com). If you want to tailor the look and feel of the survey for your fans, then you may wish to use the pay sites SurveyMonkey (surveymonkey.com) or Zoomerang (zoomerang.com).

THE NUMBER-ONE WAY TO FIND OUT WHERE YOUR FANS HANG OUT

The best place to market yourself is to get your message where fans of similar artists to you hang out. Start with one who is famous, but also track artists playing venues within your reach in your region if you play live, or a similar up-and-coming online artist if you don't.

Once you identify them, do some deep research—far more than the first page of web search results. Learn how they describe themselves on their websites. Check out any articles that cover them and venues they play at. List all sites, message boards, forums, subreddits, Twitter feeds, and social media where their fans hang out. Also consider tracking them on Google Alerts and similar tools so you can get more ideas as they continue to get covered and market themselves. Getting these alerts will give you a constant stream of fresh ideas as you piggyback on their successes. We talk about tools you can use in chapter 18, "Your Release Strategy."

STRUCTURING YOUR COMMUNICATION CHANNELS

Your marketing campaigns should reach your target audience directly (through your channels such as your website or social media) or influence people who your potential fans are paying attention to. You should develop your own channels so you can communicate to fans directly, and you can use PR techniques to influence others to cover and promote you in their channels.

Here's a list of all the communication channels you can develop to promote you and your music:

1. Owned media.

Owned media includes the presences you've set up that are outposts for fans to discover you and powerful communication channels to message your fan base. Because of this, these presences should be the first place you should market and promote yourself. This can include your website, blog, podcasts, online profiles, streaming channels and playlists, audio content hosts, patronage and crowdfunding presences, mailing list/newsletter, and public/online business materials (includes your bio, fact sheet, press kit, booking kit, press releases, and so on).

2. Shared media.

Shared media, such as your video channel/vlog and/or streaming video channel/shows and your social media, is designed for user-generated circulation. The content you post is built to be shared, to be commented on, and to invite participation. This also includes your engagement with fans on these media platforms. While your owned channels can be posted to your shared media networks, usually using the automation we covered in chapter 7, "Your Online Presences," content on your shared media is a conversation rather than a broadcast.

3. Paid media.

Paid media channels—like advertising including online and offline ads as well as physical advertising materials, such as posters and flyers—are also known as advertising, where you pay to get your message out to your audience.

4. Earned media.

Earned media, which publicity or PR falls under, happens when you get other people to cover you in press and media outlets. This is about influencing your target audience's influencers to cover you. As we cover in chapter 15, "Promotion and Publicity," you will need to have your promotional materials ready to go, including your music and/or videos, bio, press kits, fact sheets, and press releases.

This can include coverage by:

- Traditional third-party press/media (including terrestrial television and radio, magazines, newspapers, news sites, music review and discovery sites, MP3 blogs, social news and entertainment websites, other websites, and so on).

- Other third parties (including blogs, video channel/vlog and/or streaming video channel/shows, newsletters, streaming playlists, podcasts, social media, and so on).

- Your network, such as friends, family, team, and partners (including their blogs, social media, word of mouth, and so on).

- Your fans (including their blogs, social media, word of mouth, and so on).

Keep in mind, as we discussed in chapter 13, "Advanced Income Techniques," your owned and social media messaging channels can be monetized via sponsorships, endorsements, product placements, and other advanced techniques. As your fan base grows, businesses want to get *their* messages out to your audience, and since you control these channels, you can charge money for this access.

CREATING MARKETING GOALS AND PREPARING YOUR CONVERSION TOOLS

Although making goals and a marketing plan for small businesses have a lot of soul-searching to define them, musicians have just a few categories of goals that nearly every musician wants to do, and most have tools ready to go to help you convert your audience and succeed at your marketing plans. We've listed the most popular ones below to make it easy for you, but always be on the lookout for other goals worth doing and new tools to drive engagement. Once you've chosen the tools to use, keep them handy, since you'll be making them a part of nearly every marketing message you send. In fact, you should treat your channels like a stage at a show; you don't know who might have just arrived in the room and need to be told about these conversions, so use the tools often.

THE TOP SEVEN MARKETING GOALS YOU CAN SET FOR YOUR CAMPAIGNS

Good marketing plans will usually set a numeric target for each goal by a certain date—for example, to get a thousand new followers on Twitter by December 1. This can drive how to go about your campaign. Use one of the below concepts and conversion tools, or make one of your own for your campaigns:

1. Follow/subscribe to my communication channels.

These goals have a target of getting your audience to follow you on your mobile and social presences so you can communicate with them in the future and increase your income from future releases of music, merch, and shows. The number of followers is also proof of your popularity. For example:

- Twitter: Twitter Follow button.

- Mailing list: Mailing list subscribe form.

- YouTube: Subscribe button.

- Eventful: Demand widget.

- Facebook: Facebook fan page Like button.

2. Listen to my music and watch my videos on platforms that generate royalties.

Drive listens and watches of your content on revenue-generating platforms that generate royalties or ad share revenue. The tools can be as simple as linking to a YouTube video on your Twitter feed or a Spotify widget on your website. For example:

- YouTube: Embed the video in your website or post it on social media.

- Spotify: Spotify embedded widgets, Spotify codes, or link to the song, album, or artist pages.

- Apple Music: QR codes, or link to the song, album, or artist pages.

- Amazon Prime Music: QR codes, or link to the song, album, or artist pages.

3. Buy my music and merchandise.

Drive direct sales of your music and merch by giving your fans a way to buy it with a click or within a widget. Nearly every communication should drive these, since it's simple to provide a sentence in a blog post or social media with links to your music and merch available for purchase. For example:

- Digital music sales: Linking to directly purchase a song on digital is the most effective tool and should be an affiliate link if possible. (See chapter 13, "Advanced Income Techniques.") Also, many stores have embeddable widgets.

- Merch sales: Linking to merch from an image is the most effective tool; also include merch sales widgets into your web presences.

- Physical music sales: Links to the purchase page for CDs, vinyl, USBs, cassette, or other versions of the music.

4. Buy tickets and come to my shows.

Boost your draw by creating marketing goals around your live show attendance. These would target marketing channels appropriate for your location-based audience. For example:

- Drive ticket sales: Create links to directly purchase a ticket for your shows. This is even more effective if you can show how many tickets are left.

- Drive show attendance: If you don't have ways to handle ticket sales for a show where you only get the door, try creating a downloadable expiring discount coupon for merch, which can be used at the show.

5. Fund, tip, or financially support me.

Use your marketing to drive your crowdfunding, patronage, and tips. Fortunately, these platforms have many tools to help you do this, and the services themselves drive engagement if you can get your fans to go there. For example:

- Crowdfunding campaigns: Create links, images, and GIFs to drive fans to your crowdfunding page. Videos are also effective tools for these. Marketing messages should also show how much you have left to go to reach the goal to drive engagement.

- Tips: Tools include links to a tip application, or sites like PayPal.Me (paypal.me).

- Patronage: Make links to your crowdfunding page. Custom images with your material next to the patronage website's logo can be effective for this. Videos are also a great choice for this. Plus, you can mention patronage in each video.

6. Promote me to others.

Your fans can be the best promoters of all, considering their social reach, especially if you give them the tools. For example:

- Share my post: Make buttons or links to share your message when you put out new posts. Tools like Sharethis (sharethis.com) or Shareaholic (shareaholic.com) can be embedded to make this easy.

- Retweet/reposting: Make sure retweet or reshare buttons are available on each site for letting fans help spread your message.

- Share videos: These tools are often built into the platforms, but a marketing message asking for a share of your video can trigger more shares.

- Word of mouth: Asking for word of mouth can help drive promotion, including asking them to bring friends to shows.

7. Do business with me.

If you license your music, book shows, or do other business-to-business activity, your marketing communication to those audiences also needs to convert them. In this case, the goal is almost always to get them to contact you.

- License my music: For some artists, besides direct contact info, licensing can be handled by web services that have fixed fees and that provide links to the pages with your music.

- Book a show: For bookers, include a way to download or view a booking kit, and include contact info or a contact form.

- Other business activities: Phone number, email address, or contact forms should be available in all marketing messages, plus a call to action to get them to do business with you.

CREATE AND BROADCAST YOUR MARKETING MESSAGE

Once you know your audience, marketing goals, communication channels, and conversion tools, you're ready to put together a targeted marketing message. Each message should have an intent of promoting one or more of your goals.

The secret to creating a marketing message has a simple formula with four components, which you can remember easily with the acronym AIDA (Attention, Interest, Decision, Action). We'll go through these step by step:

1. Get their attention.

The more attention-grabbing your message is, the more likely it'll be heard and shared. It's easier to do this with images than words, which is why shareable images work so well on social media. Here are other ways to get their attention:

- Use self-identifiers: Try starting your marketing messages with the words your target audience uses to identify themselves. Are they metalheads? Ravers? Wrestling fans? Their eyes will snag on any message that includes words that are part of their identity. The most direct self-identifier is a person's own name, which you can do in email lists.

- Use eye-popping colors, fonts, and graphics: Words aren't the only thing that grab people's attention. Use all the aspects of a visual message to get noticed. Animation also works: GIFs are a much more effective way to get a message noticed than a static image. Try sites like Giphy (giphy.com) to make them.

- Put the message where they are not normally found: Find ways to make the actual content of the message stand out compared to other messages that the audience usually sees.

2. Catch their interest.

Getting someone's attention is one thing, but if they don't read to the end, your marketing won't be effective. Use these techniques to maintain their interest:

- Make targeted messages: The more the message is aimed at the person reading it, the better chance you have of holding their interest. Choose the smallest, most niche audience for each marketing message. This is where the "conquer-a-niche" strategy from below comes in.

- Ask your audience a question: Asking questions causes the person reading the message to try to answer it. This keeps them engaged and interested.

- Tease them: A tease compels people to want to read on to find out more. For example, blog entries with titles like "Five Ways to Improve Every Marketing Message You Send" causes readers to want to find out what those five ways are and satisfy their curiosity.

3. Get them to make a decision.

Your message must make it easy for them to decide they should take the action you determined in step 1. Decisions can be made easier by doing the following:

- Make the decision simple and singular: Simple decisions are more likely to succeed, such as to use one of your conversion tools, click a link, enter their email, or buy your song. Also, the decision should be for *just one action*. If you give them options, it increases the chances that they will get confused and ignore it. *Don't make them think.*

- Make the decision reversible: People are afraid of commitment. Because of this, many businesses offer a free trial that allows you to cancel within the trial period. Use this technique by reminding them they can always unsubscribe from your email list if they want to.

- Make the decision compelling: Limited time, limited quantity, or limited opportunities make the decision far more likely. Also, try to give the message a value. For example, adding a link where they can get a discount for "only a limited time" means they lose something if they ignore it. This also helps all the other AIDA parts of your marketing message.

4. Create a call to action.

Do the following to increase the likelihood they'll take action to make all of this come together:

- Use conversion tools: Your conversion tools are usually the easiest way to make sure your audience takes the action, especially if it's a single-button click.

- Make the actions achievable: If you try to get someone to buy something and they are on their mobile devices where they are in a bad position to whip out their credit card, your marketing message won't be effective. There's too much friction that prevents the purchase. For example, a physical poster is not a great place to put a link, because there's another step of taking out phones or devices and typing it in (but a QR code makes that easier). It's a good idea to assume that every message online is being seen on a mobile device.

- Tell them what to do: Don't assume that your audience knows how to do what's necessary. The action message needs to direct them: "Click this link." "Buy this song." "Pledge on Kickstarter." Be clear with your instructions.

- Make the action step stand out: Don't bury the action step under a lot of text or extraneous information. While the other parts of AIDA require text, if you don't highlight the action, they might miss what they need to do. This is where visual elements come in to help it stand out. For example, graphics artists may use advancing colors underneath buttons to attract people's eyes to the buttons that they need to push.

5. Broadcast your message.
Track your messages over time and see how well they are received, and then verify it against your marketing goals to see how your campaign is proceeding. You may have to adjust over time or try multiple messages through multiple channels to meet those goals.

Be aware of the marketing aimed at you, then notice the components of AIDA in the marketing messages you see. Determine what messages work on you and why. Then borrow these and apply them to your own messages and put them in your broadcast channels.

THE TOP FOURTEEN $0 MARKETING STRATEGIES
Making money with music and turning a onetime listener into a fan requires active promotion. Fortunately, many marketing strategies are free and within every musician's reach. Of all the over two hundred articles we've released over the last few years, our marketing strategies have received the most views and attention, and some of the best success stories from musicians we've heard when we go to conferences have been in applying these strategies below. Consider the following $0 marketing strategies for your releases:

1. The standing-out strategy.
Don't start promoting your music on big music sites or publications. They are the hardest place to get covered and have the most competition

to get their attention. For instance, National Public Radio's *"All Songs Considered"* receives two hundred to three hundred song submissions *each week* and they only feature eight. Even if you're featured, they are sandwiched in between other songs and played *just once*. The same is true with music reviews. Although they are good for getting quotes for your press kit, unless it's for a major publication and you're featured, it likely won't get you many new fans, since your review would be one of many.

Instead, think in terms of where your audience hangs out and then target those sites—especially if they don't normally feature music. For example, consider that one of the biggest sellers in the early days of CD Baby was an album about sailing. Instead of sending the album to music magazines to get reviewed, the artist instead sent the album to a popular sailing magazine.

The sailing magazine, *which wasn't used to receiving music*, ended up featuring and reviewing the album. Why? The album spoke directly to their readers. By submitting the album for review to a magazine that didn't normally receive or review music, the artist didn't have to compete against tons of other music submissions. They stood out and were noticed in a big way. Because the magazine had a large distribution, the album got a great review, and because they published exactly how readers could get the album, sales shot through the roof even though it wasn't a music magazine.

2. The piggybacking strategy.

One of the quickest ways to get noticed is to piggyback on something that's already popular and has been marketed by others. There are two easy ways to do this. First, listing other popular artists that you sound like on your website can help give new listeners a clue as to whether you're worth checking out. Second, cover a well-known song that can start out being your biggest seller but also acts as a gateway for the listener. If they like your cover, they typically check out your other music.

You can also piggyback on popular culture. For example, our own band, Beatnik Turtle, wrote a song called "Star Wars (A Film Like No Other)," which summarized the original *Star Wars* trilogy in one song. Around the same time, StarWars.com released a video mashup tool, and so we decided to make a video with actual movie clips for the song, using their tool. The video ended up becoming one of the most popular on the site, getting played over fifteen thousand times thanks to the active community. That popularity led to it getting picked up by Atom.com as a featured video, which in turn led to it being licensed to air on Spike TV to celebrate the *Star Wars* thirty-second anniversary.

Current events also provide opportunities. When a topic is hot, many people will be searching the web for information about it. With a little thought, you can be there to catch the trend, whether through the title of your blog or YouTube video, or hashtag on a well-timed tweet.

Charities are another form of piggybacking. Many artists team up with a charity to not only raise money for a good cause but also to help introduce themselves to new audiences. They do this through special live performances or albums where part of the proceeds goes to the charity. Besides teaming up with a charity, services like ReverbNation's "Music for Good" allow artists to sell songs and split revenue between a charity and the artist.

And finally, one of the most effective piggybacking strategies is to use the popularity of holidays. For example, our band's un-holiday take on Christmas music called "*Santa Doesn't Like You*," with songs such as "Coed Naked Drunk Xmas Shopping" and "Smokin' the Mistletoe," continually sells every year in December despite being over a decade old—and we don't spend a cent on marketing it. The songs naturally come up when people search on keywords like "*Santa*" or "*Christmas*."

3. The borrowed audience strategy.

Use the borrowed audience strategy to get onto a channel that already has eyes and ears paying attention to it so you can grow your own fan base. PR campaigns can get your music featured in front of that channel's audience. Others include being an opening band for a popular group, getting your video liked by a popular channel, getting on a TV show, getting in front of another artist's fan base, getting your video into a popular website, and more.

Chapter 17, "Get Heard and Seen," lists dozens of channels with borrowed audiences, and it's a great place to get ideas, but keep thinking creatively about new ones to reach and how you can get your music covered there. Most importantly, note that sometimes very large audiences can be reached by using the standing-out strategy. Any place can post a video, and sometimes, very popular websites will post yours if you can match their interests, getting you in front of their entire audience.

4. The fan street team strategy.

Today's artists are more connected with their fans than ever. And in these days of social media, every fan you have has their own followers of hundreds, if not thousands, of people for each tweet or Facebook post. Sometimes, all you have to do is ask in order to get their help to spread the word.

The key to a successful street team is to be explicit in asking what it is you want them to do, and make it easy to share your work. Videos on You-Tube are the most sharable media type. Second best are songs that are posted to music platforms that allow for easy sharing. Give your fans clear direction; ask them to post your work to their social networks—both directly or in the descriptions of the songs and as a callout at the tail end of videos.

Keep in mind you don't know what opportunities your fans may be able to create for you, and all you have to do is ask if you'd like to get the word out and make it a single click to tweet or post to get a message out there.

5. The conquer-a-niche strategy.

Yesterday's world was organized around geography; you needed to find someone physically close to you to interact. Today's internet world is organized around interests. Each niche has websites, forums, and social media that serve its community. Some have a very dedicated base of people looking for writing, media, and music that are aimed directly at their niche.

Just because a particular niche is focused doesn't mean that it's small. Soccer fans are just one niche in the world of sports, yet there's a huge community of soccer fans in the world. But the more focused the niche, the more dedicated the fan base. Because the internet allows people to organize this way, it makes it much easier to reach each niche and introduce your music to them. And if your music matches their interest in any way, you can use it to build new fan bases.

The artist Jonathan Coulton did this in his early days, because he wrote the kind of music the geek community around the website Slashdot enjoyed. With songs about mathematical concepts like "Mandelbrot Set" or music about computer programming like "Code Monkey," his music was often featured on websites related to these concepts. And as he conquered the geek-internet niche, he was able to build still larger audiences that transcended his original listeners—partly from help from fans within the niche who were employed at video game companies, through NPR, who wrote for music review sites, and more. Opportunities sprang from this, and his music later became used in video games, licensed to TV shows, and played on the radio. From there, he started to tour worldwide and sold-out venues.

6. The borrowed credibility strategy.

When your name isn't well known yet, you can have a hard time getting people to even try your music. To boost your chances, it helps to have your music associated with someone or something that is already well known and has credibility to make people take notice of you and your music.

The simplest way to do this when you're starting out is to use any accolades, music review quotes, mentions, awards, well-known places you've played, or other achievements to show potential fans that other people think you and your music are worth their attention. This technique works for the business side of your music as well. For live music, you'll want to talk about other venues you headlined, major artists or DJs you've opened for, or festivals you've played. For music licensing, you'll want to talk about licensing to well-known shows, movies, and productions.

7. The agent strategy.

Most independent artists represent themselves by getting their own gigs and deals and then negotiating for themselves. But one trick that's helped us and many other scrappy artists is to get someone to represent, sell, or negotiate for you—even if you're just starting out. Why? It's human nature to think more of someone when there's a third party acting on their behalf. Plus, the agent is one step removed from you and your music, and this frees the person to genuinely sell and promote you.

Plus, having an agent is even more useful during negotiations because they can be as tough as they need to be without tarnishing your image. If you negotiate for yourself and you give the other side a difficult time, they may not be able to separate the business from the artist.

Normally, an agent only makes a cut if they make you money, but keep in mind you don't need to hire a professional for this strategy to work; just have a friend or family member act on your behalf when dealing with journalists, bookers, licensors, or businesses. You'll find that you'll get better responses and that they'll be more likely to give you honest feedback about the music or the submissions that you make, which allows you to improve them in the future.

8. The cross-selling strategy.

All the musicians we've interviewed over the years share one thing in common: they don't just rely on playing live, selling albums, and selling merchandise; they do things outside of music. They have podcasts, record videos, write blogs, perform in other bands, create apps and games, write books, create comics, and more. Instead of compartmentalizing projects that they work on and jobs that they do, successful musicians often find ways to use every part of their life and all that they participate in to promote their music in an authentic way and find new business opportunities for their music.

As a creative person, it's likely that you too are working on other projects in other media. No matter what they are, find ways to tie them together. This is especially true if you are working with other creative people that have projects. Once you have done some work to develop an audience in any venue or project, find ways to cross-sell to them your music. Once they are familiar with some of your work, it's likely they will want to check out other things that you've done, and sometimes, you can bundle sales between your businesses.

9. The cross-promotion strategy.

Once you have an audience, you can start exploring cross-promotion possibilities with other artists, creative people, and businesses—after all, everyone is looking to reach new audiences, and you can become a borrowed audience for them. To do this, offer to promote their names and work to your fans in exchange for exposure of your music to their audiences.

This cross-promotion can be done via links to each other's work, but it becomes even more effective when you collaborate on something creative. For example, this happens in nearly every release of the Epic Rap Battles of History, where the musicians, comedians, or actors who participate in creating the song and episode get a credit at the end of each video, including links to their YouTube channels.

But it doesn't just have to be online. Our band became the musical accompaniment for a sketch comedy group called the Dolphins of Damnation, at Chicago's Second City. Besides playing behind musical sketches and in between scenes, we played a song or two in the middle of the show, similar to *Saturday Night Live*. One of the reasons the comedy group won the time slot was because the band came with an established fan base. In return, we got to play in front of *their* fan base, as well as to the people that go to comedy shows at Second City—exposing our music to a brand-new audience. This was on top of adding Second City to our live show bio (the borrowed credibility strategy!).

10. The stay-tuned strategy.
When radio DJs are about to play commercials, they never go directly to the ads. Instead, they announce what they're going to play after the break to keep people from tuning out. To help keep your fan base tuned in and paying attention, always talk about your upcoming project, show, or event. This is a key part of having a steady stream of releases as we recommend and outline in chapter 18, "Your Release Strategy," which makes it easier to promote what's coming, but there are more advantages as well. Teasing what's coming shows you're active and gives listeners and fans a reason to keep tabs and stay tuned to your channels. It helps generate interest in any patronage or crowdfunding campaign you're running. When you incorporate this with your PR with the press/media, it entices them to ask about what's next and makes it easier for you to get them to write future stories. It also motivates your team and can encourage your fans to get involved, promote you, and help out.

11. The social proof strategy.
People are most likely to pay attention to things that are already popular or showing a growing trend. This is called *social proof*, and you can use it in your marketing and promotional materials. To demonstrate this for your fan base, show any videos you have with a large number of views, social media with a lot of followers, newsletters with a large subscriber list, and other popularity numbers. For your business, list the number of customers you have. For playing live, post the large number of fans you've played to. For press, show the number of stories written about you. Each of these can demonstrate that many other people already consider you or your music worth paying attention to and makes it more likely they'll take a look. If you're just starting out, at that stage, use trends instead

of raw numbers, as that is easier to show impressive numbers. For example, if you go from one hundred to two hundred followers, your social media is growing by 100 percent.

12. The snowball strategy.

Each success gives you a reason to reach out to people, channels, and outlets who haven't covered you yet, especially if you're in the middle of a release campaign—and it's proof that you're worth paying attention to. Many musicians emulate the major labels and try to create something that will get them noticed in a short time frame. But while major labels used the one-hit-wonder business model, most other business use a much longer-term strategy: they build their name over the long term and eventually grow consistent income over time. This is not just true for making money with music; it also applies to building your fan base. With each release, album, video, or promotion you do, you can grow your audience a little bit more each time.

Also, as you get each success, add it to the chronicle we talked about in chapter 3, "Your Persona," because it adds weight to your history. Although your chronicle will have a list of every success, you can bundle your successes together into a single number after there are enough to become an impressive addition to your persona as well. For example, if you've played over one hundred shows, that shows a depth of your performing experience, and it can be useful the next time you reach out to venues to get booked and journalists to get coverage for your shows.

13. The time pressure strategy.

People respond to limited time offers, discounts which disappear, and upsells or bundles which expire. Each time you put a message in front of your customers, you can include a deadline for your products, tickets, deals, and paid events, making your messages to them valuable because they are worth money. Every communication you send out can make your fans feel like they are losing out if they don't act now to take advantage of the offer.

14. The remove barriers strategy.

In his talks, Martin Atkins tells musicians "Be more awesome than a pasta restaurant." He explains: "Olive Garden had a deal where they would watch your kids for two hours while you had dinner and drank wine. If you're wondering why you only have 14 people showing up at your show, it's because you weren't as awesome as a pasta restaurant." While taking care of their kids might bring young families out, you need to angle your marketing towards your audience. For example, Porn and Chicken in Chicago is an adult EDM show which packs the venues on Monday nights, probably the toughest night to get an audience. Each week, they feature music and a stage show around a different theme, buckets of fried chicken to eat, and (yes, really) porn (which we know doesn't work for everyone but the theme brings people in the door in their case). By blending food and entertainment they make it easy for fans to spend the weekday evening with them after work. Barriers you can remove for shows include: transportation/access to the venue, timing and availability for your shows, taking care of kids, and planning around big events and holidays. But this isn't just true for shows—think of the barriers your customers deal with for each thing you do and how you can remove those barriers within your marketing.

UNDERSTANDING METRICS AND HOW IT POWERS DATA-DRIVEN DECISION-MAKING

When generating ideas for your music business, you will likely start with your gut instincts, but any good businessperson will tell you once you try out your ideas in the real world, your decisions should be guided by real data and metrics. Without it, you will only be able to guess if your ideas are working.

Metrics can also tell you when new opportunities make sense to pursue. For instance, when our band, Beatnik Turtle, gave a demo of a song called "Were All These Beer Cans Here Last Night?" to an independent board game company who inspired it, they asked to let their fans hear it. We posted a link to a copy on our website and moved on to other projects, but once we saw it had been downloaded fifteen thousand times, we realized we had something special going on. The result was a brainstorming session that led to us creating an entire album in partnership with the company, illustrated by a well-known artist associated with them and distributed by them to their customers.

Try to capture as many of the metrics and stats listed below. Review them frequently (at least monthly) to see how your ideas are working.

1. Sales and financial metrics.

Make sure to capture your sales figures from every distribution channel and place you do business with. Anytime you have sales figures and a check, pull it in. These are the most important metrics to start with because they have a direct effect on your income.

- Distributor partner sales and streams reports.

- MRCO and PRO royalty reports.

- Product and merch partner sales figures.

- Live show merch sales. (Might need to capture this by hand.)

- Affiliate sales reports.

- Any other sales reports.

2. Social and sharing site stats.

Each social presence you are on should have stats available, which should be watched often, even daily if you are in the middle of a campaign and adjusting your message and audiences. Also, stats from social sites can be aggregated to other tools, which are sometimes worth exploring. Note, for musicians, it's rarely worth the money to pay for expanded stats because it's hard to make sales or streaming income cover for the cost.

3. Website stats.

If you have a website, you can get far more detailed info than you can get off social platforms. Your website host should have stats available, but if you can build in Google Analytics, you can get a wealth of info for free, plus good information about how to analyze it from the analytics site itself.

For musicians, among the most important stats are the referrers, which are the URLs that send visitors to your site. We often trace back each one to find out which websites are sending people to our site and how they are covering us.

4. Listener and viewer metrics.

Your listener and viewer stats are the most important metrics to use for your get-heard-and-seen campaigns. Every presence you have for your music is a potential source of the info. This data often includes location and demographic info, and it can clue you in on where you are listened to on a regional basis.

Your data sources can include the following:

- Spotify for Artists (artists.spotify.com)

- iTunes Connect (itunesconnect.apple.com)

- YouTube channel stats

- Next Big Sound (nextbigsound.com)

- Your digital distributor (the sales figures often include where and when your music is played)

5. Live show attendance, ticket sales, mailing list signups.
When starting out, live artists often just collect their part of a shared door and miss getting info about how many people came in the door for them. The best venues will ask each person who they are coming in for. If the venue is not doing it, see if you can get someone to do that for you. You can also get some metrics by giving out merch discount coupons and see how many people come to your table with them.

THE NUMBER-ONE TECHNIQUE TO APPLY TO YOUR MARKETING STRATEGIES

The excellent business book *Little Bets: How Breakthrough Ideas Emerge from Small Discoveries* by Peter Sims says ideas are only valuable if you can test to see if they work in the real world. But since trying things out is expensive, you should find as many free or low-cost ways to try out your ideas before you invest any significant resources in them. Most music businesses fail not because the music is "bad" or the musician is flawed but because the musician spends too much time or money without trying out their ideas first. The time to make a bigger bet is after you find out what works. Another excellent business book, *Decisive: How to Make Better Choices in Life and Work* by Chip and Dan Heath, has a perfect concept for music marketers called "ooching." Ooches are small experiments that are easy to run and give you results quickly. For example, trying out different marketing material for a few shows to see which works best or a short run of new merch to see which sells best.

Not only should you do these small experiments often, you can structure them as "A/B" testing (trying out two ads to see which works better). Or you can set a "trip wire"—an objective trigger you determine in advance that tells you when things aren't working so you can back out before you have sunk in too much money and time. Another method is to set a time limit. Cross the deadline without seeing success, and you can switch to something else. The point is to keep the experiments small, and the success criteria should be easy to judge.

Finally, remember to keep an open mind. Sometimes the world comes to you with an idea to try that may lead to new bets to place and opportunities to seize. For example, we didn't understand licensing until Disney came asking to license one of our songs. That led to us doing a *lot* of research and eventually finalizing a licensing agreement. That started us licensing other music in our catalog, something we never thought of doing until Disney woke us up to it.

15

PROMOTION AND PUBLICITY

Goal: To promote and publicize your music business to grow your fan base, increase sales, and promote everything you do.

Team Roles and Responsibilities: Publicist, Social Media Manager, Marketer, Web Designer/Webmaster, and Manager

WHAT YOU GET OUT OF THIS
By the end of this chapter, you will:

1. Have a structured way to promote your work directly to your fans while giving them content they want to see through your social presences, mailing lists, and other communication channels.

2. Know how to create a press/media target list for your publicity campaigns, how to create an effective press kit, and how to create and distribute press releases.

3. Know ten techniques to get the press/media to cover you, how to interview effectively, and how to use the coverage you get to keep your campaigns running.

4. Know how to advertise online.

5. Know when and how to hire a publicist.

INTRO

When your marketing really connects, your messaging will get spread and shared by your fans and the press/media will take notice. As we covered in chapter 14, "Marketing," get this started by knowing your marketing goals, your audience, your targeted messages, and your communication channels. The goal of this chapter is to give you techniques to broadcast your marketing message into the world. You have four media options available to you: owned, shared, paid, and earned. Each one relies on your marketing strategy, but each one has slightly different techniques to use.

For instance, when you share your message through your owned and social media channels, which should include a bulk of your fan base, you'll want to get your fans excited about what you're doing without looking like you're promoting yourself. For your earned media, you'll use PR techniques so you can convince the press/media to cover you and your music. Getting covered through earned media requires an entirely different approach than owned, shared, and paid media. In fact, using owned or shared media techniques can backfire when it comes to reaching out to the press/media.

When you view the world through a marketing lens and the different media channels available to you, you'll start seeing the promotion and publicity angle for everything you do in your music business. You'll start thinking about everything you have planned for your music business in light of the marketing, promotion, and publicity angle. And you'll want to give yourself enough time in advance so you can plan, coordinate, and promote your targeted messages and get press/media coverage. Every business relies on both promotion and publicity to drive its success. As Ariel Hyatt of Cyber PR (cyberprmusic.com) said, "I don't care what business you're in, big or small, unless you spend forty percent of your time on promotion and marketing, you're dead in the water." If you care about the music you've created and want to grow the amount of money you can make, the work in promoting yourself and generating coverage is a necessary cost of your music business.

OWNED MEDIA TECHNIQUES

THE TOP FIVE TOPICS YOU CAN TALK ABOUT ON YOUR OWNED MEDIA CHANNELS

The most difficult part of managing your owned media channels, which are listed in chapter 14, "Marketing," is consistently coming out with fresh material to keep fans subscribing to your channels and engaging with your posts. One thing that helps is the autoposting strategy we discussed in chapter 7, "Your Online Presences," so a new post is triggered whenever you post something new. But even if you implement this, it doesn't cover to the actual content you can post. Below are some of the types of content you can post to your owned media that your fans will want to see:

1. Talk about your releases.

In chapter 18, "Your Release Strategy," every item on "The Definition of a "Release and the Near-Endless Number of Events You Can Schedule" is a perfect topic to post in all of your owned media, and it is a massive enough list to drive months of content. Basing content on your releases generates authentic and natural messages to send out. They're what your fans want to see, because each release is new entertainment (music, videos) or provides updates on your upcoming events. When covering releases, make sure to weave in your marketing messages and your conversion tools related to the release. Also note that there are other items on that list that are worth covering, including press coverage you've gotten, new gear you've purchased, behind-the-scenes posts, and more.

2. Give them an update on your personal life.

If you feel comfortable, you can share parts of your life you want to make public. If you're not feeling comfortable sharing this on a regular basis, you should consider doing this if something happens that impacts your music or your release schedule.

3. Shine a light on others.

If your fans would be interested in someone else's work, you can get multiple things out of it. First, it's good content for them, but also you can give people whom you want to work with a boost, which can make it more likely you'll work with them in the future. We cover this concept in the social media food pyramid below, but this is also good for your owned media.

4. Talk about your genre, scene, or topics your audience is into.

Discuss topics your fans are into, such as your genre of music, local scene, and other topics they want to hear about.

5. Share resources or services that can help them.

If you understand your fans, you'll also know the kinds of things they will want to know about, and your posts can help them and provide value.

While these are good topics to cover, keep in mind each can be messaged through different media, such as video, photos, memes, animated images, audio, and more. Plus, you can share the same content in different ways and media. Lastly, be sure to weave your marketing messages into your content.

HOW TO USE MAILING LISTS TO PROMOTE YOURSELF DIRECTLY TO YOUR FANS

A mailing list is a powerful tool in messaging your fans and keeping them up to date on your activities, releases, events, products, merch, and more. According to the latest research, email lists are still one of the more effective ways to communicate directly to your fan base and have a higher engagement rate than other channels you control, including social media. Plus, your mailing list is still the best place to promote your live shows, so making sure it captures where they're located is important. Most mailing list services, which we discussed in chapter 7, "Your Online Presences," can track this. Having this data allows you to target your messages even more directly to your fans.

Here are a few key steps to using mailing lists for promotion purposes:

1. Use a template and customize it for your needs.

Mailing list tools provide many features, including templates to make your messages pleasing and engaging. You'll want to make sure the look and feel reflect your persona and match your brand. People respond to visuals, so embed graphics, photos, imagery, and videos when appropriate.

2. Release on a schedule.

Find a balance for your release schedule. Mail your list too often and they may consider it spam and unsubscribe. Mail your list too infrequently and they may forget about you. A rule of thumb is to schedule a mail out once a month. This allows you to consolidate everything you've done in the last month as well as what you have planned coming up. But keep in mind, your messaging schedule should also be in sync with your release strategy, since it will tie your messages to planned events, which qualifies as news and is usually appreciated by fans (see chapter 18, "Your Release Strategy"). Of course, you can also use it for "breaking news," such as events that weren't planned or your music getting placed in a film or a last-minute show.

3. Provide a mix of interesting material for your readers along with your promotional content.

Apply the list of topics above when creating messages to your mailing list. You should include a mix of shining a light on others, resharing interesting content, and material of interest to your fan base, which can work well with your own updates. People are much less likely to unsubscribe from your newsletters if you provide entertainment or info they want to see.

4. Keep building your list.

Most importantly, always be building your list. Naturally, you'll use your website to get sign-ups, but use all your channels to encourage people to subscribe. But also don't waste in-person and real-world opportunities to grow it as well. Ask people to sign up at your shows, while networking, and more. With smartphones, everyone is connected and can sign up anyplace, anytime.

5. Try to get press and media contacts on your list.

Encourage press and media contacts who covered you to join your mailing list as well. Some of them like to keep track of the groups they've covered or want to cover. Your scheduled messages might be able to spark coverage in the future.

SHARED MEDIA TECHNIQUES
HOW TO PROMOTE YOURSELF THROUGH YOUR SOCIAL MEDIA WITHOUT SPAMMING: THE ONLINE FOOD PYRAMID

Once you have pulled together social media platforms for your music, which we covered in chapter 7, "Your Online Presences," you will want to promote yourself without it looking like self-promotion.

If you follow the recommended release strategy outlined in chapter 18, "Your Release Strategy," you'll have natural reasons to engage your fans and followers on all your social channels on a regular basis. The messages you'll send will be what your fans want to see, because you'll be giving them new entertainment, music, videos, merch, or events. These are authentic messages themselves, and there will be no need to sneak them into your feed.

As for your other marketing messages, you'll want to follow the advice from the marketing chapter about making a marketing goal, including a call to action in the message, and using the AIDA structure for these marketing messages.

But this doesn't answer *how* to interact on a regular basis with your fans so these promotional messages don't turn them off. For this, we recommend using the social media guidelines as outlined by Ariel Hyatt, who is an expert at social network promotion. Her "Social Media Food Pyramid" outlines an effective way to engage your fans and followers so you don't overpromote yourself or your music. Here's her recommendation:

- **Direct engagement (three or four posts out of ten).**
Use three or four out of ten posts engaging directly with your followers.

- **Shine a light on others (three out of ten).**
About three of ten posts should be reserved to cross-promoting other artists or creatives. You can do this by sharing their posts or call them out in a fresh post. This type of engagement is flattering, and they'll more likely talk about you.

- **Share relevant links (two or three out of ten).**
About two or three posts should share articles, blogs, or other links you think your followers may get value out of.

- **Share photos, images, and memes (two out of ten).**
About two in ten posts should share photos and images you like. It's especially good to share photos of things you do as a musician your followers don't normally see, such as recording in the studio or setting up backstage before a show.

- **Shine a light on yourself (one out of ten).**
By the time you've done the above, your one post promoting your latest track, video, merch, or upcoming show will not turn your followers off. In fact, it'll make sense in light of everything else you talk about and gives

your fans something to repost (and if you've been shining a light on others, it's more likely to get picked up). Note that your posts don't need to be words, and if you can make an image using tools like Canva (canva.com) or animated picture instead using tools like Giphy (giphy.com) it's more likely to be shared.

PAID MEDIA TECHNIQUES
HOW TO USE ONLINE ADVERTISING CHANNELS TO PROMOTE YOU AND YOUR MUSIC

Advertising yourself and your music online is another promotional option now within reach of every musician, including those on a tight budget. To get your paid-for ad, promoted post, song, or video in front of the right eyeballs, you'll want to carefully plan. Here are steps to follow and some of the key points to consider:

1. Make an income-based marketing goal.
Since ads cost money, there's a risk you may spend more money on the advertising than the income it generates, especially because selling music is a low-margin sale. To help mitigate or moderate the amount of money you spend, you should set a threshold amount to spend and an advertising goal. You'll then want to monitor the advertising stats and your sales, streams, views, or other goals to see if it's achieving what you set out to do (discussed below). If it doesn't, it probably makes more sense to avoid using ads and use the free methods from chapter 14, "Marketing."

2. Choose your marketing channels.
See "The Top Six Places to Advertise" below for a list to target.

3. Limit the ads to your targeted audience.
Most advertising platforms today allow you to target and limit ads to specific segments of the population. If you've narrowed down your audience based on your work from chapter 14, "Marketing," you can plug this into the ad tools and make a message directly aimed at them. Depending on how advanced the advertising platform is and the data they have, you may be able to target specific subsets of your demographic, particular locations, or closely related audiences.

4. Create targeted advertising messages.

Using the work you did in chapter 14, "Marketing," create ads that speak to your audience and drive engagement and interaction. Note that you might make multiple ads for each audience you're targeting or for A/B testing (below). Some platforms will help you create variations or optimize your ads based on their data and expertise.

5. Test your ads for effectiveness via A/B testing.

Advertising platform tool sets today often allow you to test different ads at the same time so you can see which ones work better. This is known as A/B testing and is worth doing if you've created multiple ads.

6. Use the metrics and adjust your campaign over time.

Most online advertising services provide detailed metrics so you can keep an eye on your advertising campaign and see if it's living up to your goals. It pays to research the terminology and understand how these platforms work so you can understand the data they're reporting.

THE TOP SIX PLACES TO ADVERTISE

Below are just a few places you can advertise. There's a nearly endless array of places to do so, but these are good ones for musicians to check out.

1. Google AdWords.

Google AdWords (adwords.google.com) can get your website to come up among search results that might match your music. There's good value in getting your name to appear even if it doesn't get clicks because it gives you further legitimacy as you grow your fan base to achieve the first page organically.

2. YouTube video ads.

YouTube video advertising (youtube.com/yt/advertise) can get your video ads shown targeting your demographics. Considering many people use YouTube for watching music, it's a potentially good place to target.

3. ReverbNation Promote It.

ReverbNation Promote It (reverbnation.com/band-promotion/promote) can get you advertising and promotion on a group of music-related outlets all at the same time, including Spotify, Amazon, MTV, Pitchfork, Rolling Stone, and more.

4. Facebook.

Facebook allows you to do good targeting due to the enormous amount of information they have on each user. They also charge you to reach the full number of followers to your fan pages, which are the most targeted groups you can choose.

5. Twitter promoted tweets.

If you are a Twitter user, a Twitter promoted tweet (ads.twitter.com) could be the perfect place to run an ad to get followers and exposure.

6. Offline ads.

Naturally, you can also use ads on magazines, newspapers, billboards, and more. Reach out to each source's ad department to find out how to place these. Note that these are likely to be more effective at increasing your revenue if you can establish yourself as an entertainment destination for your town, coordinated with other campaigns.

EARNED MEDIA TECHNIQUES
UNDERSTANDING TODAY'S MEDIA LANDSCAPE

With smartphones everywhere, more and more people are consuming mass, new, and social media more frequently than ever. In the past, people could only tune in when they turned on the TV, flipped on the radio, or grabbed a newspaper. But today, people are reading, listening, and watching media at all hours of the day and during activities that never were possible before, such as during work or while walking down the street.

Plus, the lines between new and traditional media are more blurred than ever. The mainstream and traditional media outlets now have extensive online and social media presences while some new media has the authority of the mainstream media. There have been two major shifts in media. First, the internet lowered the barrier to entry, increasing competition. Second, the media business model increasingly relies on online advertising as a key source of revenue, making these companies focus on increasing page views, video views, and click-throughs to justify their advertising fees. This means those making the choices of what to cover—editors, journalists, bloggers, reporters, media personalities, and more—are competing for fresh, exciting, and human-interest content to constantly grab eyeballs. It also means some seek sensational headlines, human drama, or controversies to spark commenting (and clicks) on their sites.

This means more media is within the reach of more musicians than ever before. If you want to get noticed and generate publicity for what you're doing, you need think in terms of what these gatekeepers behind the scenes want: engaging human-interest stories, fresh content and scoops, and stories that generate conversation or controversy. Your goal is to give them the kind of stories, entertainment, and images that can catch their attention—the right kind of story you pitch to them about you and your music or the right type of video, song, or social media update you post can catch their interest. And, if it does, they'll shine their spotlight on you, getting you in front of the audience they cater to, and possibly growing your following and generating additional revenue. Plus, you'll rack up another publicity success to snowball into yet more coverage.

And, when it comes to the mainstream media and major publications, one of the secrets they haven't told you is that their online blogs typically have less editorial oversight. This means the bar for getting covered by an established media player is even more in reach than ever before. Get your music covered on those and it can carry the same weight as if you were covered in the main publication or channel itself.

THE TOP TEN TECHNIQUES TO GET THE MEDIA TO COVER YOU

Once you understand the media landscape, you can write more targeted emails, press releases, and posts aimed at their needs.

1. Getting publicity is still about who you know.

Your personal relationships are the best place to start to get stories. In fact, the primary reason people hire professional publicists is to leverage their existing relationships. This is also why it helps to designate a team member to be your publicist, as they will start building those relationships over time.

2. Keep your emails short and clearly ask what you want.

Many musicians (and some publicists) write lengthy and meandering emails, which confuse the press and media contacts they're hoping to influence to cover them. As Michael Molenda, editor of *Guitar Player* magazine, who receives fifty to a hundred email submissions from musicians *a day*, said, "I'll get emails that blather about their influences, what car they drive, but I swear I'll scroll down three paragraphs and have no idea what they're asking me to do. This transcends talent. You may have a great song that deserves to be covered, but you lost me by not getting to the point." Use the same AIDA writing techniques we discussed in chapter 14, "Marketing." Keep your emails short, and spell out your ask in the subject line. Use the second or third sentence to spell out exactly what you want them to do. Provide links or MP3s to the exact song you want them to review or video you want them to discuss.

3. Give them a scoop and special access.

Press and media contacts love breaking a story before anyone else as well as getting access to knowledge, information, music, and content the public doesn't have access to yet. One way to use this to your advantage is to reach out to them before your release to give them an exclusive look before anyone else. Sharing prerelease material or providing artist access for interviews to your media contact can be an incentive for them to check you out. Also, don't forget to add them to your guest lists of your shows.

4. Solve *their* problems by aiming the content at *their* readers.

Put yourself in their shoes. Press and media contacts are looking for angles on stories that fit their publication and their readers' interests. Most think in terms of clicks and views for their target demographic. Your press and media list research (see the section below) should give you an idea of the types of stories the press or media contact you're targeting covers. Match their style and content in your request, and write a brief, targeted email pitch.

5. Use polite persistence.

Press and media contacts are extremely busy people. They often don't write back because they're staring at hundreds or thousands of emails in their in-box. Many times, as Michael Molenda noted, emails can go ignored for two reasons. First, they come into the same in-box as his work emails, so your email may compete against his other work and deadlines. Second, some days he doesn't have the time to dig in and when the next day hits, your email winds up two pages back in his in-box. So you can't take it personally when a press or media contact doesn't respond. Instead, "go until a no." Very often, it's the second, third, or fourth email that catches their attention. Keep sending follow-up emails until they call you off (or if their submission policy asks you not to). Also, the unanswered emails keep them aware of what you're doing, even if they don't respond; don't assume that they are not reading them just because they didn't answer, but also make sure your subject line has what you want them to know in case it's all they read. That said, if they do say no, it doesn't mean "no forever to everything you do," just that one pitch. Polite persistence also means you will want to submit new stories in the future and never resubmit the one they rejected.

6. Never make them wait.

Whenever a press or media contact responds or reaches out to you for an interview, music review, or story, don't make them wait! They're likely trying to hit an imminent deadline. Be responsive and get them what they need, when they need it, or you might miss out on coverage.

7. Snowball and ladder up.

Once you get coverage, send the link or clipping to other press and media contacts you're trying to work with, since it might trigger them to cover it. Also, you'll want to snowball coverage success in other areas you're working on. For instance, a good music review can help your get-heard campaign, and radio play could spark a music review or interview. Also use the ladder technique: reach up to bigger outlets after you get coverage, with the first rung of the ladder being the blogs of major publications, which tend to have less editorial oversight and need a lot of content. Coverage in these blogs can add a major name to your press list, which lets you ladder up to even larger outlets.

8. Send a thank-you and follow-up after getting coverage.

A simple thank-you message to the person who covered you makes a big difference after you get press coverage. That person is more likely to cover you in the future, especially if you keep the relationship warm.

9. Two steps forward, one step back.

After getting coverage, you might get a spike in traffic to your website or video views but know the traffic will drop down once the story ages out of people's attention. But even though the attention drops, each one can get you new fans, subscribers, and followers. This is a great way to grow your fan base. This is all the more reason a sustained publicity effort is necessary.

10. Two ways to get coverage: press campaigns and being easy to contact.

At first, you'll be actively pursuing and contacting the press and media to cover you, but once you're established and known, they will contact you. Be easy to reach, responsive, and available when they decide to cover or interview you. If you're well known, you'll likely need a publicist or team member to act as one for you so you don't miss anything and filter out the ones you don't wish to talk to.

HOW TO CREATE A PRESS AND MEDIA TARGET LIST FOR YOUR PUBLICITY CAMPAIGNS

Building your own press and media target list is important, not only for knowing who specifically to reach out to but for keeping track of who covered you and for building your relationships with the media over time. Use these steps to generate ideas on where you can get covered:

1. Add media outlets that have covered you before.

Outlets that covered you in the past are the most likely to cover you in the future. Download a copy of each coverage for archive purposes and pull out the best quotes for your press kit. And make sure to also capture the names of the individuals who wrote the story, did the podcast, or recorded the video so you can research them (as we talk about below).

2. Add media outlets you or your team and network are connected to.

Go through your media list and see if you're connected to any people at the outlets you listed. Check with your bandmates, team, friends, family, fans, and anyone else in your network to see who they might know. And, if you use it, don't forget LinkedIn, which can show you if you already know someone who has a connection to them. Once you have this, ask them to introduce you.

3. Add media outlets that have covered artists similar to you.

Follow the steps outlined in "The Number-One Way to Find Out Where Your Fans Hang Out" in chapter 14, "Marketing," on artists who sound similar to you so you can see where they've been covered and who wrote about them.

4. Add media outlets from additional sources.

Sources like the Indie Bible (indiebible.com) provide a list of press and media outlets and contacts interested in covering music. These are sorted by outlet type, location, and genre so you can better augment your list. Also, the list of forty-five categories from chapter 17, "Get Heard and Seen," includes universes of publications, blogs, podcasts, TV options, radio options, magazines, and more, which can be a good list to generate ideas for your press and media research. The research you do for your get-heard-and-seen campaigns can help here, since many places to get heard also review music, interview artists, and are looking for stories.

5. Research the people themselves, not just the outlets.

Using the list you compiled of any press or media contact who covered you previously, do some research to help you angle and pitch future stories, since they're most likely to be interested. Besides, if you want press or media contacts to be interested in you, start with being interested in *them*. Since many are freelancers, you may discover they write for other outlets. This can be one way to expand your coverage fairly easily. Also, people in the media move around within the industry frequently, so you'll want to follow their careers and see if they'll write about you in their new outlets. Explore their social media, websites, and LinkedIn profiles. Read their other published stories and find out what they've covered before. Discover the audiences they tend to write for and the kinds of stories their blogs, podcasts, videos, or outlets normally cover. Then compose a message using some of the marketing techniques we discussed in chapter 14, "Marketing," to increase your chances once you reach out.

HOW TO MAKE A PRESS KIT

You still need a press kit in today's media landscape because it provides a single source where press and media contacts can learn more about you. Since they're often time-strapped, they want an easy way to put together a story. Your press kit can give them all the necessary background they need to write about you, including paragraphs they can lift wholesale into their story. Having your pictures, bio, and info in one place ensures they have what they need. Your press kit should have the following:

1. An online home.

You should have a single place online for journalists and anyone who wants to cover you to get the contents of your press kit. You can do this through your website; sites like ReverbNation (reverbnation.com) or Sonicbids (sonicbids.com); or non-music press kit sites like Presskit.to (presskit.to).

2. Artist bio.

We talked about bios in chapter 3, "Your Persona," and the one for your press kit should be ready to cut and paste directly into an article about you. It needs to include the kind of details they would write themselves as if they had done the research and should be aimed at readers of entertainment sites as an audience.

3. Press-ready photos and multiple versions of your logo.

You need multiple press-ready photos and logos, high and low resolution, ready to download and use. Include the photographer info, since the press and media are required to credit photos and images in their story. What you'll want to give them, as much as possible, is not only the story to write but also the photos that go along with the story, all of which are needed for them to add a new story to their site. Also, don't be afraid to share animated images. Some news outlets like using those as well.

4. Press clippings and interviews.

Press quotes, clippings, and interviews provide real-world, objective proof of your success. Plus, the right clippings can make members of the media feel as if they've been missing out on something great they should cover for themselves. Choose the best quotes and snippets. If you have a feature article about you, include it in its entirety, and consider adding a scan of it so they can see it in context of the website that covered you. Note that fan reviews and quotes, also known as testimonials, are also fair game, but should be a secondary choice.

5. Praises and accolades.

Share any praise from notable people. Also share any accolades like awards, contest wins, or best-of lists you're on. This should be captured in your chronicle to make it easy to write about in the future.

6. Info sheet.

Make writing a story about you easy by providing all your details in one place. Your chronicle can help provide the material for this. Include your name, genre, artists you sound like, one-sentence bio, your website, date founded, hometown, discography, band members, radio plays, live show info, press quotes, and upcoming projects. Include any impressive summary numbers from your chronicle, such as social media stats, number of views for your top videos, major sales figures, and any other numbers that stand out. Review your info sheet monthly and add to it as you get more press, plays, and media exposure.

7. Your music.

Provide links to your music and videos so they can hear and watch your material. Depending on the outlet, know they may share these links as well, so make sure you only include your best tracks. You can use tools like Songlink (song.link) to make a page that links to multiple places to hear your music.

8. Your videos.

Share and embed your best videos. This will often be the first place they will go to experience your music.

9. Press releases.

Add prior press releases to the kit so they can see what you've done before.

10. Show calendar.

If you play live, post your prior show calendar to demonstrate your live credentials.

11. Online ads, PDFs of flyers, and posters.

Any material you use to promote yourself can also be good material for your press kit. For online materials, it's even better if they are animated.

12. All your links.

Provide links to your social media, websites, blogs, YouTube channels, and every web, social, and mobile presence you maintain. Make a special section for the links to every way they can subscribe to you and follow you, plus a way to subscribe to your mailing list if you have one. The more journalists keep up with you and your music, the more likely they'll want to cover you in the future.

THE TOP SIX TECHNIQUES TO USE IN PITCHING COVERAGE OF YOUR MUSIC

Below are concepts that can help you write your stories and run your publicity campaigns. These can angle how you plan your releases with promotion in mind:

1. Think publicity, always.

If you think publicity whenever you plan your upcoming events, releases, content, and the music you'll be creating, you can build media appeal into everything you do. This is what marketers do, and it makes a publicist's life that much easier. Each thing you do should have a publicity component so it helps you keep a steady stream of potential stories you can pitch to your press/media list (which we discuss below). For example, our band, Beatnik Turtle, generated press by releasing one song every day for a year. While the artists in us focused on the music, the businesspeople in us couldn't help but think of the project with publicity in mind. The challenge we put on ourselves was unique enough to generate coverage and interest both when we began and when we ended the project successfully. Note that even if your story doesn't get covered, the stream of engagement to the media will make them more aware of you and might result in future coverage.

2. PR is an ice pick.

Although your instinct might be to angle your stories toward as broad an audience as possible, make your story narrow and targeted to give it the best chance to be covered. You might end up writing the same story in many different ways to angle it at different media outlets, but this will raise your chances of getting covered.

3. PR is a Crock-Pot, not a microwave.

PR takes place in people-time, not internet-time. This means that publicity is usually a campaign rather than a single effort. It usually takes sustained efforts over a period of time to get coverage rather than a few all-out attempts, partly because it takes time to get your name known. But those initial contacts are what start the name recognition, which pays off later as you keep up your media efforts.

4. Controversy and sex.

As the book *Trust Me, I'm Lying: Confessions of a Media Manipulator* by Ryan Holiday revealed, the press may not admit it, but it wants stories about controversy, sex, and anything that will make great clickbait. He would use self-described "underhanded" techniques such as "leaking" information to them about controversial topics so he could get coverage in their outlets. For instance, in promoting films for his entertainment clients, he'd share arguments, lewd details, and crooked behind-the-scenes stories to generate interest in writing a story about the movie coming out. These techniques worked, because the media knows these types of stories get clicks, and he could deliver them. The history of music coverage is filled with stories like these, and because the media still looks for it, you should be aware this type of angle may work for you and your music, if you feel comfortable using them based on your persona.

5. Add a deadline to the story.

You'll have an easier time getting the press and media to pay attention to you if there's an expiration date to your story. This adds a sense of urgency to covering you and your story. Live events and tours have built-in ticking clocks. And if you follow the release strategy, your scheduled releases and other planned events will help create a sense of urgency with the media contact, since you can say with confidence your release or event will happen on a specific date.

6. If you didn't get covered, it didn't happen.

While you can write about things that you've done in your own blog or web presences, it's far more effective to use what the press has said about you and provide a press clipping for each notable event instead.

HOW TO WRITE A PRESS RELEASE

Press releases are not used by all entertainment-focused publicists, who often use more informal messages to try to get coverage. One of the more effective ways to get their attention is to simply make a short video using your phone, and you may want to explore that before making a formal press release. But if you achieve a certain level of success and notoriety, you'll be submitting stories to more mainstream media outlets, and many need a formal press release. To write a press release, follow these guidelines:

- **Length.**
A press release should be one page long.

- **Contact information.**
Include a name, phone, and email and URL at the top of each page.

- **Release date.**
If there's a date the story should be released (such as the release date of an album), put it at the top. Otherwise, add "For Immediate Release."

- **Headline.**
The headline, often written in all caps, should be designed to catch the press and media contact's attention as well as their readers. It's a good idea to write a title that teases the story.

- **The lead (or lede).**
This lead is the first sentence or two of the press release. A news release should answer the questions who, what, when, where, why, and how. A feature story should have a hook or story that is of human interest, attention-grabbing, controversial, or amusing.

- **The press release text.**
Tell your story briefly and succinctly, and make it as compelling as possible. Make it cut-and-paste ready so they could run with the story as is.

- **Call to action.**
The best press releases have a call to action.

- **Mention recent and future projects.**
Near the end, it's a good idea to mention recently finished projects as well as future ones. You never know what the press will pick up on.

- **Provide high-quality photos with attribution.**
Include press-ready photos with attribution with your press release, and it will make it even more likely they'll cover you. Journalists need to in-

clude photos with stories, and if you can give them the whole package, you'll increase the chances of coverage.

- **Have someone else proofread it.**
Spell-check and grammar-check the release, and get other people to look at it to find any mistakes.

- **Submit it to PR newswires.**
Start with free press wires you can use, such as Music Industry News Network (mi2n.com) and Free Press Release (free-press-release.com). You can also use paid services like Story Amp (storyamp.com).

Rather than writing your own, you can also hire a press release service to write them for you. If you are looking for help, besides sites like Upwork (upwork.com) and Fiverr (fiverr.com), you can also check out Mi2N's Press Release Copywriting Service (mi2n.com).

HOW TO PREPARE FOR INTERVIEWS TO MAXIMIZE YOUR MESSAGE

Interviews are much like stage performances: you need to practice for them just as you'd practice for a show. The difference is you will never be exactly sure what questions you'll be asked. Here are some techniques that will help you prepare:

1. Research the interviewer.
A few minutes of searching the web on the person interviewing you can reveal a lot, including their point of view and the kinds of stories they write. If you can find their blog, you can see what they have been up to lately and can bring this up when you first meet with them. And Twitter feeds and social media can give you up-to-the-minute info about them. This can give you an instant connection that can make the interview go well.

2. Know what to expect.
Your interviewer usually has an idea of the story that they want to tell. Most of the time, they are interviewing you to fish for original quotes that will match their story (which they often have partially composed—sometimes in their head) and perhaps fill in some details that weren't

covered in your press release or press kit. It's rarer to get a feature story, where they'll interview you to learn what you're really about. Your goal during the interview is to give the interviewer what they're looking for while blending in the talking points you want to get across.

If it's not a Q&A-style piece about your music, you'll be lucky to see more than two actual quotes from a one-hour interview. You don't have much control over these stories except for how you answer questions and the points that you manage to squeeze in. Unfortunately, it's pretty common to be disappointed in how they're presented and the quotes they choose to use. Also, the press and media are human and so often get at least one thing wrong in every article or interview they do. For instance, they may misspell your name, get your website address wrong, tell the story out of order, or take something you said out of context. This is also why you will normally just take one or two quotes out of the article for your press list. The good news is you can combat some of these problems with talking points and sound bites.

3. Prepare talking points and sound bites.

Talking points are short, prepackaged statements that focus on the messages you want the interviewer to include, which can help control the message and get them to cover what you wanted them to say. You'll want to prepare these ahead of the interview and rehearse them. Also, you'll want to prepare short answers to common questions, such as "Who are your influences?" and "Where do you get your ideas?" If the interview seems to be getting off track, you should try to help by pulling it back to your talking points, because you'll have that ready to go.

4. Prepare stories and anecdotes.

Have stories ready to go for interviews. Engaging, dramatic, or engaging stories can give the interviewer a hook to use to build the story. You'll want your stories to align to your messaging and persona. Stories make live media like radio and television truly memorable.

5. Give them fact sheets and follow-ups.

When the interview is done, you should send your interviewer a thank-you and reiterate some of the key messages you discussed. You can also include some additional points and offer to clarify anything you think was unclear. Beyond increasing the accuracy of their stories, it also will help cement your relationship with the interviewer, which is another important objective, since you want more coverage in the future.

THE TOP SIX THINGS YOU SHOULD DO ONCE YOU'RE COVERED

When you get covered, consider doing these actions each time so you can snowball your efforts and make it easier for the next publicity campaign.

1. Write a "thank-you" and establish a relationship.

The places most likely to cover you in the future are the ones that have already covered you once before. If you get a positive mention such as a review or comment, consider doing the following:

- Contact the person to acknowledge the coverage and send a "thank-you." The sooner the better. Then save the email, as you should use this thread in the future to promote your next event/release.

- Add the person to your press contacts for future publicity campaigns, since people who write about you are the ones most likely to write about you again in the future.

- Send the person some music or a sneak preview of your next release.

2. Save a copy of the coverage and keep an archive.

If you have a story that's online, it might be gone next week. You have no guarantee that it will hang around on the web. Since we've been around for over twenty years, many of the review links of our music no longer exist (even some of the publications don't exist anymore!). Save the story when it comes out. We prefer using tools like Scrapbook for Firefox (addons.mozilla.org/en-US/firefox/addon/scrapbook), which captures not only the text but also the web page and all the images. We also use tools like Evernote (evernote.com) to save the text as well as to store downloaded podcasts or video coverage we received.

3. Update your press kits, quote pages, and public presences.

Now that you have coverage, update all your press materials online and off. Also, consider talking about it in your blog, Twitter, Facebook, or any of your web presences.

4. Keep an eye on any website coverage's comments.

The comments on stories can often give you very interesting feedback or even more quotes. Sometimes, you can even get in touch with commenters and make a relationship with them by reaching out.

5. Share your coverage with other outlets and snowball the coverage.

Snowball the coverage by using it as an excuse to reach out to your press and media contacts who haven't covered you. It's also an opportunity to break into press and media outlets that haven't covered you yet. Send them a link to the coverage you received and highlight some quotes from it. Remember, go upward as well as sideways to other outlets. For example, you can use press coverage to try to break into a new target for your next get-heard-and-seen campaign (which we'll discuss in chapter 17, "Get Heard and Seen").

6. Send the coverage to your fans and social media.

Reward any outlets that cover you by sending your fan base there and increasing their traffic. Cover it on your social media, blogs, newsletters, and any of your other communication channels. It's great content for them. You can also share your social media posts with the journalist that they may want to see.

HOW TO HIRE A PUBLICIST

Publicists can provide some key services, such as help you assemble a press kit and edit your bio, pitch stories to their press and media contacts and get you coverage, run and follow up on press campaigns, create press releases and submit them under their name, collect press clippings for your press kit, and set up and coordinate interviews. To hire a publicist, do the following:

1. Figure out your budget.

Like advertising, there's a risk you could spend more money on publicity than the income it generates you in return, since the benefits of publicity are often hard to measure. To help mitigate this, you should set a threshold amount to spend and set publicity goals. You'll then want to monitor the publicist's progress to see if the publicist is achieving what you set out to do.

2. Choose a publicist.

Search for a publicist in your area or use services like Cyber PR (cyberprmusic.com). Note that many publicists have skills and services that include marketing, persona creation, and more.

3. Share information and use the publicist effectively.

If you hire a publicist and are comfortable with their approach, experience, and contact list, there's quite a lot you've developed that you can share with them so they can help you. First, send them your current press kit, which should include your best music and videos. Second, share your press list, since a good publicist will be better able to use every connection you've already made. Third, share your release strategy and all the upcoming events and releases you have scheduled. Lastly, they may be interested in your brand style guide you created in chapter 3, "Your Persona." Each publicist will have their own working style, but once you hire them, you should make them a key part of your team, connect with them often, and keep them updated on your plans so they can help you think publicity, always.

16

GET GIGS AND PLAY LIVE

Goal: To create a killer live show and plan, book, and promote your live events so you can get more fans, sell more music, and boost merchandise sales.

Team Roles and Responsibilities: Booking Agent, Live Show Promoter, Live Event/Tour Manager, Live Music Producer, Store Clerk, Live Sound Engineer, Lighting Engineer, Roadies, Video Producer, Cameraperson and Microphone Operators, and Manager

WHAT YOU GET OUT OF THIS

By the end of this chapter, you will:

1. Create an effective booking kit and plan for getting gigs, as well as have an understanding of the numerous live show opportunities available today.

2. Know the six things you need to do to put together a killer live show.

3. Have a structured plan for running a live show, including eleven things to do before, thirteen things to do during, and ten things to do after the show to ensure you're booked again, maximize exposure, and promote your music.

4. Know the eleven places to promote each show to boost your draw.

5. Run an engaging merch table that draws a crowd and maximizes sales.

6. Know how to livestream your performances to generate revenue or use as a special reward to fans.

MONEY MAP

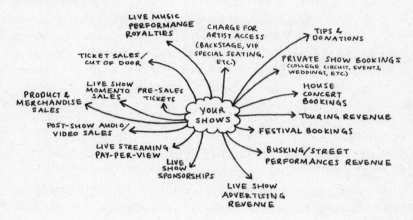

INTRO

There is huge income discrepancy between sales, streaming, publishing, and touring in the recent *Billboard* breakdowns of the revenue for the highest-paid musicians (billboard.com/photos/7865108/highest-paid -musicians-2016-money-makers). The article also examines the biggest source of income between sales, publishing, streaming, and touring. Touring almost always provided the most income by far.

With streaming revenue low and digital download music sales dropping fast, it's live sales that provide the most consistent source of income. After all, a show can't be pirated or stolen. Plus, people want experiences and are willing to pay for them. The question is: Can you grow your own shows into experiences? Will it be more than you just performing your music on a stage?

Playing live is one of the best ways to get new fans and promote yourself. We asked both Jim DeRogatis, music editor for *The Chicago Sun-Times* and cohost of NPR's *Sound Opinions*, and Todd Martens, a music writer who has written for *Billboard* magazine and *The Los Angeles Times*, how they find out about new bands. Their answer: live shows. After all, the larger venues want to get people in the doors, and if you are playing at one of them, you are worth checking out. When these music editors couple the "buzz" they hear on the web and through their personal connections with seeing the band's name playing a show, they check them out.

Getting to those venues takes time, but it's no secret: you need to put on great shows. Shows that connect emotionally with your audience. Shows that create big moments. Shows that leave the audience hungry for more. How to build a great show to do that is part of what we'll discuss in this chapter, but we can boil it down to one sentence: you are there for the audience, not the other way around. Your audience wants to be entertained, and even transformed, and you can do this by connecting with your audience, leaving a lasting impact so they become fans.

KEY CONCEPTS
FIVE KEY CONCEPTS MUSICIANS NEED TO KNOW ABOUT BOOKING AND TOURING TODAY

The internet and services for musicians have changed everything for how musicians can tour today. From using tools to choose the best places to hold their shows, to giving ways for their fans all over the world to experience a streamed version of their live shows, there are better options than ever to organize, plan, and execute your live shows. Use these concepts to angle your shows and the income streams generated by them:

1. You can go to where your fans are.
With the wealth of demographic information available to you about your fans, you can plan your tour around where they are located rather than touring in concentric circles around your home city to build a fan base. For example, using tools like Tweepsmap (tweepsmap.com), you can map your Twitter followers. And Eventful (eventful.com) gives you widgets to build into your website to let fans demand you play in their area, plus a notification tool that lets them know when you head their way. There's a broad array of other fan info tools, and any time you get locations with your fan demographics, use it to help plan your tours and target their locations. The most personalized form of this is house concerts.

2. Your fans worldwide can also be part of your live performances.

Let your fans worldwide take part in your live shows by streaming your performances. Many of the venues you would play at have at least Wi-Fi if not camera setups available, and you can live-stream your shows using the techniques we share in this chapter. This is a big change, because you are a worldwide artist from the moment you make your music available on the internet and on streaming services. You should give those fans the opportunity to experience your live shows too. This can be as simple as using Periscope with a phone or as fancy as a multicamera setup. You can monetize these shows as well as we discuss below.

3. Let your posters, flyers, and merch sing through QR codes.

Any poster, flyer, or piece of merch can be an audiovisual experience through QR codes. They should include music listening options, such as a Spotify code, and QR codes to your videos to let them see you play live.

4. Give your whales, dolphins, and minnows what they want.

As we talk about throughout this book, you should segment your audience into how much they pay, and give each of them what they want. For live shows, this means minnows usually only pay door; dolphins buy merch and bring friends; and whales pay for VIP seating, backstage access, and after-show hangouts and want premium, high-end merch. Your shows should have something for each of them so you can make the most income from your live performances.

5. Be skeptical about "pay to play."

There's a growing trend for musicians to have to pay to play at venues. This means the venue wants you to purchase a number of tickets, which you're responsible for selling. When you treat music as a business, ask yourself if spending this money will make you more money afterward. This rarely is the case for these shows. The only exception might be if you're just starting out to get your first show.

PREPARING TO GET BOOKED

HOW TO CREATE A BOOKING KIT FOR YOUR BAND

Unless you're booking at a tiny venue, the talent buyer will want to see your booking materials. They will want to know where else you've played, what kind of music you play, your draw, and whether you are reliable, since nearly every venue has had musicians flake on them.

Press kits have migrated from physical stacks of paper to being purely online. You can build one on your website or use services like Sonicbids (sonicbids.com), ReverbNation (reverbnation.com), myPPK Power Press Kits (powerpresskits.com), or ShowSlinger (showslinger.com). You can also use broker services like Afton (myafton.com).

Remember the marketing goal of a booking press kit is to get you booked, which is very different from your regular press kit, which has a goal of trying to convince an audience of journalists to write about or cover your band in a story. You may need to adjust your stories, bios, and materials to angle it toward what a booker wants to know and make it as likely as possible they'll book you.

Your booking kit should include:

1. Your contact information on every single page.

Your contact info is the most important part of the booking kit because your goal is to get talent buyers to reach out to you. Make that simple by making sure your contact information is easily found everywhere. Add it to every page of your paper kits, since they often get separated. If online, it should be along the side, top, or bottom of the page.

2. Your band bio.

Your bio should focus on the live aspect or your music and show off your value as a band.

3. Music samples.

Include links to your music (Spotify codes or QR codes are a good idea on physical pages) or, if they insist, a CD of your latest album.

4. Press clippings.

Press clippings and quotes are effective ways to get venues excited about your act. Sometimes, it also helps to have a list of prior show dates to convince a new venue you're an experienced band.

5. An eight-by-ten photo.

Include an eight-by-ten-inch band photo with the photographer attribution, as this is the size most often used by venues. It's a good idea to provide a color and black-and-white version, as they sometimes do make print ads out of it.

6. Live videos.

Possibly the most effective part of your press kit would be YouTube videos of your live show, which can prove, better than anything else you can provide, your band can perform.

7. Testimonials.

Providing testimonials to talent buyers can provide just what they need to see to make the commitment.

8. Set lists.

If you're a cover band, provide a list of songs you play. If you play only originals, you can provide it if your songs are well-known enough to be recognized. If they aren't, just stick with the streaming and video versions of your music.

9. Live requirements, stage chart, instrumentation, booking/pricing info.

Provide any further info needed by the engineers, stage crews, or talent buyers.

BOOKING GIGS AND TOURING

HOW TO BOOK LIVE SHOWS

Booking gigs is another of those art forms that could fill a book by itself, but we will cover the most important steps below:

1. Designate a booker.

Assign a single person to handle bookings, whether you do it yourself, use a pro booker, or choose someone on your team to do it. You don't want any problems when two different bookers lock down shows on the same date or create confusion among the venue bookers over whom they should talk to. Great bookers love people, have a thick skin to deal with rejection, and are persistent.

If you decide to get a booking agency, you may need to choose an exclusive or nonexclusive agreement with them. In an exclusive booking arrangement, all your bookings go through the agency, the booker will be listed as your main contact, and your booker will get a cut of every gig you get whether they found it or not. In a nonexclusive agreement, you can still find bookings through others. Either way, you should have a clear, signed agreement with your booker that includes an out clause: an agreed way to terminate the relationship if it doesn't work.

2. Make a list of target venues.
Make a target list by finding similar artists to you in your city, and search where they've played to try to get a gig in the same venues. Even better, try to open for them or play a show with them. Otherwise, you can use venue listings like the Indie Venue Bible (indievenuebible.com), Indie on the Move (indieonthemove.com), and GigTown (gigtown.com), or tools like Sonicbids (sonicbids.com) to find open bookings. For events and parties, try out sites like GigMasters (gigmasters.com). And if you want to talk with other musicians to see if you can cross-book with other artists, check out the forums at Just Plain Folks (jpfolks.com).

3. Use scheduling tools.
Create an online calendar and clearly mark the dates you've already booked for your booker. If you have a band, mark down all dead dates that cannot be booked if any band member is busy. Google has one of the better free, shareable online calendars for this. If you have a larger show, try more advanced tools like Master Tour (eventric.com/products/master-tour), and if you need to coordinate merch to arrive too, check out atVenu (atvenu.com).

4. Setting a price and getting paid.
When setting prices, consider how much you *need* to do the show, rather than how much you think you're *worth*. This will give you a solid basis for your price quote. You'll also have a better idea of how far you can bend on the prices that you set.

Make sure you are clear on any cuts of your merchandise sales the venue demands, if any. And be clear if merch sales are available at all, since some venues, such as colleges, may not let you sell any.

5. Working with fans to help you book gigs.

Your fans know the venues in their local area and can actually do the footwork for you if you ask them. All you need to do is deal with the final booking details. For example, fans were always demanding that indie artist Jonathan Coulton tour in their hometowns. When he realized he had to travel halfway across the country to Seattle at the last minute for a personal matter, he blogged that he'd have one night free and could play a show if something was set up. Fans in Seattle—who didn't want to pass up a rare opportunity to see Coulton live—immediately took up the challenge and, within twenty-four hours, had arranged a respectable venue. All Coulton had to do was contact the place to cement the details. Twenty-four hours later, he was onstage playing to a packed house.

The Brobdingnagian Bards have gone a step beyond and requested that their fans make the arrangements for them. This worked out so well that they eventually put together a list of steps for their fans to take to help book them. Of course, another advantage of fan booking is that fans don't usually ask for a booking cut. They just want you to play in their area and are happy to get you to come to their town.

6. Use the snowball technique.

Use each booked gig to get you more bookings by asking for another date after a successful show and capturing press clippings, show reviews, and any other media that talked about your show. Use each one to convince talent buyers who haven't signed you yet to pick you up. Also try to get testimonials/references from the venue if you had a great show.

7. If starting out, use open mics and other techniques to get that first booking (and then snowball it).

The easiest first shows are open mic nights, opening band slots, or smaller venues that host a new-artist night. You'll want to impress them with your draw, so invite all your friends and even offer an after-party to boost your first draw. Note that when starting out, you can also offer to be a fill-in act in case anyone cancels, which can get you early bookings and more experience playing. One final method to consider if none of the other ideas work is to play a single pay-for-play show to establish yourself if you think it can lead to future gigs.

8. Network to get subs and other artists to play shows so you never have to cancel a gig.

Don't cancel gigs if you can't make them and put the problem on the talent buyer; it's your responsibility to find a replacement. Create and tap your network of other artists to fill in the date. If you can make enough connections, you can offer entire evenings of entertainment for the talent buyers rather than making them come up with who plays in each time slot. You'll want a large enough group so it's not the same show every time.

THE TOP SEVEN TYPES OF SHOWS YOU CAN BOOK

There is a long list of types of bookings you can put together for your live act, each with their own techniques and factors. Here's a list of types of bookings you can make, with details on each:

1. Playing live music venues and touring.

Your standard live music venues are the places that most artists begin their careers at and are the main focus of most musicians. You will need to convince the talent buyers to book you. Once you have a history, leverage this up into larger music venues.

2. Festivals and conventions.

Many artists focus only on *music* festivals or conventions, such as South by Southwest (sxsw.com) or the National Association of Music Merchants convention (namm.org). This is a mistake, since there is so much competition for play slots, and some of these music conferences charge the band to play because of the opportunity of playing for "music industry" folks.

Remember that every type of festival or convention can have music. For example, Carla Ulbrich makes a good living playing conventions, especially medical conventions, because some of her music is based on her experiences as a patient. But your music doesn't even have to be related to the convention to provide musical entertainment and get a paid gig. Besides contacting the festivals in your area directly, try Festivals .com (festivals.com) or Festing (festing.com), but note that getting into festivals and conventions is definitely more of a "who you know" activity. On top of this, it can sometimes take multiple years of trying to break in. Once you do, and you're proven, getting return bookings can be made much simpler. You will want to use a warm handoff if you can find someone who already knows the committee rather than sending it cold.

3. College tours.

Some artists make most of their living off college tours, so this can be a major source of income if you don't mind being on the road for these types of events. To do this, join campus activity organizations like the National Association for Campus Activities (NACA) (naca.org) and the Association for the Promotion of Campus Activities (APCA) (apca.com), which are organizations that help colleges find entertainment for their campus events. It costs money to join these groups, but the costs are usually recouped within about three gigs. NACA and APCA hold conventions all over the country every year, where the activity committees from hundreds of colleges go to find and book acts. Get to know the committee members personally if you can, because that is the best way to sign them up.

Also, don't forget that venues near colleges are always looking for bands to bring in the student crowds. You might be able to book extra gigs, and if you have to travel, this will make your trip more worthwhile.

4. Corporate events.

For corporate shows, the bookers are usually employees, secretaries, executive assistants, or someone in the human resources department. You can also use sites like Sonicbids (sonicbids.com) or GigMasters (gigmasters.com).

5. Charity events.

Charity events deliver a lot of benefits to bands that play them. Usually, all proceeds are donated to the charity, but the events usually have their own press releases and the event gets media attention.

6. Weddings.

Many bands play weddings to supplement their income. It's an area with its own pitfalls, but those who can successfully navigate it can secure a dependable source of gigs. George Hrab boosts his indie music income with steady work playing with a wedding band, the Philadelphia Funk Authority (phillyfunk.com). And one of Chicago's top wedding bands is the High Society Orchestra (highsocietyorch.com), run by Allan Heiman, who has been in the booking business for decades (in fact, he used to manage Curtis

Mayfield back in the day). Heiman started his wedding band with a splash. He rented out a hotel ballroom and catered an evening for wedding planners, hotel-venue managers, flowers, music, catering, and others in the wedding industry to enjoy the band. That one event, along with an advertising campaign in bridal magazines and other publications, got him fifty-two bookings that first year. The people to win over are wedding planners and the hotel-venue managers who recommend bands and DJs. In fact, you may want to give them a bounty or cut if they do.

7. Parties, bar mitzvahs, family events, and more.
Live artists and DJs are needed at all kinds of events, and they are all opportunities to make another set of income from your music if you want to play them. Each of these has a different set of places to find potential bookings. Consider having a page on your website or web presences for each of them, separately, that talks about why you're great for the particular event to improve your chance of being booked because each buyer type has different needs.

HOW TO BOOK HOUSE CONCERTS
Thanks to the internet, house concerts, which are small shows hosted at people's residences, have continued to grow in popularity. Just note that there are real legal issues and sound ordinances to contend with for house concerts due to zoning laws. For more information about house concerts, we recommend the books *Host Your Own Concerts* by Joe Taylor Jr., or *No Booker, No Bouncer, No Bartender: How I Made $25K On A 2-Month House Concert Tour (And How You Can Too)* by Shannon Curtis.

Do the following to book house concerts:

1. Book gigs using your fans, or visit websites that help you book house concerts.
Most house concerts are booked with your fan base. If you want to put your music out to the world in general, try sites like HouseConcerts.com (houseconcerts.com) or Concerts in Your Home (concertsinyourhome.com).

2. Ask your hosts to guarantee a minimum payment (or play for a flat fee).
What you get paid shouldn't have to depend on your host's ability to bring in people.

3. Make sure you have the right equipment to put on your own show.

Of course, houses don't have PA systems, so you'll have to come up with your own amplification if you need it.

4. Be aware of sound laws in each area.

Just be aware it's very possible for a show to get shut down or know you might need to turn down your volume knobs.

HOW TO BUSK (STREET PERFORMANCES)

Performing your music in public for donations, or "busking," is not for everyone, but it can pay off. In fact, busking can generate income and interest and can grow your following more today than those who busked in the past. The key is to leverage all the tools available, since there are ways to get paid beyond having passersby toss coins in a guitar case, including selling your digital music directly to them or getting digital tips.

Each town might handle street performers differently, and there may be many rules to follow, including licenses, ordinances, and restrictions. Here's how to go about playing live on the street:

1. Obtain a street performer license.

Make sure you have a license if your town requires it. You might need to pay a fee, and some towns even require you to audition. Also, you might need many licenses depending on where you play. In our hometown of Chicago, you need a separate license for street performances and the subway (where you need to contact the Chicago Transit Authority and Metropolitan Transportation Authority directly). Since licenses cost money, we suggest letting your audience know by showing a sign with the license and how much you've paid to entertain them, because it encourages donations to help you pay for it.

2. Create a space to perform with a poster and the right equipment.

Part of setting the mood for your music includes creating a space, which you can do by putting down an inexpensive rug along with blocking an area by your instrument cases and a battery-powered amp so you can be heard. You'll also want to put up a sign or poster to promote shows, your mailing list, your social presences, and more. In fact, most people have smartphones, so add QR codes, Spotify codes, Snapcodes, and your Twitter ID to your posters and signs so it's easy for them to follow you.

3. Set out a tip jar or donation box (and seed it!) and have products to sell.

The best choices for your tip jars are large containers, like a guitar case or box, so people can easily toss in money from a distance. Seed your tip jar with a twenty-dollar bill or two if you have them, which are the most common bill people have in their pockets thanks to ATMs. You'll want them to think it's perfectly normal to toss in a twenty rather than try to make change. Also, consider taking tips using things like PayPal.Me (paypal.me); mobile apps like BuSK (busk.co) or ShowSlinger (showslinger.com); plug your patronage page using a QR code; or using a device like a DipJar (dipjar.com). BuSK can also help you sell music when they donate to you, or you can have physical products on hand, such as CDs or USB drives for the music. And you can write something clever to make people more likely to tip ("Only sexy people tip!").

Consider grouping your songs into small sets of just two or three songs, and leave room to ask your fans to tip or buy something. Also, whenever anyone steps within ten feet of you as you're performing, you should physically acknowledge their presence with a nod or smile. This draws them into your orbit and encourages more tips.

4. Video-stream your performance to your online fans.

A smartphone, a good phone data plan, and a video-streaming app like YouTube (youtube.com), YouNow (younow.com), Periscope (pscp.tv), or Snapchat (snapchat.com) can turn your local street performance global. Simply lean your smartphone against something so your camera captures your performance, and instantly, your internet fans can enjoy your street performance too. In fact, because you'll often be playing for long stretches of time, it's your online fans who may engage more than the people on the street, since passersby often need to move on or get on trains. This is a great way to build a following on the internet, and you can also highlight your tipping, music store, and merch methods.

THE LIVE SHOW

UNDERSTANDING THE IMPORTANCE OF BEING
THERE FOR THE AUDIENCE

Musicians often argue the issue of "staying true to the music" versus "pandering to the audience." This might make an interesting debate over beers, but it's not useful when it comes to putting on a show. In the end, you're there to entertain the audience. Of course, you need to follow your aesthetic tastes—which might include a dark, brooding look or a screaming spandex serenade—but don't forget: *you are there for them.*

Having the attitude that your audience is "lucky to hear you" will *not* result in a good show. David Bloom, one of Chicago's jazz gurus, captured it best: "Don't reduce music to the size of your ego. It's a lot bigger than you. It was here before you, and it'll be here long after you're gone." If you look up to music, the audience will look up to you. But if you look down at the audience, they probably won't be there next time you play.

If you want to win fans, the size of the audience you play to doesn't matter. Every show counts. As Brian Austin Whitney, the founder of the music community Just Plain Folks, says, "Don't worry about playing to twenty people; play like you're playing to twenty thousand. If you make the best music you can and play the best you can play, you will grow your audience."

THE TOP SIX THINGS YOU NEED TO DO TO PUT
TOGETHER A KILLER LIVE SHOW

Think back and try to relive one of the most memorable live shows you've attended. Why exactly do you remember it? Did you feel involved? Connected? Energized? Were you transported to another place? In other words, did you *feel* something—not just *hear* it?

In the best shows, the band and the audiences connect.

Tom Jackson (tomjacksonproductions.com), a musician and one of the leading live music producers for tours, showcases, and shows, has spent decades figuring out what makes audiences connect to musicians and what keeps fans coming back for more. He's boiled it down to three reasons: audiences come to be captured and engaged, to experience moments, and to experience change in their lives. While this might sound lofty, there's no question that music can do this for people. What Jackson does for a living is to teach musicians how to *create* this connection in their own shows.

A live music producer acts like a sports coach does with his athletes—teaching the skills, testing out the "plays," and getting the individual parts to work together as a team. It's not about developing your musical chops (which you should do on your own time); it's about developing your show for the stage. This may mean having the lead singer walk to the side of the stage at a certain point, having the lead guitarist come forward when it's his time to solo, and rearranging the song in ways that work best for a live show to get an audience involved. These are the same techniques that bands like U2 and Prince used to pull off such spectacular shows.

As Jackson says, "Just because you learned how to play music doesn't mean you automatically know how to perform in front of an audience." If you want to win fans, your live performances must be more than just taking your recorded music and playing it really well onstage. According to Jackson, a live show is 15 percent technical, 30 percent emotional, and 55 percent visual. Most musicians spend their time practicing the technical part but neglect the other 85 percent. Since the visual part of a show is the most important, think about your own set. Even though it's likely that each of your songs *sound* different, be honest: do they *look* different onstage? As Jackson says, "Audiences get bored and disconnect when all your songs look the same."

Here's a small sample of the advice that Jackson gives to help build that connection with the audience:

1. The performance should visually match the song.

You can't control the audience's eyes, but you can control what you do onstage. Give the audience *visual* cues that match moments in the song. When one musician has a solo, she should be forward, and the others should step back "out of the picture." If a song builds, bring musicians forward as they add their parts. The audience's view of the stage changes dramatically depending on where your band members stand, so always let the audience know where they should focus their attention.

2. What's good for a recording isn't necessarily good for the stage.

Abandon the idea of reproducing your radio-friendly, three-minute-long track at the stage door. In a live show, three minutes goes by so fast that most audience members don't even know what happened. They didn't pick up on that cool riff or harmony vocal. Jackson will often work with musicians to find the highlights of songs and then retool those parts for stage performance. Techniques include extending intros and outros to songs, repeating the cool licks or hooks that sound great on the recording but go by too quickly onstage, extending a bridge or solo, or breaking down a part and vamping on its underlying rhythms.

3. Less is more.

Most bands try to pack a set with as many songs as they can, but the point is to make the songs you play special and memorable for the audience. Applying the techniques above lengthens the songs, meaning you'll play fewer songs in a set, but each will have more impact.

4. Learn how to move onstage.

If you watch the top musical performances, you quickly realize movement is just as important a part of a performance as playing the notes. This is not just for the U2s of the world, and to the extent that you can bring it into your performances, your shows can become electrifying. The biggest moments of your music are not likely to come out with you standing behind your microphone for the full forty-five-minute set; instead they should match the visual part of the performance. This isn't dance choreography, and these are not mysterious skills. In fact, Jackson suggests that there are four different ways to get around onstage: walking, running, skipping (think AC/DC), and walking with authority (walking like you own the stage). Each can be used to match the song and needs to be rehearsed, because even if you can do it in your living room, what about when you're in front of an audience playing your guitar and singing? Football players practice footwork, and musicians should practice the fundamentals of movement so that they can marry it to the music.

5. Create moments.

The times in our lives we remember have qualities that you can generate onstage to create something special for your audience. In their book *The Power of Moments: Why Certain Experiences Have Extraordinary Impact*, Chip and Dan Heath claim the moments that stick with us have one or more of four key qualities: elevation, insight, pride, and connection.

The more of these you can build into your show, the more likely it is to be the type of event that impacts your audience. Each one of these qualities can be part of a show depending on the kind of music you play and the show you design.

6. Plan and rehearse.

Just as you practice your instrument and the songs you play, you must spend time practicing your live performance and planning your set. As Jackson notes, all those live shows of your favorite big-name bands looking like they're making it all up as they go along are really planned. Your practices should reflect this. Jackson recommends to first learn the music on your own; next, practice as a group in a circle to learn the songs; and finally, practice as if onstage. This includes practicing the produced song—moves and all.

HOW TO DO A SOLID SOUND CHECK

The sound at a show is the most important part of it that you can't directly control. The sound engineer can never make a bad band sound good, but they can definitely make a good band sound bad. If you don't have your own sound engineer, make friends with whomever is running the board. And, most important, *do not skip the sound check*.

In our experience, sound engineers tend to be an unusual breed, and it's always interesting to get to know them. One of them that worked the boards for our band would get drunk, hit on our female friends, and do a lousy job with the sound to boot. Another did great work but posted a note facing the stage: "Do not play 'American Woman.'" Naturally, we announced that we were going to play it in the middle of a set. He made this hilarious hand-waving motion as if he were trying to get a plane to stop landing on a runway that was mined to explode. Of course, our audience missed the joke while the band cracked up all on the stage.

Here's how to make the most of a sound check:

1. Get to the venue early.

We know. This never happens. But do it if you can.

2. Provide your microphone chart and instrumentation so the sound engineer can see where things go.

This will make the setup go so much more quickly.

3. Designate one band member or representative to work with the sound engineer.

Have one person answer the sound engineer's questions and tag along with them throughout the check to make sure things get resolved quickly and correctly. Every band has some oddities with its microphone setup, so it pays to have someone there to make sure the sound is right.

4. Be particular about the sound, especially monitors.

If you need more volume or a different mix, take care of this now. It's impossible to change the monitor mix much during the show. The best you'll usually get is yelling, "Turn it up!" or "Turn it down!" during the show.

5. Let each vocalist try his or her mic.

If there are a lot of harmonies, make sure that each vocalist can hear the others during the check.

6. Have the member with the best ears stand in the room to double-check the sound.

This is exactly where you can catch the mistakes of a bad sound engineer.

7. Tell the sound engineer about any planned instrument changes.

For example, one member of Beatnik Turtle plays sax, sings, then plays flute. He often gets one mic for saxes and one for flute *and* vocals. When he switches between flute and vocals on that mic, he needs the levels adjusted between songs.

8. Buy the sound engineer a beer or give him a tip.

Make friends with your sound engineer. Offer free merch. This gives them an incentive to make you sound good, and if they wear your shirts, it could spark interest in your music. Also, the sound engineer is usually connected to other venues in your area, and that connection might just get you more shows. They can put you in touch with other musicians and otherwise expand your skill and opportunity networks.

HOW TO HANDLE ONLINE TICKET SALES

Even if you are playing smaller venues, you can still sell tickets and make money off the ticket sales. The biggest issue you'll run into is how to take the sales online, and this, fortunately, can be handled by some services that can handle this problem for you. To do this, use the following steps:

1. See if the venue accepts tickets, or work with them to accept your tickets.

If the venue provides online sales, see if they have affiliate sales so you can get an extra cut for the purchasers you send there. The small venues that don't have ticketing might not want you to use your own, since you'll have to handle the money and get it to them, which they might not trust. They tend to like to keep it in their own hands. Still, if you can work with them, you might be able to show them you can get more preorders with your mailing list.

2. Choose online ticket sales tools.

To handle online ticket sales, you can handle ticketing yourself using tools like Topspin (topspinmedia.com), Music Glue (musicglue.com), Ticketleap (ticketleap.com), Limited Run (limitedrun.com), or Songkick (songkick.com).

3. Try creating sales bundles.

Once you can sell online tickets, you can combine it with online bundles to offer digital products with the tickets to boost your draw, or coupons for merch and other offerings to give your ticket sales more value. It can also drive up merch sales. Platforms like Music Glue (musicglue.com) and others allow you to create these types of deal bundles.

RUNNING AND PUBLICIZING A LIVE SHOW
THE TOP ELEVEN PLACES TO PROMOTE EACH SHOW

Use this section as a checklist to get your show promoted through all the channels available to you. Make sure to plug your shows multiple times, starting long before the show and all the way up to the show date so your fans can plan to go.

1. Your event calendar.

Maintain a show calendar, and enter gigs as early as possible so fans can plan ahead. Calendar tools can automatically update your online presences. Although there are many sites that track shows from musicians, the ones that make it easy to export include Eventful (eventful.com), as well as ReverbNation (reverbnation.com), Bandsintown (news.bandsintown .com), and JamBase (jambase.com). Eventful allows your fans to demand that they play in their town, which will let you know where you should tour, and then lets you contact them when you have any show dates in their town.

2. Your social presences.

Besides automated messages triggered from your automated show calendar, make sure to plug your shows via social presences. These are even more effective as online poster images, which are easier to share.

3. Your mailing list.

Mailing lists are perfect places to promote shows far in advance, as well as in targeted mails to the people in each region in the dates running up to the show.

4. Show posters.

Show posters in the venue you'll be playing are still a great place to promote your show, because anyone at the venue is likely to come back to see other acts. Plus, if you've played there before, a random poster viewer might have seen you. The best posters have the music included using QR codes, Spotify codes, and links to videos so your promotion becomes a full AV experience. If you're on tour, you can consider options like Bandposters (getbandposters.com), which will print and ship them to the venues directly so they can put them up.

5. Flyers.

Flyers can be handed out on the street or put up at local stores and venues in the neighborhoods around your venue. These are most effective when you give them a value, such as a discount or free drink of some kind. If you can work out a drink deal with the venue, that can work best, but if you have to, give away something at the venue or money off the door or ticket. Use the QR codes on the flyers as well to make them more of an AV experience.

6. Street team.

Having friends or a street team personally hand out flyers to passersby right before the gig is a surprisingly effective way to boost your draw. One other technique we learned from Las Vegas strip escort promoters involves tapping the stack of flyers twice quickly against your hand when people walk by so they can hear it, and hold it out to be picked up. They'll often take it from you. Really. Try it.

7. Promoters.

In many cities, there are event promoters who specialize in packing the house with people. While they take a cut, they are often very good at getting people in the door and can be worth the price.

8. Local radio.

As covered in chapter 17, "Get Heard and Seen," local radio shows, college radio, and radio appearances are all within reach of musicians. Playing gigs in their area makes it more likely they'll pay attention to your pitch to be on their show, especially if it's a large venue.

9. The media.

Only try to engage the media if you have more of a story than "Local musician plays show." But if there's an event of some sort, such as an album release, charity tie-in, or other interesting angle, engage them. Use the techniques in chapter 15, "Promotion and Publicity," to perform a media campaign. Especially try to get coverage in new media, which is more accessible to indie musicians.

10. Contests and giveaways.

With tools like Woobox (woobox.com), Wishpond (wishpond.com), and ShortStack (shortstack.com), you can run contests or giveaways and use them to promote your live show.

11. Your van or car.

Try putting show posters on the side of your vehicle; with a QR code, you can also send people to your tour calendar. We knew one band, the Locals (localsrock.com), who would also put giveaway magnets on their van.

THE TOP ELEVEN THINGS TO DO PRIOR TO YOUR SHOW
Use the items below as a preshow checklist. Some of these happen long before the show, including promotion, and others happen the day of.

Each can affect the amount of money you make, so it's' worth taking the time to get them right.

1. Lock down the booking.

Before you even promote the show, confirm your show is booked properly. We once showed up for a three-act night, and six artists showed up. We only resolved it by showing that we and two other acts were advertised in the paper, and the other three were not. It was ugly, and the venue didn't resolve it—the artists had to fight it out.

2. Promote the show (see above).

Use the promotion ideas and channels we list above to promote your show and get as much of a draw as you can.

3. Make the most of your guest list.

Your guest list is your best way to invite local media, journalists, music reviewers/writers, and bloggers to write about you. Also, don't forget local talent buyers, city event directors, festival bookers, college music event bookers, and other influencers who can get you future gigs. Even if none of these invitees come, they are seeing your name in their email and can see you are playing in their town. It can still help you get future coverage and bookings. Make sure to send all these all your tour dates no matter where they are located so they can see everywhere you're playing. This makes it easier for them to write a story about you or book you in the future.

4. Sell presale tickets.

If you can sell tickets for the show, promote this on all your channels, and use ideas like bundling it with other digital products or merch offers to entice them to come, giving each ticket purchase more value than a simple ticket buy.

5. Work with the venue to create specials or tie-ins for the show.

If your venue is okay with it, see if they'll offer specials or other promotions. The best time to ask for these types of promotions is as you're being booked.

6. Lock down your set list and print/write them up.

If you're rehearsing the songs as well as the transitions, it's better to come up with the set list ahead of time rather than at the venue. As you grow to much larger venues, your lighting and other aspects will need to be locked down even further in advance.

7. Prepare your merch.

You'll want to know what you sold when done and make sure you have enough of everything to sell at the shows, so pack up the merch table before going to the venue. At the venue, make the merch table as attractive as possible, set up lights, and lay out the table as we discuss in the section below.

8. Set up your cashbox and credit card app.

Don't lose a sale because you can't make change or lose *a lot of sales* because you don't have a way to take credit card transactions.

9. Give T-shirts to sound people and venue staff to wear.

If you can start out the day or night by giving the people you're working with something, you'll almost always get better treatment. Plus, these merch items will advertise for you.

10. Sound check the venue.

Use the steps in the "How to Do a Solid Sound Check" section above.

11. Check live video feed (video and audio) and lighting.

If you are live-streaming the event, use the sound check to test all these aspects of your live show.

THE TOP THIRTEEN METHODS TO EFFECTIVELY USE YOUR MERCH TABLE TO SELL AND PROMOTE

Below are all methods that can improve your sales at your merch store. Mix and match these for your own shows and keep which ones work the best.

1. Get someone to run your store.

If possible, always get someone to run the store for you. It's a fairly easy job, but it's hard, and less effective, to sell from the stage. We once teamed up with other local bands and did an exchange program where we ran the stores at each other's shows. (And we promoted the other bands' shows as well.) You should do everything you can to get people to help out the band in this way. Offer your friends incentives like free CDs and T-shirts, free shows, or anything else that would entice them to help you.

2. Make the table attractive, inviting, and engaging.

Presentation matters, and you will want your table to be both attention-getting and inviting. Make sure people notice the table by using lights; there are endless options for this, including Christmas lights, electroluminescent (EL) wire, and others. You can also use projection lights pointed to the floor near the table, even better if the lights are in motion to draw people in. And giveaways or cheap items like glow bracelets are easy and get attention. The merch table should be inviting by laying out merch so people can see and handle it, and there should be a clear path in front of it. And it can be made engaging by including conversation pieces, such as a leg light or art pieces or displaying video.

3. Prepare payment options.

First of all, make sure that you have enough singles and fives for change. You don't want to miss a sale just because you didn't have enough. Second, people will often spend all their cash on beer, so make sure you can take credit cards. We provided options for this in chapter 2, "Your Music Business."

4. Give away swag.

Give away stickers or other inexpensive items to get them to walk up to the table, even if they don't buy anything. This draws them in. You can also give those away as something extra for the purchase. Also have your flyers available to hand to anyone who buys something.

5. Encourage mailing list signups.

Your mailing list signup or a tablet to let them do it should be available at the table. Offer to do it for every customer.

6. Offer discounts and coupons.

Offering everyone who enters the door a coupon for some percentage off a product or merch to get them to come to the table can increase your sales. When you come up with a discount, don't let it take out too much of your margin.

7. Roll your T-shirts.

Martin Atkins, drummer for groups like Ministry, Pigface, and Killing Joke, goes out of his way during his "How to Make $100,000 a Year in Music" talk to explain that T-shirt rolling is a critical factor in selling more merch. If you have a line that is too long, you will lose sales, and rolled shirts are easier to grab and sell. Make sure they're rolled so you can see the size and the logo on the front so you know which one to grab. They are also easier to throw from the stage as a giveaway.

8. Put out a tip jar.

If you decide to put out a tip jar, make a big deal about it. Your jar should be seeded with twenty-dollar bills, and you should have fun with the sign.

9. Present merch options for whales, dolphins, and minnows.

Apply the whales, dolphins, and minnows concept from chapter 2, "Your Music Business," to your merch table. If you have a $1 sticker, your minnows will have a chance to contribute something, but have higher-priced items all the way to the high-end $100+ items. You should also offer bundles so they can buy music, a shirt, and a sticker for a single price.

10. Offer patronage options.

Use your physical presence to grow your monthly patronage income. Instead of trying to just get a single sale, try to get someone to sign up to be a patronage supporter as well. For example, you can have special merch items that are only available if they sign up at a particular support level every month. Make a QR code pointing to your patronage page available to make it easy for them.

11. Offer limited-availability merch, and put a sign up to let them know.

Always offer limited-availability merch if you can, and when you do, put up a sign to let fans know how many are left. Cross them out with a marker and keep writing in how many are left. This will tend to make those items sell out, and it's attention-grabbing.

12. Put up a display rack.

Display racks improve your sales. Once fans have something in their hand, they are more likely to buy it rather than put it down.

13. Promote next shows.

Each show is a chance to get people out to the next one. Make sure you have flyers and signs that promote upcoming shows.

THE TOP TWELVE THINGS TO DO AT THE SHOW

Consider doing these things at each show to get more sales, bring more people in to future shows, and give people a better experience.

1. Announce your name frequently.

At every show, there are probably some in the audience who don't know who you are; plus there are often new people walking into the room all the time. Ideally, bring a sign or banner onstage.

2. Build your mailing list.

Make sure you create a mailing list and ask people to sign up. To maximize signups, have a giveaway (but don't give away anything that you are selling at the merch counter or you could hurt sales). Make some entry slips with spaces to put in their contact info. Audience members are more likely to give their contact information if there's a chance of winning something.

3. Pitch your merchandise.

Every few breaks, remind people about your merch table. Your audience might just need a reminder as an extra push to get them to make the purchase. Plus, some people might have just walked in the door.

4. Moderate the live-stream chat and answer on behalf of the artist.

If you are live-streaming your event, it helps to have a team member talk on behalf of the artist to the chat. They can also forward requests or give info, and they can remove offensive posts and audience members.

5. Be active on your social presences.

During the shows, it's a perfect time to post pictures, video snippets, audio, and all kinds of posts about the event to excite the fans who couldn't be there about the show. At least one team member who is not in the show can help with this.

6. Tip jar (in person and online).
If you have a tip jar, you'll need to remember to put it out and pitch it from the stage and keep an eye on it to make sure no one is taking any money out.

7. Promote all your media.
Turn audience members into followers by showing banners or talking about your social presences, shows, video channels, website, or other places for them to follow you.

8. Take photos of the crowd.
Use at least one break between songs to take a picture of the audience. These can be some of the best promotional shots for your social media as well as talent buyers.

9. Have others take photos of you while you play.
Your shows represent action shots and great content for all your channels. You'll want to get some every show to get many different pictures of your live shows.

10. Get a video recording of the show for your own game tapes.
If you have a live stream, you'll already have this, but otherwise, it helps to see your show afterward to get an idea of what you can improve and to see what worked even if you have one camera pointed at the stage.

11. Promote future shows.
During the performance, announce your next shows and upcoming projects to draw people in. If you have a poster for your next show, place it at your merch table.

12. Put your logo on everything.
Your logo should be on all your instrument cases, gear cases, and onstage equipment. Each time you appear in front of people, you have a chance to reinforce your persona.

THE TOP TEN THINGS TO DO POSTSHOW

After the show, there are more opportunities to make money, get more bookings, and bring your fans back to see you again. Don't lose these opportunities:

1. Thank the sound engineer and anyone else who helped you during the show.

So few people thank the staff, which is a mistake, since they are a big part of your success. You should always give them a shout-out at the end.

2. Sign off from the live video stream.

Don't forget to shut off the feed. No reason to let them watch the venue tear down the stage. But you can also let the feed follow you, the artist, around as you interact with fans.

3. Interact with fans immediately after the show and do a final plug of the merch table.

This is a perfect time to give autographs, which you can charge for when you put out your merch. Some artists do selfies for free, and others and charge for it if they have enough of a draw.

4. Sell postshow impulse-buy merch.

Your broken drumsticks, snapped guitar strings, discarded set lists, and even clothes you wore onstage are worth something when you have enough of a draw. Autograph them, and they become perfect mementos for your fans. You can also sell immediate postshow recordings or videos to your audience using tools like Set FM (set.fm). It's also a time you can sell your fans access to the artists in a VIP postshow after-hours event.

5. Tell your happy fans to talk to the venue.

If any of your fans rave to you about your show, tell them the venue wants to hear from them. Point them toward the talent buyer or whoever is running the venue and tell them to spend a minute to tell them. More fans are willing to do it, and it's one of the best ways to get booked again.

6. Send fans to your social presences by tagging them.

Each picture is a chance to send fans to your social presences channels if you tag them. This gets your name out to all their friends, which they will hopefully bring out to the next show.

7. Collect the door proceeds, thank the venue, and try to book your next gig.

Send your booker or designated venue contact to collect the funds and try to get another booking on the spot. This is one of the most effective times to book.

8. Inventory your products and merch by tallying up what sold.

Take a final inventory of your merch either at the venue as you pack up or afterward. You'll use this to adjust your merch strategies.

9. Turn in your set list for live show royalties.

As we discussed in chapter 12, "Licensing and Royalties," PROs like ASCAP and BMI will allow you to submit your set list so you can collect performance royalties from your shows. Make sure to track the venue, date, and songs played.

10. Capture the ads, live show music reviews, and other coverage about the show for your booking and press kits.

These can not only help get you future gigs, they can add to your press campaigns. We once made a collage out of the ads with our band name in it to visually demonstrate all the shows we'd played.

LIVE-STREAMING YOUR EVENTS
HOW TO RUN A STREAMING EVENT EFFECTIVELY

The live-streamed versions of your events can be a free offering to your remote fans or could be something you charge them for access. It can even be a reward option for your patrons or crowdfunding campaigns. Depending on your needs, you need to get the right tools and services to help you put this together.

Use these steps to run a live-streaming event effectively:

1. Promote your streaming even the same way you'd promote your shows.

Live streaming is a live event, and so it's worth the buildup, promotion, and postshow coverage.

2. Choose the right cameras and equipment.

From leaning a phone against a bar with a view of the stage to having multi-camera setups with lighting, you have a lot of options to put together the camerawork for a live-streaming show. The equipment and apps for this regularly updates, and you will want to evaluate what can work for you to put this together, and test and plan it out. If you have a more elaborate setup, you should have a team dedicated to doing it right.

The most important part of your setup is probably not the cameras or the lighting; it's the sound. You should get a direct feed off the soundboard if you can and put it through some decent filters, EQ, and mastering if you have the opportunity.

3. Choose the right services.

There's a bewildering array of places to stream, including YouTube (youtube.com/live_dashboard), Periscope (pscp.tv), Twitch (twitch.tv), Livestream (livestream.com), and Facebook Live (live.fb.com). Add to that services that can pay you for participating, such as YouNow (younow.com), Stageit (stageit.com), Concert Window (concertwindow.com), or Street Jelly (streetjelly.com), and it should be clear you will want to research the space carefully depending on your needs. Note that some of these have built-in payment options, and this can make a big difference for your income.

That said, with services that allow you to multistream like Crowdcast (crowdcast.io) or Restream (restream.io), or tools like Open Broadcaster Software (obsproject.com) or Wirecast (telestream.net/wirecast/overview.htm), you can stream it to multiple services at the same time, which is a good option if you have a large audience and you want to provide a nonrestricted, free stream.

4. Provide the stream afterward for video sales.

Most every live-stream service provides a recording of the event, but you don't need to leave them up there. These are perfect reward extras, videos to sell, content for your YouTube Channel, or freebies. They are also excellent content for your booking kit. The audio alone might make great content for a live album.

GET HEARD AND SEEN

Goal: To get your music heard and videos seen by as many people as possible to grow your fan base, get publicity, and generate royalties.

Team Roles and Responsibilities: Promoter, Publicist, Marketer, and Manager

WHAT YOU GET OUT OF THIS
By the end of this chapter, you will:

1. Know forty-five *categories* of places to get your music heard and your videos seen.

2. Have a structured get-heard-and-seen publicity campaign plan for researching, submitting, and getting your music heard and videos seen.

MONEY MAP

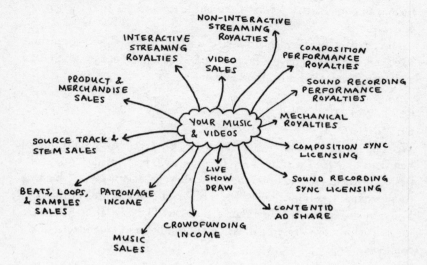

INTRO

There are more places to get your music and videos "out there" and discovered by people than ever before. Thanks to the convergence of computers and media, people can listen to your music in more places than was ever possible in the past: on their computers, phones, tablets, watches, home speakers, TVs, gaming console platforms, and more. In fact, we've cataloged *forty-five categories* you can target to get your music heard and videos seen. These range from digital streaming and social music services to MP3 blogs, podcasts, vlogs, radio, TV, and more. In this chapter, we'll cover each category where you can get your music heard and seen, plus give you the general techniques on how to target them so you get plays and views.

The main thing to understand as you begin your get-heard-and-seen campaigns is that the success you find in getting your music noticed has nothing to do with the quality of the music, although it's a factor. Your goal is to see if your music can find an audience. For example, for many years, NPR syndicated *"The Annoying Music Show"* across one hundred stations that highlighted nearly unlistenable music and played to people across the country. The show only ended when the quirky curator passed away, but while it was going, it even created compilation CDs, and the show had fans all over the world. Although it's likely none of the songs on

357

the show would have been featured on Pitchfork or played in any other forum, this music still attracted an audience and got into the ears of millions.

If you spend time understanding which fans, stations, blogs, or forums like your music, you have a better chance of having your music find an audience so you can build your fan base.

KEY CONCEPT
GETTING YOUR MUSIC HEARD
We'll go through all forty-five categories of targets to get your music heard and videos seen, but keep in mind each is a world of possibilities on its own. For example, the MP3 blog aggregator Hype Machine (hypem.com) has hundreds of MP3 blogs of every genre, worldwide. You can do an entire campaign around MP3 blogs alone. Because there are so many possibilities, you should spend some time to do some planning.

- Research and find the specific stations, services, shows, and sites that fit your music's genre and style.

- Target the channels your potential fans listen to (see chapter 14, "Marketing," for ideas on getting to know who your fans are and where they hang out online).

- Follow the "Executing a Get-Heard-and-Seen Campaign" steps below or incorporate them within the release strategy as detailed in chapter 18, "Your Release Strategy.")

As you do your research, capture who to contact and the submission guidelines (including what type of file to send). You'll also want to track where you sent your sound recordings and when, whether you followed up, and whether you sent a thank-you.

Keep in mind you don't have to target all the below categories! In fact, it may be enough to target just one or two and get just a few places to play your music at first, and then use these successes to target others.

Finally, note that the best places to get played are often the ones that aren't normal music channels and don't have submission guidelines. For example, getting your music video about soccer on a popular soccer site might just mean sending your video to the website owners and could get you in front of millions of visitors if they post it.

UNDERSTANDING ALGORITHMS AND AUTOMATIC SUGGESTIONS

Fans pick up new music in today's world via suggestions through video, streaming, and store platforms. In today's world, there's a saying: "Algorithms are marketing." These are the search results and automatic suggestions platforms like YouTube and Spotify make for music and videos. For example, when a person listens to a music video on YouTube and the autoplay brings up the next suggestion, you want it to be your video.

The strategies to influence these algorithms change over time, and these platforms keep the formulas secret because they don't want people to be able to cheat the system. Still, it's necessary to keep track of the latest strategies to make it more likely your music will be suggested when uploading your music and videos to the platforms discussed below to make sure your keywords, descriptions, settings, and marketing around your content matches what the platform wants to see. Uploading isn't enough; it should be as friendly as possible for the platform.

There is one aspect that all the algorithms use, however, and that is based on the popularity of the video or track. All the other techniques found below will help this aspect of your content and can help the platforms suggest your music and videos more often.

WHERE TO TARGET GETTING YOUR MUSIC HEARD

THE TEN RADIO CATEGORIES TO TARGET

When you think about getting your music heard, radio is not the best first choice in today's music world, because it is so closed off to most musicians. That said, there are some methods to get heard on radio stations within reach of independent artists, especially college/university radio and public radio. Here are the radio categories you can target for your music:

1. Commercial radio station rotation.

Commercial radio does not work the way it is portrayed in some movies and TV shows. They don't accept unsolicited submissions, and a commercial radio campaign can cost anywhere from tens to hundreds of thousands of dollars. Part of that money goes to independent promoters, who control access to the stations and block any music that doesn't pay them for that access. Your best bet for getting into a commercial radio station's rotation is to hire a radio promoter/plugger who specializes in commercial radio. But the money doesn't guarantee results, only submissions, and it doesn't guarantee your music will get played. This is rarely affordable for most independent musicians, and most indie bands avoid commercial radio altogether.

That said, if you happen to be in a country that promotes local artists, such as Canada, organizations like CRTC (crtc.gc.ca/eng/home-accueil .htm) mandate that a certain percentage of music needs to be local musicians, and you can use that to get on commercial radio rotations.

2. Commercial radio syndicated shows.

Some commercial stations air syndicated shows that specialize in a certain type of genre that accept submissions. These syndicated shows are similar to local music shows in that the show host typically decides what to play. Unlike the local music show, syndicated shows span multiple markets and have a broader group of listeners. Examples include *Little Steven's Underground Garage* (UndergroundGarage.com) and the long-running *Dr. Demento Show* (DrDemento.com).

3. Commercial radio local shows.

Some commercial radio stations have shows that feature local artists, such as WXRT's *"Local Anesthetic,"* hosted by Richard Milne, out of Chicago. These shows will accept submissions from any local band. Unlike what's played throughout the day, the host of the show chooses the music that will be featured. If they are anything like Milne's show, the host may ask a band or artist to come in for a live interview or in-studio performance.

4. Commercial radio talk shows.

Talk shows are another way to get played on commercial radio. If one of your songs is on a topic being discussed, they might just play it if it's brought to their attention. A play on a talk show helps make your music stand out more than one in a standard music rotation. This happened to us when we sent our version of the Irish song "Tell Me Ma" in anticipation of Saint Patrick's Day to Jonathon Brandmeier, who had a morning show in Chicago.

5. University/college radio station rotation.

College/university radio works the way that most people think commercial radio should work: you send them your music, and if they like it, they'll play it. It's uncomplicated and far less expensive than dealing with commercial radio. But this doesn't mean it won't take hard work to get your music played. It simply requires time, effort, and follow-up by sending your songs to the music director for the stations.

6. University/college radio station shows.

University radio stations let their students create their own radio shows on a genre, theme, or topic. The host/DJ chooses all the show's music separate from its music in its rotation. Shows that fit your music style are all potential targets for getting your music played and in front of potential fans. These shows usually have their own web pages or social media and may or may not have submission guidelines.

7. University/college radio station live on-air performances.

Live-music shows typically run during the day and feature in-studio performances and interviews with bands and musicians performing in the area that night or weekend. Getting on the air in this way works out well if you link it to a tour so you can arrange appearances when you're in their town.

8. Public radio syndicated shows.

U.S. public radio often features new music through syndicated shows such as *All Songs Considered* (npr.org/sections/allsongs). Get your music considered by following their submission process, and also look for other syndicated shows on public radio that might feature your music.

9. Public radio local music shows.

Most U.S. public radio stations have local shows that feature events, news, and culture in their town. These shows often cover music from local artists and might have their own submission guidelines. For the BBC, try the BBC Music Introducing (bbc.co.uk/introducing).

10. Satellite and cable radio.

Satellite radio works like satellite television, the signal being beamed from orbit rather than from local towers. Satellite radio services like

SiriusXM (siriusxm.com) require a subscription fee but have been chipping away at terrestrial radio's listenership. Additionally, SiriusXM will take submissions of music through its Music Programming Department. To submit your music, go to the contact page for SiriusXM (siriusxm .com/contactus) and get the latest info for the Music Programming Department on where to send your recordings.

THE FOUR STREAMING CATEGORIES TO TARGET

Streaming has taken over how people listen to and discover music. The platforms themselves recommend music, and both users of these platforms as well as the platforms create playlists that match all kinds of criteria that your music could be a part of. To get onto these platforms so your music can be heard, use the techniques described in chapter 9, "Distribution and Streaming."

1. Noninteractive streaming services.

Noninteractive streaming doesn't allow the user to control the songs being played other than to choose a station or style of music. Examples of this include Pandora (pandora.com), which creates a "personalized" music station that plays music matching the tastes of the listener based on the Music Genome Project. Getting your music on this service can help people discover your music when listening to established artists in your space and can be done by your music distributor or you can submit to them directly. Other noninteractive streaming sites act like radio stations, such as Live365 (live365.com) and iHeartRadio (iheart.com). Each station might have its own submission guidelines and DJs.

2. Interactive streaming services.

Interactive streaming services like Spotify (spotify.com), Apple Music (apple.com/music), and Deezer (deezer.com) allow their users to listen to any piece of music on the system. They have automated music discovery methods that try to match their music recommendations to each listener. These mechanisms are not public, however, and they tend to recommend mainstream music more often than independent music. The keys to getting the system to notice your music include getting many listens, adds to people's personal libraries, and additions to playlists.

3. Your streaming playlists.

Interactive streaming services allow you to create your own public playlists to let other people listen to the songs on the list. If you can create a popular playlist, you can feature your songs along with others in the space. The streaming services also allow you to feature playlists from your artist page, and these can help drive listens of your music. We cover this in "How to Promote Your Music on Streaming Services by Creating Playlists" below.

4. Popular streaming playlists.

Popular playlists run by other users of interactive streaming services, or the official playlists by the platforms themselves, can feature your music and get you noticed and played by other users. You can reach out to the organizations or people who run these popular playlists and submit your music to them, much like submitting your music to a radio station or playlist. We cover this in "How to Promote Your Music by Getting on Other People's Playlists" below.

THE FOUR PODCAST CATEGORIES TO TARGET

Podcasting is "internet radio on demand" and one of the better ways for musicians to get heard and discovered. They are shows about a particular topic that anyone can put together, upload to the internet as an MP3, and make available for people to download. The audience size of podcasts varies from small to large, and production values vary greatly as well. Some podcasters use state-of-the-art recording and production techniques, while others sound as if they recorded their show with a cassette recorder while cooking dinner.

The advantage of getting your music onto a podcast is that these shows are available as long as the podcast exists, so unlike a radio play, the music is always available as the listeners go back through older episodes and listen.

1. Podcast music shows.

Podcasts are a natural place for people to discover new music, and there are numerous podcasts out there you can target. You can find music podcasts based on your music genre, a specific topic, and even podcasts that highlight musicians in your town. You'll find a list of music podcasts at

Podbay (podbay.fm/browse/music), iTunes (itunes.apple.com/us/genre /podcasts-music/id1310?mt=2), or Podbean (podbean.com/music -podcasts) as examples.

2. Podcast talk shows.

Podcast talk shows need music as well, and it's often easier to get them to play your music, since musicians don't usually submit music to them. For example, we reached out to a podcast for coffee drinkers with our song "Coffee," and they played it, and it only took a few minutes to search to find a matching podcast and send them an email. Note that these shows often need theme songs, bumpers, and beds, and they will usually link to you after featuring your music, which can gain you new fans. To find these podcasts, just search the podcast directories, such as Podbay (podbay.fm), iTunes (itunes.apple.com/us/genre/podcasts /id26?mt=2), or Podbean (podbean.com), or search the web.

3. Your podcast.

If you have the production capability of recording music, you'll have an easy time creating your own podcast. This gives you a platform to promote your music as well as everything else you do. It's also yet another method to build your audience.

4. Make your music pod-safe.

Podcasters know using music without permission on their podcasts is infringement, and the more aware ones are always looking for music licensed under pod-safe terms. Once you do this, podcasters are more likely to play your music. Creative Commons licenses are pod-safe, but others will serve as well. To make your music available, you can list your music as pod-safe and host it on your own website or audio hosting sites.

THE SEVEN THIRD-PARTY COVERAGE CATEGORIES TO TARGET

These third-party coverage sites don't have a single method to get your music covered and heard by each, but they represent some powerful ways to get your music in front of new potential fans. Read the submission mechanism with each to know how to make use of them.

1. Music review, discovery, and magazine sites.

The top music review sites include Pitchfork (pitchfork.com), NME (nme.com), Billboard (billboard.com), Earbits (earbits.com), Amazing Radio (amazingradio.com), and NoiseTrade (noisetrade.com). They are some of the hardest to break into, but coverage at each can mean a lot of attention. Because of this, these are not good places to start a campaign, but they are excellent targets to hit after you have a solid social media following and proven coverage to show them. Also, make sure you are sending your music to the right journalists and outlets to cover your type of music.

2. MP3 blogs.

MP3 bloggers are essentially freelance music reviewers. The main differences between MP3 bloggers and traditional music journalists is that they provide an actual copy of the song they're reviewing (as an MP3), and they tend to only write about the music they like and are deeply passionate about. The audience sizes for MP3 bloggers vary from a handful up to tens of thousands of listeners. MP3 bloggers often get inundated with submission requests, so follow their submission guidelines carefully. The best place to start is to explore the MP3 blog aggregator Hype Machine (hypem.com) and search their massive directory to find blogs in your genre.

3. Social News and Entertainment Websites

Sites like Reddit (reddit.com), StumbleUpon (stumbleupon.com), Slashdot (slashdot.org), Funny or Die (funnyordie.com), Break (break.com), and Dailymotion (dailymotion.com) have discovery and sharing features that can introduce your music to potential new fans and help get it discovered. There are a variety of ways to get your music onto these sites, so you'll have get to know each before submitting, but the communities behind sites like these can be quite large.

4. Live DJ playlists and charts.

Live music DJs have their own websites, stores, and music sources they pay attention to. Getting charted on Beatport (beatport.com) or Traxsource (traxsource.com), for example, is a great way to get played by DJs all over the world. Sites like these usually only accept music from labels they work with, so to sell your music through these sites and get charted, you will need to work with existing labels or create your own label and start a relationship with these companies.

5. DAW, synth, and plug-in vendor features.

Vendors are often eager to show artists doing cool stuff with their software and hardware, and they will highlight musicians they think will highlight their products. There are more opportunities to get featured than it seems. For example, the Ableton "One Thing" video series (you tube.com/watch?v=dPWhjh0F05E&list=PLoh4MB-kbBmJCGq 34lLYsMQ12b3nqjOae) lets producers show one technique they find useful in their creative process and feature a different producer each video. To get covered this way, see if there is already a place you can be featured, or simply talk with them if you think you can help highlight their products and offer to work together.

6. Specialty stores.

Mainstream music stores are hard to break into to get featured, usually needing major label support to get featured, but specialty stores love highlighting artists that fall directly within their niche. For example, Interpunk (interpunk.com) for punk artists, and Bleep (bleep.com) for genres like experimental, grime, and braindance. Each represent not only a sales channel but also a place to get your music featured.

7. Non-music websites.

Don't forget that any site on the web can share videos or music. Blogs, message boards, forums, news sites, charities, organizations, and businesses can and do post related music. There are some advantages to this: your music stands out on non-music websites, and there are usually no formal submission guidelines. If your music fits the site, these are excellent ways to get played and can help you reach entirely new audiences. In our case, we've gotten tens of thousands of plays of some of our songs from posts on non-music websites.

THE SEVEN SHARING AND SOCIAL CATEGORIES TO TARGET
Sharing and social media sites have a mix of sites that are primarily under your own control (other than others' social media, which you can influ-

ence), which gives you a lot of access to these channels. Still, some of them come with user agreements that require you to share the music perpetually, so read those agreements carefully.

1. Your social media.

You should promote your music to your hard-won social media followers as much as possible. Don't assume they have heard your latest track just because they are following you. They may have followed you because they saw a funny post of yours. Treat it similarly to a live show: you'll want to announce who you are and talk about your music as if some of your audience just walked into the room.

2. Others' social media.

When you make a release or have something to promote, ask the people you know to help you cover it. A mention in a popular person's feed can mean a lot of coverage and retweets.

3. Your website.

Your website is a premier place to get your music heard and should have a main menu item where fans can experience your music and music videos. It should also promote sales and licensing, since you have full control of the content on your website and can drive these income streams in a way you can't on other categories.

4. Your audio content hosts.

Sites like ReverbNation (reverbnation.com), Bandcamp (bandcamp .com), and others do more than just host your music; they have music discovery features.

5. Remix sites.

If you like the idea of remixing, consider remix sites, which allow musicians all over the world to get ahold of your source tracks to make their own versions of your music. You can use these sites to both play music and share your own. Try out ccMixter (ccmixter.org), but if you put your music up there, be prepared to put it under a Creative Commons license. Some musicians put songs out on sites like these and then release albums of remixes done by other musicians.

6. Recorded music archive sites.

Music archive sites like the Audio Archive (archive.org/details/audio) and Free Music Archive (freemusicarchive.org) catalog and store music so it can be downloaded and shared. Your music can be discovered here, although if you submit it, expect to put it under a license that allows users to download and share it.

7. Live music archive sites.

Sites like Etree (etree.org) allow users to find and listen to a growing catalog of live music recordings. This is affiliated with the Bands That Allow Taping (btat.wagnerone.com), which catalogs musicians who allow live recordings of their shows to be made and uploaded. If you play live your music and sign up, your music might be discovered here.

THE THREE CHALLENGE, CONTEST, AND AWARD CATEGORIES TO TARGET

Challenges, contests, and awards have a competitive element to them, which attracts potential fans. And awards shows have an event associated with them that gives you press opportunities before, during, and after if you are nominated, whether you win or not. For each of these, most are within the reach of every musician and are worth exploring to see if there are any in your region or for your genre.

1. Song and album challenge sites.

Song and album challenges help you write and record music as well as give you exposure. Each is an opportunity to participate in a songwriting and recording challenge to write and record music within a time limit.

If you want a weekly challenge, try out the website Song Fight! (song fight.org), which gives you just one week to write and record a song based on a word or phrase for each week's challenge. Once the week is up, the songs are published on the site for anyone on the internet to listen to and to judge the entries. The winner gets a mention on the site rather than a prize, but the public who votes on the songs gets exposed to the music.

If you want to take on a bigger challenge, try writing and recording an entire album in a month. The better-known album challenges include the Record Production Month Challenge (rpmchallenge.com), February Album Writing Month (fawm.org), and National Solo Album Month (nasoalmo.org). Each of these contests is free and has different rules on length and submission requirements. And each of these challenges shares the music to listeners. Some get media attention; for example, the RPM organization usually gets coverage for their artists on National Public Radio (NPR).

2. Songwriting contests and battle of the bands.

Songwriting contests can give you exposure to both potential fans and people within the music business. There are innumerable songwriting contests you can enter, with perhaps one of the most famous being the John Lennon Songwriting Contest (jlsc.com). Lists of songwriting contests can be found at the Muse's Muse (musesmuse.com/contests.html). Also, both online and live battle-of-the-bands contests pit artists against each other to win bragging rights and sometimes prizes. Note that many of these contests require a fee, and you should beware of contests that exist merely to get money from musicians. Research them to make sure they are reputable.

3. Awards and awards shows.

Awards can give you exposure for your music and are not limited to the GRAMMYs. There might be awards for your location, genre, and more. Even being nominated for an award can give you material for your press materials, and winning can be a reason to get some coverage for your band. Awards ceremonies can also be a great place to perform.

THE FIVE TELEVISION CATEGORIES TO TARGET

There are many advantages to getting on television as an artist. First of all, you get in front of a new audience, but it's also a perfect thing to add to your bios and your chronicle. The good news is that there are television outlets within reach for new artists through established ones, so you can target the best one for your level. Your publicist can help you with these.

1. Public access television.

Public access television started as a legislated requirement for cable companies to provide a local TV station for the municipalities they operate in. Although most stopped their funding of these stations, they often continued as privately funded organizations and broadcast to cable subscribers. They are often simulcast to video-streaming services to get broader coverage. Each has their own local TV shows, which are good targets to get some live-TV experience and a great place to start out because once you've "been on TV," you can use it to get access to higher-level outlets. Find the websites or social media for music or culture-based shows on your local public access television station and reach out to the show producers to get covered.

2. Local television shows.

Most television markets have morning and evening shows that highlight local entertainment and will often cover artists. If you have major shows or events in the area, you will have an easier time getting the attention of show producers. The most common placements are an invite to their studio to play a song or to a stage run by the TV show during a festival or at an event. Reach out to the producers to get invited to a show.

3. Syndicated national/international television shows.

Syndicated television shows get played in local markets all over the world and are much harder to get featured on. If you have an established following and proven experience, you can target higher-end national shows. This is easier to do when you or someone on your team has the connections to get you in touch, as these producers are harder to reach. Perhaps the most famous show that features music is *Saturday Night Live*, but there are plenty of choices in this area to explore.

4. Talk shows.

Nearly every evening talk show features music, and all of them are fair game to target. Similar to the syndicated shows, they are harder to get into but worth targeting once you've hit a high level of success and coverage.

5. Music video channels.

Although it's been a long time since MTV featured only music, networks such as Music Choice (musicchoice.com) have stepped in to fill in the gap and provide over fifty channels of music based on genre. Networks like this do accept submissions, and you should carefully follow all instructions for it considering the volume of submissions they receive.

THE FIVE ONLINE VIDEO CATEGORIES TO TARGET

Online video has transformed the internet and is one of the top ways fans run into new music. You should always put videos of your music online, even if it's a waveform video, as fans expect to see your music there. Consider the following video categories for your music:

1. Your video channel and shows (YouTube, Vimeo, Facebook).
As we discussed in chapter 6, "Your Videos," and chapter 7, "Your Online Presences," your video channels are some of the best places to promote your music. Those chapters go into detail on how to create and promote those channels, and we discuss integrating video throughout the book.

2. Music video festivals.
Once you've made a music video, you can submit it to music video festivals taking place all over the world. It's a great way to get your music in front of new listeners, and if you win or are even nominated, you will have material for your bio, chronicle, and press materials. To find festivals to submit your videos to search for ones in your area or for your genre, or check out sites like FilmFreeway (filmfreeway.com) and limit the searches to music festivals.

3. Your streaming sites and shows.
Live streaming is as easy as clicking on an app and pointing your phone at whatever you want to broadcast. You can put on a concert from your bedroom. We covered how to put on a live-streaming show in chapter 16, "Get Gigs and Play Live," as well as how to monetize it and get the most out of it.

4. Others' video channels and shows.
Your music and video material can be featured on anyone else's video channel, and the more popular the channel, the more you'll get out of the coverage. You could get coverage in a vlog, as a "reaction video" (where they watch it and show them making commentary and reacting), and more. To target others' channels, get a feel for what they normally talk about, and reach out to the owner if your music is a good fit. Many don't have formal submission mechanisms, so it might be as simple as sending a friendly email. Each bit of coverage can help you get more in the future.

5. Others' streaming sites and shows.

Since live streaming on YouTube, Facebook, YouNow (younow.com), and more is so easy, there are many shows with good followings you can target to get coverage for your music or videos. Similar to #4 above, the submissions to these shows might be informal and just need an email to the right person, but if they have formal guidelines, follow them carefully.

THE NUMBER-ONE TARGET TO HELP PEOPLE DISCOVER YOUR MUSIC

The music discovery application Shazam (shazam.com) allows music fans to hit a button to scan the audio playing in the place they are in and find out song info, including the title, album, and artist for the song. It also allows users to purchase the song on the spot if they wish or add the song to their streaming playlists automatically if they tie it to their streaming accounts. This is a great way to let new fans discover you and drive sales and streams. To get into Shazam, use a digital music distribution partner that has Shazam as a target. See chapter 9, "Distribution and Streaming."

EXECUTING YOUR GET-HEARD-AND-SEEN CAMPAIGNS
WHAT TO DO BEFORE STARTING A GET-HEARD OR GET-SEEN CAMPAIGN

When you decide to tackle your get-heard campaign, there are a few key concepts to understand before you dive in and send your music out:

1. Aim for targets that play your genre instead of "independent music."

First, consider how you want to classify your music and note that "indie" or "independent" doesn't tell anyone what the music sounds like. It only tells them if the artist has signed a contract with a label, and fans don't care about that. Instead, they search for genres they like. You want your music played alongside the top music in that genre.

2. Make sure the site is targeted at music fans rather than musicians.

If the front page of any site that plays music is aimed at musicians, it's unlikely to have genuine music fans listening to them. Fans want to see info about the genre, artists, and songs they want to hear. The ones that start with a claim that they can get your music heard without even wanting to listen to it are rarely effective and are not aimed at fans.

3. Check out if there's an agreement to sign.

Some sites that play music force you to sign an agreement that gives up some of your rights. Read these agreements carefully before signing them and decide what you feel comfortable with.

4. Consider using research sources.

Sources like the Indie Bible (indiebible.com) cost money but are a handy way to find many places to get your music reviewed, heard, and sold. They also provide a note about their submission guidelines, which can save significant time. If they have a free trial option, use that to determine if you think it's worth it before paying.

5. If you want to hire a promoter/plugger, do your research.

Unfortunately, the music world is filled with unethical people who take advantage of musicians. The legit promoters put their reputations on the line when they recommend music and will not just accept any musicians without listening to their music before accepting them. It's best to search their name and along with the word *"scam"* to see if anyone has said anything negative. If you're going to commit a significant amount of money, find other clients they've handled and interview them to see where the promoter got them played and if they did a good job.

HOW TO PROMOTE YOUR MUSIC ON STREAMING SERVICES BY CREATING PLAYLISTS

If your music is on streaming services, playlists are one of the best ways to get your music discovered and heard. First of all, most interactive streaming sites allow you to feature playlists on your artist profile. Second, although most services no longer allow users to communicate with one another, public playlists are discoverable via the search, and if you use searchable titles, other users might subscribe to your playlist. In general, a playlist should have twenty-five to thirty songs, but it can always be longer. Also, customize your playlists with images and descriptions if your steaming platform allows you to.

Use the below steps to create playlists that fans will enjoy and subscribe to in order to promote your music:

1. Create playlists for your artist profiles.

Since you can feature playlists on your artist profile, it makes sense to create playlists featuring your music. Ideas for these playlists include:

- An intro or "best of" playlist with your music.

- A playlist of your entire catalog.

- A "greatest hits" or "artist favorite tracks" playlist.

- Commentary playlists (a playlist with commentary tracks).

- A "What I'm Currently Listening To" playlist that includes your tracks.

2. Create public playlists to entice other people to subscribe to them.

The best public playlist titles match song titles, other artist names, moods, or activities that they are searching about so they will come up in a search. You will want to add your music in with other artists. Ideas for playlists include:

- Genre playlists that include your music between other popular music in the genre. For instance, our band put together a "Geek Rock" playlist to highlight our music in between other geek rock classics.

- Inspiration, which features your music and the artists you are inspired by.

- Bands you've toured or played with.

- Your place of origin (city, state, country).

- Instrumentation.

- Mood (happy, sad, melancholy, and so on).

- Theme of what your music is about.

- Activity to do while listening to the music: party, quiet evening, workout, yoga, coding, and so on.

3. Promote the playlists.

Promote them via your social media and web presences and through any marketing channels you have.

4. Refresh the playlists on a schedule.

Keep the playlists fresh by changing them up on a schedule, especially if you have a lot of followers. This also gives you a chance to highlight other songs from your repertoire.

HOW TO PROMOTE YOUR MUSIC BY GETTING ON OTHER PEOPLE'S PLAYLISTS

Other people's playlists are a great way to get your music heard by fans, especially if those playlists already have a lot of subscribers. The most popular ones boast thousands or tens of thousands of subscribers. While these are the best ways to get heard, most streaming platforms do not allow fans to communicate with each other, and it is not always possible to communicate with the playlist owners to get your music played. Aside from these, your fans and other contacts are within your reach and can help promote you by creating playlists of their own to develop their own following.

Use the following steps to get your music featured in playlists:

1. Find popular playlists that match your music genre, style, topic, activity, or feel.

If you can find popular playlists that match your music and discover who curates them, reach out to them to see if they're interested in adding your music. Use the steps from "How to Execute a Get-Heard or Get-Seen Campaign" below, especially the follow-up steps.

2. Ask the influencers and musicians within your reach to put your music into playlists.

Each addition of your music is another seed that can pull in a new fan, and since it's easy to ask the people within your influence and control to add your music to public playlists, don't forget to reach out to them. Other ideas include collaborative playlists or local artist playlists.

3. Ask your fans to put your music in playlists.

You can either use your social media to ask your fans to do this directly or ask them to send you their playlists so you can subscribe to them.

Since this takes just a few minutes for fans to do, it's a simple way for them to help promote you. You can also use creative ways to influence them to create playlists with your music, such as playlist contests, or asking them to create playlists about your genre, activity, topic, and so on (which we discuss in the section above) with your music. Also, don't forget to reach out to your fan base and ask them to introduce you to playlist curators they may know to get your music added.

4. Get covered by MP3 blogs, music writers, and influencers to get on their playlists.

Some of the same people you'll be making a part of your get-heard campaign will also put up curated playlists. This can include music bloggers, radio stations, magazines, authors, creatives, online personalities, brands, and even other artists. Make sure to make them part of your get-heard campaign, which we talk about below, and also make it part of your research of those sites to see if they have playlists in addition to the coverage you can get from them.

HOW TO EXECUTE A GET-HEARD OR GET-SEEN CAMPAIGN

Once you've done the research and are ready to run a campaign, here are all the steps you need to follow:

1. Prepare your content correctly.

• For your music: Name, ID3 tag, and prepare your music files so they advertise you when people use the files. Very often they will lose the email and other materials and will only know who you are based on an MP3 filename and the ID3 tags. See chapter 5, "Your Music," for how to do this properly.

• For your video: For video, make sure to upload it to your channel with all the right descriptions and other material, including buy links for the song, so you can get the most out of it. See chapter 6, "Your Videos," for the steps for this (and preparing your video channel).

2. Make sure all your credits, copyright, and royalty registrations are completed.

• For your music: Complete your copyright and royalty registrations so any plays on radio, TV, or elsewhere generate royalty income for you. See chapter 12, "Licensing and Royalties," for more information on how to do this for audio. And see chapter 5, "Your Music," for the steps to register the information about your credits so fans can use it to find more about you if they like the music.

• For your video: See chapter 12, "Licensing and Royalties," for more information on how to register your music with Content ID to get video royalties.

3. Make sure your distribution partner has your sound recordings available for sale.

• For your music: Your music should be available for sale at major outlets like iTunes and Amazon, and it should be on the streaming platforms. If you've done the hard work to get your music played, you will only get the resulting sales and royalties if your music is ready to buy and stream when they hear it. See chapter 9, "Distribution and Streaming," for the steps.

• For your video: If you are selling HD versions of your video content, make sure it's available for sale before getting it covered. See chapter 9, "Distribution and Streaming," for how to do this.

4. Prepare your online presences.

As people discover and listen to your music or watch your video, they'll want to learn more about you. Make sure your web presences are up to date and your conversion tools are ready to go so you can capitalize on any listens you get. See chapter 7, "Your Online Presences," on how to do this.

5. Choose your targets based on your research.

Explore the dozens of categories of places to get heard and seen above, and, based on your listeners and music, choose the best targets for your campaign. Note the submission guidelines if they have any, or, if they don't have any, research to get to know them well so you can write a convincing pitch to them.

6. Make a plan based on your release date.

Your release date might drive which targets you choose and when you'll release it to them. Some make sense to send prerelease material, while others may need to get it after the release. You have a choice: you can promote your music or videos on an ongoing basis (promoting it for years afterward), or you can use the release strategy outlined in chapter 18, "Your Release Strategy," to drive your activities and maximize promotion around the release of your track, EP, album, or video. Even if you tie your music or video release to a release campaign, you can always keep a get-heard or get-seen campaign going as long as you want.

7. Submit your music or video and follow any submission guidelines.

Use the submission guidelines to get your music or video to each target. If it's an exclusive prerelease, call it out. Get to know the outlet well and the people making the choices about what gets played. Communicate directly with the music director or decision-maker if you can—the best promoters use personal relationships to succeed. And if the submission guidelines require you to send a CD, DVD, or tape by postal mail, see if you can get in touch with them first to make sure, and then write *solicited materials* on the envelope to improve your chances of getting it considered.

8. Follow up and use polite persistence.

You should "go until a no" on your campaigns rather than take silence as a rejection. Many places won't even look at new music until someone has tried to get in touch two or three times, so don't give up until you've tried at least that many times (unless their submission guidelines clearly tell you not to contact them). If do get a rejection, don't use it as criticism. If you want feedback about your music, go to other musicians or producers.

9. If you're played, capture it!

Once you get played, send a thank-you. Record it in your chronicle and—if it's a major bit of coverage—in your bio. If it's a music review, capture any good quotes to use for marketing. Also, if you have other songs or albums, reach out and see if they want more music or if they want more music in the future when you do another release.

10. Snowball your successes.

A successful get-heard or get-seen campaign builds on every success. If you get played at one or more of your targets, collect them together, make a set of links, and send them out to all the places that haven't replied yet to show the momentum your music or video is generating. This can be the trigger that causes them to take a look at the music or video and cover it. It's credible objective evidence that your music or video is worth checking out. This is also why it's a good idea to start out with get-heard or get-seen targets within your reach before reaching out to ones who don't know you yet.

HOW TO PAY TO GET HEARD AND SEEN

If you've got the money, there are numerous ways to pay so your music is heard or videos seen, and we'll share a few here. However, you should always be skeptical about services that ask for money to get you played, so you'll want to do your research, since some services may be questionable.

If your music isn't available for sale yet, you should hold off spending any money to get your music played (unless you just want exposure and are not worried about sales). To pay to get played, follow these steps:

1. Use pluggers or promoters.

Legit promoters put their reputations on the line when they recommend music and the best ones are choosy about which musicians they promote. Make sure to do a web search for their name to see if they represent artists you like, and also see what other people think of them before signing on.

Consider services like Ariel Hyatt's Cyber PR (cyberprmusic.com), which has good relationships with many new media outlets that have large audiences. Others include Team Clermont (teamclermont.com) or the Syndicate (thesyn.com).

For video, you can use YouTube's Fan Finder (youtube.com/yt/fanfinder) or try services like Hip Video Promo (hipvideopromo.com) or Rive Video Promotion (rivevideo.com).

2. Use automatic submission services.

Some services will blast out your music to many different outlets in hopes that they will play the music or use it in a radio show or webcast. Since these are less personal than promoters, the success rate is lower. Examples include MusicSUBMIT (musicsubmit.com) and SubmitHub (submithub.com).

3. Target and pay influencers.

You can pay influencers—celebrities and social media celebrities—with large followings on Twitter, Instagram, YouTube, blogs, and more. These are done on a one-on-one basis with the influencer, so you should research them to see if their rates and influence are worth it.

YOUR RELEASE STRATEGY

Goal: To effectively schedule multiple releases throughout the year to keep your fans engaged, create promotional and publicity opportunities for you and your music, increase patronage and crowdfunding income, and generate revenue.

Team Roles and Responsibilities: Manager, Marketer, Publicist, Promoter, Web Designer/Webmaster, Social Media Manager, Video Producer, Product and Merchandise Manager, and Live Event/Tour Manager

WHAT YOU GET OUT OF THIS
By the end of this chapter, you will:

1. Have over sixty ideas for creating engagement for your fans throughout the year (it's not just about releasing music).

2. Create a workable schedule by sequencing your releases to excite your fans and generate press/media opportunities.

3. Have a structured plan for coordinating activities before, during, and after each release for you and your team, including incorporating other campaign plans we've discussed in previous chapters, such as the live show publicity campaign, get-heard campaign, get-seen campaign, and crowdfunding campaign.

4. Track and measure the effectiveness of your release campaigns so you can adapt your plans as needed.

INTRO

The web and social media world create an unending hunger for new activity. Today's busiest sites, like Reddit, Facebook, Instagram, and You-Tube, engage audiences with endless new content on a minute-by-minute basis. Your potential fans and customers expect constant entertainment and news and have an insatiable hunger for something new. A minute of downtime on the corner waiting for a stoplight is a minute of engagement with content on their smartphone. Content consumption is now a habit.

Because of this, audiences reward consistent, scheduled updates, and this has changed everything. Your music release plan should match your audience's expectations instead of secluding yourself into the studio for months and then emerging with a ten-song album a year later.

In fact, your videos, shows, new merchandise, and more can be planned out across the year to make it easier to promote, market, and engage. Plus, when you release multiple events over time in a consistent and regular fashion, you increase the odds of snowballing your successes, growing your exposure and fan base, and generating revenue so you make more money with music.

KEY CONCEPTS
THE BENEFITS OF PLANNING AND RELEASING ON A SCHEDULE

Social media notifies people when there's a new post; streaming services notify followers when there's new music. To take advantage of this, and considering singles comprise nearly 70 percent of all listens on these streaming music services, you should release your album as a series of releases that eventually work its way to the final album. You'll also satisfy your fans, who are always looking for fresh material. This may mean putting together one or two single releases, a couple of remixes, and finally, at the end of the cycle, the complete album. Breaking up releases in this way creates eight to twelve events over the year and keeps bringing your fans back to your page.

Each release can keep you on top of mind with fans. In fact, planning a steady stream of releases on a set schedule drives the following benefits:

STEADY BEAT OF RELEASES

1	2	3	4	5	6	7	8	9	10	11	12	13	14	15	16	17	18
RECORDING/MIXING/ MASTERING								SINGLE	SINGLE	VIDEO	EP	SINGLE	VIDEO	SINGLE	EP	SINGLE	SINGLE	ALBUM
						PRODUCTION/ DISTRIBUTION		★	★	★	★	★	★	★	★	★	★	★
									MARKETING/PUBLICITY/PRESS								
									GET HEARD/GET SEEN CAMPAIGNS								
SOCIAL MEDIA																	
														TOURING/GIGS			

- Drives natural promotion activities and regular engagement with fans through your owned and social media.

- Gives you reasons to launch and drive your get-heard or get-seen campaigns.

- Drives publicity and earned media activities, which generates buzz and media coverage.

- Boosts patronage engagement and can support crowdfunding campaigns.

- Generates streams, sales, and royalties for new releases, but also your back catalog as it gets discovered and explored.

- Creates snowballing effects and may generate future opportunities (licensing opportunities).

In the end, the goal isn't to substantially change how you *make* your music—you still need time to create and produce the music—but instead structures how you *release* it.

PLANNING YOUR RELEASE SCHEDULE
HOW THE WORK YOU'VE ALREADY DONE WILL
HELP YOU PLAN YOUR RELEASE SCHEDULE
When you build and plan out your release calendar, you'll prep step
activities from other chapters. For instance:

1. Getting your team, partners, network, and services to plan and
run your business (chapter 4).

2. Building your persona and brand elements (chapter 3).

3. Creating and preparing your music for release (chapter 5).

4. Creating and preparing your videos for release (chapter 6).

5. Registering your music, videos, and other works so you can make
royalties off them (chapters 8 and 12).

6. Creating your products and merchandise (chapter 10).

7. Preparing your online presences for promotion (chapter 7).

8. Preparing your patronage, crowdfunding, and other methods of
raising money (chapter 11).

9. Getting your music and videos distributed worldwide (chapter 9).

10. Knowing your audience, marketing plan, and planning out your
promotion and publicity (chapters 14 and 15).

All of this work will come in handy as you plan your release and sequence your events into a calendar to structure all the activities. This includes mapping out the steps of the various campaigns before and after
the release date. You may also want to schedule a live show publicity campaign (chapter 16), get-heard campaign (chapter 17), get-seen campaign
(chapter 17), or crowdfunding campaign (Chapter 11).

THE DEFINITION OF A "RELEASE" AND THE NEAR-ENDLESS
NUMBER OF EVENTS YOU CAN SCHEDULE
Fans stay in tune and engaged in what you do when you consistently release
new content. This will not only make your fans happy, it will give you natural
reasons to promote and publicize yourself and help you make more money.

But you don't have to just release music. There are a huge number of possibilities you can schedule for your release calendar. Use this list for ideas:

- **Music.**
  - Single
  - EP
  - Album
  - Streaming playlist
  - Repackaged previously released music (greatest hits, topic albums, reissues, remasters, and so on)

- **Videos.**
  - Music video
  - Vlog
  - Music used in someone else's video

- **Products and merchandise.**
  - Single, EP, or album for sale
    - *CD*
    - *Vinyl*
    - *Tape*
    - *USB*

  - Limited print items

  - T-shirts and clothing

  - Items from live events (broken drumsticks, set lists, and so on)

  - Book, photobook, or ebook

  - Repackaged previously released products or merchandise (bundles, mystery bags, reprintings, reissues, throwbacks/ nostalgia, and so on)

  - Other merch

- **Live music events.**
  - Tours (multiple live shows)

- Specific live show (a.k.a. live show publicity campaign—chapter 16)
  - *Concert or festival appearance*
  - *House concert*
  - *In-studio radio, video, or other live-streaming appearances*
  - *In-your-studio concert*
  - *Any streaming concert*
- And more . . .

- **New or updated online presences.**
  - New social presence created (and ask fans to follow or subscribe)

  - New or updated launch of website

  - New website feature

  - Latest blog entry

  - Latest podcast entry

  - New photos shared from latest show

  - New gear or instrument purchased

  - New or updated studio

  - Family or other life event milestone (band member married, graduation, child, and so on)

- **Snowballing press/media coverage.**
  Post about any coverage in:

  - Music review sites

  - Podcasts

  - MP3 blogs

  - Curated streaming playlists

  - Video channels or shows

- News, magazines, or other sites
- And more...

- **New raising money or other achievement/milestone.**
  - New patronage reward
  - Patronage milestone achieved or nearly achieved
  - Crowdfunding goal or stretch goal achieved or nearly achieved
  - Crowdfunding completed and project to start
  - Crowdfunding project delivered
  - Music licensed for film, TV, advertisement, or movie trailer
  - New sponsor
  - New endorsement of product

- **Fan engagement.**
  - Contests (incentives for creating artwork, merch ideas, raising money, generating publicity for you, getting you booked in a new venue or covered in the media, and so on)
  - Polls (questions to your fan base, naming EPs and album)
  - Mailing list newsletter updates

- **Music production events.**
  - Behind-the-scenes stream while making or recording music
  - Behind-the-scenes stream while making or recording videos

- **Other live events.**
  - EP or album listening party
  - Video viewing party
  - Film-, TV-, advertisement-, or movie-trailer-watching party that your music is licensed in
  - Online hangout sessions

- Video game sessions (Twitch)
- Party bus event
- Party boat cruise
- Travel event
- Local hangout event
- And more ...

This list is just the start of what's possible. Keep in mind you can drive even more engagement by staging a prerelease event to drive sales in your releases. In other words, don't just think release, think prerelease and add a separate prerelease event to drive sales and excitement—not just for music but also for merch or other products. To do this, use the following techniques:

- Bundling merch, digital downloads, and extras available only to fans who preorder the release.

- Getting fans to presave albums on Spotify using services like Show.co (show.co).

- Driving people to order limited-run merch and products before they run out.

- Making early preorders only available to funders on patronage or crowdfunding rewards to let them go "first in line" for limited-run products.

HOW TO PLAN OUT YOUR RELEASE CALENDAR
To plan out your release calendar, you'll need to:

1. Decide on the number of events you're comfortable executing through the year.
Divide up the fifty-two weeks of a year into consistent releases. We recommend one of the following:

- Fifty-two releases = one event a week (or forty-eight if you leave out holidays)
- Twenty-four releases = one event every two weeks

- Twelve releases = one event every month

- Or some combination or releases between twelve and fifty-two

You don't need to start your schedule immediately or at the beginning of the year. Plan it out based on when your music, videos, and content are ready to go.

2. Brainstorm on the types of events, and prioritize by level of effort.

List all the music, videos, shows, and other events planned for the next year. Keep in mind not all your events should be major work efforts, and you'll want to mix the low- or medium-effort events with the high-effort ones, such as videos, EPs, albums, or shows.

3. Sequence your events across your calendar.

Schedule your events around your time, resources, and goals. For instance, we consulted a musician who sequenced two single drops as well as videos through the year. These were the high-effort events, and he interspersed them with low-effort events to give him the space to get it all done.

4. Schedule time for the pre- and postrelease steps.

Determine what needs to be done *before, during, and after* each release date. This is where you may find you need to adjust the timing of some or even all your release dates based on the work that needs to occur around the release.

For example, if you release a new song, make sure you have enough time to perform the twelve registrations we discussed in Chapter 12, "Licensing and Royalties," since you want it to generate royalties for you on day one. Also, add in the date you need to have the final mastered copy and when it needs to be uploaded to your distribution partner. Also schedule any prereleases to your patrons, fan club, or supporters.

But that might not be all. If physical merchandise is part of your release, you'll want to leave time for manufacturing and shipping. And if you want to run a get-heard campaign, work backward from the release date to give yourself time to get your song heard. If you're planning on getting it some media attention, you'll need to give yourself a couple of weeks to reach out to your press and media contacts. You'll also want to update your website and other promotional channels so they're all promoting the same thing to your fans.

Fortunately, much of this work can happen in parallel. For example, you can do many of the get-heard steps, publicity steps, and website updates at the same time.

5. Start executing, but always know you can adjust the calendar once you start.

Stay flexible and don't be afraid to adjust your calendar if you have unforeseen issues. Just keep in mind a calendar is less flexible if there are outside groups involved, such as a venue, show, or publicized event.

While this is a lot to track, there are tools and software that can help you do this—tools like Jammber (jammber.com) or project management solutions, including free options like Trello (trello.com) or Freedcamp (freedcamp.com).

EXECUTING ACTIVITIES AROUND EACH RELEASE
HOW TO PROMOTE AND PUBLICIZE YOUR RELEASE

For each release, use the below as a checklist to make sure you've done everything you need to promote and publicize it. Remember, you should delegate these tasks to your team or publicist to make it easier for you to appear before your audiences.

1. **Before the release date.**
   - Update any of the following you have:
     - *Your website, including your front page, your blog or announcement page, your calendar and event log*
     - *Your social presences*
     - *Your mailing list/newsletter*
     - *Your video channel/vlog*
     - *Your podcast*
     - *Your press, fact sheet, booking kits (depending on the type of event)*
   - Email or contact your team, friends, and family to spread the word of the event to their networks.

- If you're doing a preorder (physical or digital products, merch, and ticket sales), announce this now and point them to the service's conversion tools.

- Research and prepare your press and media target list.

- Create your publicity tracking spreadsheet.

- Create a press release or video announcement for the press and media.

- Create an email cover letter for your press and media contact with links to the video announcement or press release.

- If the event is live, offer to add your press or media contacts to your guest list so they know they're special (and it increases the chances they'll attend).

2. **During the release campaign.**
   - Retweet or repost fan shares of your announcements or fan comments about your upcoming event.

   - Share real-time behind-the-scenes preparation for the event through your channels to promote continued engagement and awareness.

   - Send reminder announcements, plug preorders (if applicable), and so on.

   - Follow up with the press and media contacts who haven't responded.

   - If you get any initial coverage, snowball that coverage with those who have not yet responded or covered you.

   - Update your publicity tracking spreadsheet to help you keep track of who you contacted and when, if you got coverage, and if they said "no".

3. **On the day of the release.**
   - Be sure to make one final announcement through all your channels (mailing list/newsletter, front page, and so on) and be active on your social presences.

- If the event is live, borrow and follow those relevant steps outlined in the "Running and Publicizing a Live Show" section in chapter 16, "Get Gigs and Play Live."

- Follow up with press and media contacts who haven't responded.

4. After the release.

Once the release is over, do the following:

- Update your social presences (retweet or share any fan comments or coverage so other fans and followers know).

- Update your website, including your front page and your blog or announcement page.

- Email or contact your team, friends, and family about the success so they spread the word about it to their networks, which can help boost awareness for your next event.

- Send "thank-you" notes to all outlets and journalists who covered you.

- Capture clippings of all coverage for your chronicle and website.

- Update your press and media target list to note who covered you, since those individuals and outlets will be more likely to cover you in the future.

- Update your press kit with standout quotes and coverage clippings.

TRACKING THE SUCCESSES OF YOUR RELEASE CAMPAIGNS THROUGH METRICS AND ANALYTICS

HOW TO TRACK AND MEASURE YOUR RELEASE CAMPAIGN SUCCESSES

One problem with any media coverage you may get is that your media contacts rarely tell you they've written a story about your band, even if you sent them a press release. The only way you'll know is if you discover the story yourself. Fortunately, there are tools to help you do this. To track mentions of your band, do the following:

While many people use search engines to search their own names, it's necessary to do this on a regular basis to find out who is talking about you. You can do this by reminding yourself to search your name every week, or you can have the search engine automatically email you when it finds new web pages and blogs that talk about you. This takes just a few minutes and is a very powerful way to keep up with anyone who mentions you. Don't skip this section—it's free, it's simple to do, and it's a very powerful feature for anyone who is in the media.

If you use it, you will:

- Find out about articles and reviews of your band that you may not know about.

- Catch message board posts that talk about you.

- See blog entries that mention your music.

- Be able to find new fans and new opportunities for your music, publicity, and marketing.

To track mentions of your band and find out the rank of your website, you will need to do the following:

1. Register and set up alerts at various search services.

You will need to create an account at the services listed below. If you already have an account, just log in. Set up your alerts at Google Alerts (google.com/alerts). You may also want to use a paid service like HootSuite (hootsuite.com) or SocialOomph (socialoomph.com), which offer some services for free. Follow each service's instructions. Depending on the service, you will get a choice as to coverage (we recommend choosing the broadest as possible), how frequently you want to be notified (we recommend being notified as they happen rather than a digest so you can stay on top of mentions), and how you want to be notified.

You can also sign up at Mention (mention.com), which is a service that tracks all search and social mentions of keywords you tell them to track—so you don't have to sign up for all the above. You can sign up for a limited free version, or you can pay the recurring fee to have it track everything.

2. Add search terms and use advanced search features.

You can add any search term relevant to you. Some to consider include your artist name and all misspellings (and if you're a band, your band member names and misspellings); your website address; the names of any music releases, such as EPs or albums; any songs you release with unique names (if it's not unique, you'll be inundated with alerts that are off the mark); and the names of artists similar to yours. Why? Because any sites, podcasts, blogs, or other media that cover them should be interested in you too.

3. Use advanced search features.

To help narrow your searches so they pull more relevant information, be sure to use advanced search features. For instance, "Beatnik Turtle" +*Chicago* will require that the word *Chicago* be found on any pages that mention our band's name. Use this if your artist name is not unique worldwide but is unique in a particular city. The - searches exclude results. The search phrase "Beatnik Turtle" -*turtlenecks* will find our band name except in pages that talk about turtlenecks.

4. Regularly check your web referrer list on your website.

If you have a website, you can check to see what links people clicked on to get to the site. These are usually called *referrers* if you have web statistics. You can use this to find stories or blog entries about your band that you didn't know about. Even better, you will be able to see how many people have come to your site from each link, so you can learn which articles are the most effective at sending you new fans.

CONCLUSION
ASSISTANCE FOR MUSICIANS AND LEARNING MORE

No one knows where the music industry is headed. As Jim DeRogatis said, "If anyone says they know what it will look like in five years, they're lying." And with the insights we've gained and the changes that have happened in the five years after our last book on the subject, he was right. But that book also predicted there would be new opportunities to connect with fans and get your music out there. And since then, the smartphone has transformed everything, streaming music services took off in popularity, YouTube grew into one of the most powerful ways to get your music discovered, patronage grew up to allow fans to directly support musicians on a regular basis, and live streaming became commonplace. By the time we write our next book, there will only be more options. The key is to pay attention and take advantage of them when they come out.

Meanwhile, we'll be helping you stay on top of all these opportunities through all our newsletter, column, articles, speaking engagements, and more by following us at MakingMoneyWithMusic.com.

HOW TO GET ADDITIONAL SUPPORT AND OPPORTUNITIES FOR GIGS, LICENSING, TOURS, AND MORE FROM CITIES

Music makes a big difference to the economies of many cities throughout the world, and many are doing what they can to nurture and grow their music economies. Based on some studies in music cities, music tourism can drive billions in revenue due to hotels, restaurants, and tourism income. A great example of this is the Austin Music Census (bit.ly/austincensus). As a result of these, cities have taken notice of their music economies and are doing the same kind of advocacy, income-generation tax benefits, and assistance that they do for other industries. Many of these cities have music offices and want to help musicians connect to jobs, licensing, and gigs, and they can be a great resource. See if your town has a music office, and connect with them to get good advice.

THE TOP FIVE PLACES TO GET HEALTH INSURANCE FOR MUSICIANS

If you're building a music business and looking to make a living through music, having your health care guaranteed through your government significantly reduces a critical business cost. Health issues can occur at any time, and if you're not covered, the costs can overwhelm your business. The good news is most countries guarantee health care for its citizens. However, if you're a musician who lives in one that doesn't, such as the U.S., then the cost to have some form of health insurance falls on you and your business. Without coverage, it's up to you to pay out of pocket, and health care bills can be significant. Unfortunately, studies continually show self-employed musicians—ones who are making a living through music—skip getting health care coverage to save costs at a far higher rate than most professions. This is a risk, since if something happens to your health, it not only can disrupt your music business and reduce your income, it also requires diverting capital to paying health care bills. Options for health coverage include:

1. A day gig.
Many jobs offer health insurance as a benefit of employment. If you have a day gig that doesn't get in the way of your music, it's a good way to get coverage, since plans become cheaper when you buy them in groups.

2. Musicians unions and organizations.
Musicians unions often offer insurance, and if you have joined one, or wish to join, you should explore their health insurance options. Also, some PROs and other musician organizations also offer insurance, and you'll want to explore each of them to see what they provide.

3. A label.
If you are signed to a label, you may be eligible for insurance through AF-TRA (sagaftraplans.org/health).

4. U.S. state and federal government.

Currently in the U.S., while the government doesn't guarantee universal health care coverage, the federal government enacted the Affordable Health Care Act, which you can join during certain times of the year. For more information, visit HealthCare.Gov (healthcare.gov). Additionally, you will want to research your local state's health care coverage options.

5. Health insurance information source.

If you're still uncertain where to go, you can contact the Music Health Alliance (musichealthalliance.com) or the Future of Music Coalition's HINT (futureofmusic.org/issues/campaigns/get-hint). Both organizations provide advice and links to additional resources, and, in some cases, assist in the face of medical issues. This advice is made possible by a grant, but they also accept donations, so it may be worth supporting or raising money for them if you're looking for a cause to support with your music, since their mission is to help musicians.

HOW TO GET ASSISTANCE IN CASE OF EMERGENCIES AND DISASTERS

When you are faced with an emergency or disaster, it's hard to know where to turn. Fortunately, there are organizations dedicated to helping musicians out during these times. These are a few places to go, but search for organizations in your area in case there is an emergency.

1. MusiCares.

The Recording Academy's MusiCares (grammy.com/musicares) organization is dedicated to helping musicians. According to grammy.com/musicares/about, it "provides a safety net of critical assistance for music people in times of need. MusiCares' services and resources cover a wide range of financial, medical, and personal emergencies, and each case is treated with integrity and confidentiality. MusiCares also focuses the resources and attention of the music industry on human service issues that directly impact the health and welfare of the music community."

2. Disaster assistance.

After major disasters like hurricanes and earthquakes, charities will often create funds to help musicians get back on their feet. For example, after Hurricanes Harvey and Irma, the Hurricane Harvey/Irma Musicians Relief Fund (sweetrelief.org/program/harvey) was founded to specifically help people in the music business. If you are caught in a major disaster, you should see if any of the charities apply to you.

HOW AND WHY TO JOIN A MUSICIANS UNION

Musicians unions can help provide many benefits to its members, including health insurance, pensions, retirement benefits, and more. In exchange, you'll be paying union dues. Each union has their own admission requirements. Also, you'll want to research each carefully before joining, as you'll want to understand their benefits as well as their rules.

You can also open up new income streams by joining a union. For example, if you are a member of AFM or SAG-AFTRA, you can collect royalties from the AFM & SAG-AFTRA Intellectual Property Rights Distribution Fund (afmsagaftrafund.org). These royalties can be generated from playing in recording sessions or for theatrical performances if you are a member. See the fund for more details.

Consider the following unions:

1. SAG-AFTRA

If you do any kind of screen or theater work, are signed to a label, or work any kind of union jobs associated with them, consider joining SAG-AFTRA (sagaftra.org). They claim they represent "approximately 160,000 actors, announcers, broadcast journalists, dancers, DJs, news writers, news editors, program hosts, puppeteers, recording artists, singers, stunt performers, voiceover artists and other media professionals." They provide insurance and many other benefits for musicians.

2. American Federation of Musicians (AFM).

On their website, AFM (afm.org/en) says the following: "80,000 musicians comprise the American Federation of Musicians of the United States and Canada (AFM). We perform in orchestras, backup bands, festivals, clubs and theaters—both on Broadway and on tour. AFM members also make music for films, TV, commercials and sound recordings." If you do a lot of session work or have the opportunity to play union jobs, consider AFM.

3. Actors Equity.

If you do a lot of live-stage theater work, explore Actors' Equity (actorsequity.org).

HOW TO PROTECT YOUR HEARING

Your hearing is one of the most important assets you have as a musician, and this book wouldn't be complete if we didn't cover how to protect it, especially because regulations to cover noise are not uniform throughout the world. One excellent resource to deal with sound as a musician is the Sound Advice website (soundadvice.info). This is a UK-based site created as a result of the Control of Noise at Work Regulations 2005, but it's great advice no matter where you are in the world.

If you are regularly exposed to loud music, you may also wish to invest in custom molded earplugs designed for your ears. Although there are kits available to do it yourself, as a professional musician you may wish to get one made for your ears by an audiologist.

HOW TO KEEP YOURSELF UPDATED ON THE LATEST *MAKING MONEY WITH MUSIC* INFO AND RESOURCES

This book has a framework and structure you can put behind your music business, but it also pays to keep up with the latest info, techniques, and news to generate new income ideas and continue to build your business. Check out the following resources we provide:

1. Subscribe to the *Making Money with Music* newsletter.

Have the latest info delivered to your in-box by signing up for our free *MakingMoneyWithMusic.com Newsletter* (makingmoneywithmusic .com/Newsletter) for articles, advice, ideas, and news. Keep yourself plugged in, and continue to get new ideas to add more revenue to your music business.

2. Read over 250 free articles and columns.

Check out our weekly column, "The DIY Advisor," at emusician.com /advisor for weekly articles on DIY Music. You can also find links to every article we've written, well over 100,000 words in over 250 articles, available for free at MakingMoneyWithMusic.com/Articles-By-The-Authors.

3. Join MakingMoneyWithMusic.com

We provide even more detailed revenue stream how-to information, tools, services, and individual guidance at MakingMoneyWithMusic.com to help you manage and grow your music business.

4. Come to our speaking events and workshops.

We travel extensively to do presentations, speaking events, and workshops. We will keep you up to date on our speaking schedule in our *MakingMoneyWithMusic.com Newsletter* (makingmoneywithmusic.com /Newsletter) as well as on our website at MakingMoneyWithMusic.com. Keep an eye out for talks in your area. Note that if you are in the Chicago area, where we are based, we often do talks out of 2112 (2112inc.com), where we are mentors.

5. See our talks at music business schools.

We've taught regularly in music business schools since 2009, but due to a busy schedule, we usually only make guest lecture appearances. If you are a teacher or student at a music school and would like us to do a livestream Q&A or short presentation for your class, feel free to reach out at writeus@makingmoneywithmusic.com, and we can see if we can fit in a talk around our speaking and writing schedule.

6. Sign up for consulting with us (very few slots!).

We occasionally take on musicians and labels as consulting clients, but our schedule is usually full, and we don't take on many clients because we prefer to write, speak, or teach to help more musicians at once. If you want to talk with us about our fee-based consulting services, reach out at writeus@makingmoneywithmusic.com. Note that because of our full schedule, we're more likely to provide you resources to get the answers you need than we are to find a consulting slot for you.

LEARNING MORE

There is always more to learn about the music business. Although we get multiple newsletters, have a huge stack of research books, and are constantly doing research on the web for our weekly column, there's always a need for more. Here are external resources we've found useful to get you the info you need. We recommend the following to get more information on the music business:

- **Books.**
  If you're hungry for even more info, like we are, we will give you a head start and take the waist-high stack of books that we used for research and

boil it down to the ones that we liked the very best at MakingMoney
WithMusic.com/resources.

• **Blogs and newsletters.**
Today's music business moves fast, and new ideas to take advantage of
the latest social networks and services appear every week. Besides our
own *MakingMoneyWithMusic.com Newsletter* (makingmoneywithmu
sic.com/newsletter), we particularly like Bob Baker's newsletter (bob
-baker.com). We also like blogs from Derek Sivers (sivers.org), Hypebot
(hypebot.com), Musformation (musformation.com), and Digital Music
News (digitalmusicnews.com). You can also come to MakingMoney
WithMusic.com/resources for clickable links and even more websites
and information that are worth reading.

• **Magazines and websites.**
Considering our regular weekly column at *Electronic Musician* (emusi
cian.com), we're aware of the great resources at magazines like *Guitar
Player* (guitarplayer.com), *Bass Player* (bassplayer.com), *Audio Fanzine*
(audiofanzine.com), and others.

• **Music business schools.**
We believe in music education because although you can pick up a lot of
knowledge from books like this one and just trying stuff out in the real
world, it helps to have a structured curriculum of everything you need
to know. Because of this, we're PAC members (board members) of SAE
here in Chicago (usa.sae.edu/campuses/chicago), and we advise them on
what students need.

Other options include online classes you can attend no matter where
in the world you live. The largest online music school in the world, and
one of the best, is Berklee Online (online.berklee.edu). The school has
extremely practical courses aimed at indie musicians that also give you
college credit. They have practical topics like concert touring, music
licensing, and music marketing. If you are interested in more than one
class, you should also look into their certificate programs, which give you
a series of courses so you can master entire topics like music business or
music production and technology. Certificates are between three and
twelve courses and have advantages beyond just covering the topics; you

will have a series of college-credit courses when you're done, as well as a certification that can help you in the music world. The mix of courses updates often. As Dave Kusek, the CEO of BerkleeMusic, says, "We survey our audience constantly so we find topics that people are interested in and then deliver it. Asking questions like where are the jobs? And if you're going on the DIY route, what is it that you need to know?"

And finally, you can always join more full-fledged music business programs. We were curious about what business schools do to keep up with today's music world, so we interviewed Don Gorder from the Berklee College of Music (berklee.edu), who not only heads the music business program but also founded it. With classes like Creative Promotion in New Media, they are staying ahead of the latest trends. Their music business program is split into three tracks—music management: covering what you need to know to be a music manager; music marketing: everything that is involved with taking a product to marketing; and entrepreneurship: covering what you need to start your own business. As Gorder says, "Not only the mechanical steps but also the mind-set you need to start your own business." He continues: "We have other classes like Emerging Music Business Models, where we give students an outlook on new business models that are developing and give them latitude to develop their own. This is the thinking-outside-the-box class."

As you can imagine, there's a wealth of other options for learning more, so come to MakingMoneyWithMusic.com/resources for links to many more options on learning more.

• **Connecting with musicians.**

Beyond options to connect online, keep in mind that there are conferences, workshops, and organizations that will allow you to buddy up with other musicians or people in this business. Organizations like ASCAP (ascap.com), BMI (bmi.com), and the GRAMMY organization (grammy .com) all allow musicians to connect with one another and run conferences and workshops that are great places to connect.

CONCLUSION
We'd love to hear your suggestions, ideas, and comments. You can get in touch with us by mailing contactus@makingmoneywithmusic.com or going to the website and using the contact form.

Sign up for the free newsletter at MakingMoneyWithMusic.com and use the site's additional resources, tools, and bonus information to make money and grow your music business.

Also, follow us on Twitter at @IndieGuide and, if you like our music, at @BeatnikTurtle.

But enough reading about music. Now go out and make it. After all, there's no better time to be a musician.

ACKNOWLEDGMENTS

First, we'd like to thank our agent, Rick Broadhead, for realizing our potential. We wouldn't be writing our fourth book if it weren't for him. Thanks for all the continual guidance, support, advocacy, and encouragement to make this the best book it could possibly be.

Thanks to everyone at St. Martin's Press for their help, knowledge, and support in bringing *Making Money with Music* to life—especially our editor, Lauren Apperson, who put in the time and energy to make it the best book it could be. Thanks also to Richard Brady for helping with the overall layout of the cover and Keith Glantz and Steve Andersen and his team for their work on the illustrations, and Ilya Zlatkin for his legal review.

Many who helped make this book a reality may or may not know it. These have been our advisers and mentors—people who have helped pioneer the areas that made it possible for musicians to do it themselves and inspired us. These include, in no particular order: Don Pitts, Peter Schwarz, Martin Atkins, Derek Sivers, Lawrence Lessig, Jed Carlson, Tony van Veen, Bob Baker, Ariel Hyatt, David Taylor II, Jonathan Coulton, Wally Lockard III, Scott Alden, Orville Kline, Brian Boncher, Coleen Spapperi, Mark Shiozaki, and many, many others. This also includes all the great people at 2112 and Fort Knox including: Scott Fetters, Amor Montes de Oca, Rob Tovar, Alex Restrepo, and the many other faculty, musicians, and tech start-up entrepreneurs who inspire us each day. Everyone at New Bay Media and Electronic Musician past and present who have influenced our writing and The DIY Advisor column including: Sarah Jones, Gino Robair, Barbara Schultz, and Michael Molenda. And some of the great people we've met on the road where we've spoken, including: Teresa Jenkins, David Messier, Christen McFarland, Kim

McCarson, Neil Padukone, Tiffany Williams, Erica Shamaly, and many, many others.

Additionally, we want to thank our first book's editor, David Moldawer, for believing in us in the first place. Without him, there would be no first book, let alone a fourth one.

Lastly, there wouldn't be a book if there wasn't a Beatnik Turtle, so we'd like to thank everyone involved in our band or thesongoftheday.com over the past twenty years!

RANDY WOULD LIKE TO THANK . . .

As always, thanks to my parents, Glenn and Susan Chertkow, as well as my sister Heather, brother-in-law John Cumings, and my nieces, Chloe and Eva. And also thanks to Jason's family, Peggy, Liam, and Brendan. Thank you to the Pegasus crew: Shannon Prickett, Andrew Crawford, and Jessica Firsow for their constant support. Special thanks to Kirk Marty, Patrick Thompson, and Gus Siefker for working around my schedule as I wrote the book. Big thanks to Debra Ann Christensen and Dietrich Horsey for keeping me physically in shape as well as the great conversations and ideas.

And thanks to you, Jason, as not only a co-author but also a friend.

And, finally, to Peggy: I wasn't sure if we could survive another book, and, in fact, I'm not sure if we did. :) In either case, he's all yours again . . .

JASON WOULD LIKE TO THANK . . .

First and foremost, I'd like to thank my wife, Peggy Mahoney, for all her love, support, encouragement, and understanding as I put long hours into this book. I'm grateful to have a wife like you! Thanks also to my two great sons, Liam and Brendan. Liam for his understanding of all the work I had to do weekends and evenings (but then, he's a published author of his own!) and Brendan, for constantly telling me to keep writing and "Just get it done, Daddy." Love you all!

Second, my parents and family for their support and encouragement—especially with Beatnik Turtle and all the musicians who traipsed across their house at odd hours of the night.

Third, I'd like to thank everyone at work for their encouragement, even though most had no idea I did this and those that did asked, "Wait, you write books?"

Fourth, I'd also like to continue to thank Jim Citrin for unknowingly inspiring me to get into this book-writing thing.

Lastly, I'd like to thank Randy for co-writing this. As always, we not only poured our all into it, we ended up with a thousand more ideas we now have to do!

ABOUT THE AUTHORS

Randy Chertkow and Jason Feehan are professional musicians, authors, journalists, public speakers, instructors, and consultants. They co-wrote two critically acclaimed editions of *The Indie Band Survival Guide* (Macmillan), *The DIY Musician* (Random House), and Making Money with Music (a 15-hour online course via CreativeLive), and are weekly columnists at *Electronic Musician* magazine ("The DIY Advisor"). They speak and consult on music business and musician revenue development at conventions, music organizations (e.g., The Recording Academy—grammy .org), businesses (Guitar Center), and in cities (New York City, Austin, Chicago), and schools (SAE, Music Industry Workshop, Columbia College). This includes speaking at venues such as Carnegie Hall.

ABOUT RANDY CHERTKOW, M.S.

Professionally, Randy is an enterprise-class IT professional with more than twenty years of experience as an infrastructure architect in Fortune 500 companies and has an IT background in engineering, consulting, and technical sales at large enterprises, major software vendors, and Silicon Valley start-ups. His technical resume reads like an acronym soup. He has a business bachelor's degree and an M.S. in Computer Science: Data Communications, with a secondary concentration in Artificial Intelligence.

ABOUT JASON FEEHAN, J.D., PMP

Professionally, Jason is a licensed attorney, program/project manager, product manager, consultant, and creative business director. He specializes in starting up or reinventing existing technology or business organizations as well as turning around, improving, and developing organizational capabilities. He's worked in a variety of industries including manufacturing, law, financial services, software development, and professional consulting services. He has a Bachelor of Science in Political Science and Psychology and a J.D.

ABOUT ARM'S REACH CONSULTING CREATIVE CONSULTING SERVICES EMPOWERING MUSIC, TECHNOLOGY, AND THE ARTS

Randy and Jason founded Arm's Reach Consulting, LLC., in 2008, a consulting firm specializing in the new tech-driven, internet-powered music and arts industry. Arm's Reach Consulting has a decade of experience consulting, educating, writing, speaking, and developing thought-leading intellectual material to navigate and succeed in the new tech-driven music and arts business. It also consults, develops, builds, and manages successful programs to increase artist and musician revenue, build fan base support, grow the overall music economy, empower culture and the arts, and bring more art and music into the world.

ABOUT THE AUTHORS' BAND, BEATNIK TURTLE

Jason and Randy's band, Beatnik Turtle, has released more than five hundred songs spanning twenty albums, licensed music to Disney and Viacom, and created music for TV, films, and theater including Chicago's famous Second City. In 2007, they released a song every single day of the year from their website TheSongOfTheDay.com.

INDEX